KV-038-035

Waking the Sleeping Giant

Waking the Sleeping Giant

The Birth, Growth, Decline, and Rebirth of an American Church

Rev. Dr. Gerald B. Kieschnick, President

The Lutheran Church—Missouri Synod

Published by Concordia Publishing House
3558 S. Jefferson Ave., St. Louis, MO 63118-3968
1-800-325-3040 • www.cph.org

Manufactured in the United States of America

Library of Congress Cataloging-in-Publication Data

Kieschnick, Gerald B.

Waking the sleeping giant : the birth, growth, decline, and rebirth of an American church / Gerald B. Kieschnick.

p. cm.

ISBN 978-0-7586-2544-1

1. Lutheran Church.—Missouri Synod—History. I. Title.
BX8061.M7K54 2009
284.1'322--dc22

2009045590

1 2 3 4 5 6 7 8 9 10   18 17 16 15 14 13 12 11 10

To my beloved wife, Terry.

Her love for Christ and His Church . . .

Her love for her family . . .

Her love for pastors' wives . . .

Are an inspiration to me and to many!

Contents

Introduction

The life of a national church body president is an intriguing one. "President" is probably not a very accurate term when understood in the context of The Lutheran Church—Missouri Synod. Dictionary definitions of the term "president" focus on describing the head of a state or nation, the highest-ranking member of an association, business, or corporation, and so on. In reality the president of our church body is a theological advisor and ecclesiastical supervisor. Yet the president is also a leader, understanding that our world is terribly complex and helping the church, its congregations, laymen, laywomen, and professional workers in the task of applying biblical truths to the contemporary context in which we live.

My life is full of many duties and responsibilities requiring prolific communications, both spoken and written, together with much national and international travel. In the course of my daily endeavors, I'm asked many questions by people both within and outside the church. Many folks have never heard of a "synod," and some who have are clueless as to what it means. The majority of people in the church have little or no awareness of the existence of a regional or national church, much less any knowledge of their role or function. Their church experience revolves around, and is pretty much limited to, the local congregation.

In our case, the national Synod is the standard-bearer, the quality-control center, the entity responsible for what all its member congregations and professional church workers publicly teach and preach. The one who serves as its president is expected to provide leadership that is both faithful and fruitful. I am keenly aware of the awesome responsibilities that accompany the role of president/servant leader of The Lutheran Church—Missouri Synod.

Many who read these words will know who I am. Others will not. It should therefore be stated at the beginning the obvious truth that I am a Christian. Born into a family of Christian parents, Christian grandparents, and Christian siblings, baptized into a Christian church, confirmed in the Christian faith, married to a Christian woman, father of Christian children, grandfather of Christian grandchildren, and ordained into the Christian ministry, I have been and still remain committed to a lifetime of service to the cause of Christ.

My personal life and professional career have been spent as a Christian child, student, teacher, pastor, regional and national church leader, all under the umbrella of The Lutheran Church—Missouri Synod, a 162-year-old national church body with international relationships and foreign mission fields in nearly 100 countries throughout its history. I was born a Christian and, by God's grace, I will die a Christian.

The Good News of the Gospel of Jesus Christ has served as the guiding force in my life. I believe that the Bible's eternal truths provide direction for life. By the grace of God as revealed in the Bible, I am confident that my life on earth, which will someday end in death, will continue to exist in heaven for eternity. These simple beliefs are difficult for many to understand and accept. But for me and for billions of others who bear the name "Christian," the assurance of God's forgiving love, made real for mankind in Jesus Christ, the Son of God, provides a sense of peace that goes beyond all understanding.

It is no great secret that I am a sinful human being, painfully aware of my failures and shortcomings as a man, husband, father, grandfather, pastor, and national church body president. I need and invite the support, encouragement, constructive words of advice, and counsel from family, friends, pastors, and others in the church. Above all, I need the prayers of people in and beyond our church body that God would continue to bless my heartfelt endeavor to be a man of the Word, of prayer, of humility, strength, courage, wisdom, sensitivity, fairness, and love. That's what a church leader needs to be and what this church leader desires to be, by the grace and mercy of God.

Preface

The major purpose of this book is to communicate to whoever reads it something of importance regarding a church body that began in America more than a century and a half ago, that in many ways has had a glorious past, and that, like most other Christian church bodies in America, is faced with many challenges and opportunities in present times and in future years.

This endeavor to express the vision not only of a church president but also of the church body itself is to encourage you, the reader, to think creatively about how you as a Christian, whether Lutheran or other, can provide faithful leadership—both biblically based and culturally sensitive. For the purpose of your congregation and church body is making known the love of Christ to a world of people who daily face fear, uncertainty, doubt, abuse, distrust, condemnation, despair, depression, loss, grief, and many other of life's realities.

While this book makes frequent reference to God, Christ, the Bible, The Lutheran Church—Missouri Synod, and other Christian themes or principles, the observations regarding life, ministry, and vision for leadership articulated in the chapters that follow are applicable to an audience not limited to The Lutheran Church—Missouri Synod.

In the chapters that follow, I share what is on my mind and in my heart as I consider the past and look toward the future, specifically of our church body, but in a general way also of Christendom as a whole. Part of what I express may sound familiar to some, for I am in large measure a product of the experiences gained in life and leadership. Some of what is written has been conceptually articulated in speeches given and articles written during the eight years of my service as president of The Lutheran Church—Missouri Synod (LCMS). The rest represents my current thinking, recommendations, hopes, and dreams. All of what is written comes from my heart, from my love for the Lord and this church, and from nearly 40 years of ministry and leadership in the LCMS.

Someone once said a leader should enunciate his vision until he gets sick and tired of doing so, but if it's the right vision, he will never get sick and tired of saying it. I'm a long way from being tired of sharing the hopes and dreams I have for the LCMS. And I'm absolutely committed to helping our church body think creatively and plan strategically how best, under God's grace, to enable these hopes and dreams to become reality. As long as God gives me life and breath, health and strength, and as long as the opportunity is presented, I will look forward in the years ahead to continue doing so.

How the Christian Church addresses the needs and longings of people whose lives have been hugely affected by the changes that have occurred in the past 150 years, even the past 10 years, will mold and shape not only the lives of people in the church but also and especially the lives of people in our country and throughout the world. That is the topic of this book.

Before proceeding, I believe it is appropriate to address a few questions that might naturally occur to the reader.

Question: Why Is the President of a National Church Body Writing a Book?

Answer: For almost the entirety of my service as president of the LCMS, I have been encouraged by many to do so, including other leaders of our church and leaders of the publisher of this work,

Concordia Publishing House in St. Louis. I believe The Lutheran Church—Missouri Synod has much to offer the Christian Church at large, including other branches of Lutheran Christianity and society in general. From the unique perspective of a national church body president, I have been blessed by God with many opportunities and experiences I am privileged to share. In addition, a book is a vehicle in which information may be shared in a way that clarifies misunderstandings and refutes misinformation about many matters, including what this church body and its president believe, teach, and confess.

QUESTION: WHY WRITE A BOOK NOW?

Answer: Experience is a great, though often painful, teacher. Much has transpired both in the world and in the church since 2001, the year I began this portion of my life's journey. The event now known worldwide as "9/11" occurred three days after my initial installation as president of The Lutheran Church—Missouri Synod. Since that day, much has changed. We live in challenging times, characterized by anxiety, concern, uncertainty, fear, and worry on the part of many Christians and non-Christians alike. I pray that my contribution to bringing a measure of "the peace of God that passes all understanding" and my experiential perspectives on the role of the church in so doing will be helpful to all who read these words. My life and ministry have been tested in the crucible of nearly 40 years of ministry in various roles in the LCMS. I believe I have something worth saying.

QUESTION: WHAT IS THE AUDIENCE THIS BOOK INTENDS TO REACH?

Answer: It is my anticipation that pastors and other leaders of the church body I serve, The Lutheran Church—Missouri Synod, will have an interest in this offering. It is my hope that other leaders in the Christian Church at large who read these words will come to know something more about the LCMS and what we believe, teach, and confess than the inaccurate perceptions or misconceptions with which our church body is sometimes caricatured. We are not a fundamentalist sect but an integral yet unique part of the Holy Christian Church on earth. In addition, it is my prayer that any who read this book without the assurance of "life in all its fullness" will be led to read further, to dig deeper, and thus to discover the peace of God and peace with God, for which all humans have a natural longing, whether realized or not. We have been blessed as a church body in America for more than 160 years and thus have much to offer.

QUESTION: WHERE DOES THE TITLE *WAKING THE SLEEPING GIANT* COME FROM?

Answer: Over the years, Missouri Synod speakers have been fond of quoting a statement originally attributed to Billy Graham, who is alleged once upon a time to have called our Synod "a sleeping giant." Our church body has been in existence since 1847. In many respects, relatively speaking, we are large, strong, and laden with talent and purpose, and yet we don't seem to accomplish as much as we might. Like most mainline church bodies, over the past few decades, we have experienced a slow but steady decline in numbers of members of our 6,160 congregations. "The Sleeping Giant" is a description of someone or something fully capable of accomplishing much, though not until awakening. For many reasons I believe The Lutheran Church—Missouri Synod, a part of the Holy Christian Church, has been for many years, even decades, a sleeping giant. I further believe that this giant is awakening, taking more time in doing so than many of us would like, but awakening nonetheless.

Indeed, the sleeping giant shows many signs of awakening! As awakening occurs, the giant, like Washington Irving's Rip

Van Winkle, will be faced with discovering the changes that have occurred during slumber and will need to see these realities not only as challenges but also as opportunities. While demographics and a changing attitude in our country toward organized religion have contributed to declines and decreases, I have much hope for our church body. Many factors contribute to this hope, which some might consider fantasy, but which I firmly believe is very real. The giant has much potential for bringing hope, health, and wholeness to many.

The only other reference I have been able to find to "Sleeping Giant" is from Wikipedia—The Free Encyclopedia. Wikipedia cites both the 1970 film *Tora! Tora! Tora!* and the 2001 film *Pearl Harbor* as portraying Japanese Admiral Isoroku Yamamoto using the phrase in the aftermath of the December 7 attack when describing the reaction he feared from the United States. The historical accuracy of this quote is in doubt, and may have been the invention of the *Tora!* screenwriter, even though its sentiment is in line with what historians know of Yamamoto's views. Still, Yamamoto biographer Hiroyuki Agawa, in his book *The Reluctant Admiral*, has an account in which the admiral is said to have used the phrase "a sleeping enemy," also expressing concern that Japan had merely awakened an enemy that would return with a vengeance.

The Bible clearly describes our battle: "For we do not wrestle against flesh and blood, but against the rulers, against the authorities, against the cosmic powers over this present darkness, against the spiritual forces of evil in the heavenly places" (Ephesians 6:12).

With that description of our enemy, the image of an awakening sleeping giant, roused and angered by the attacks and schemes of the devil, is particularly apt. We are the ones who must rise to fight the enemy. That's what Paul encourages in these words: "*Finally, be strong in the Lord and in the strength of His might. Put on the whole armor of God, that you may be able to stand against the schemes of the devil*" (Ephesians 6:10–11).

Even more forcefully is this battle described in the words of Jesus:

> *Now when Jesus came into the district of Caesarea Philippi, He asked His disciples, "Who do people say that the Son of Man is?" And they said, "Some say John the Baptist, others say Elijah, and others Jeremiah or one of the prophets." He said to them, "But who do you say that I am?" Simon Peter replied, "You are the Christ, the Son of the living God." And Jesus answered him, "Blessed are you, Simon Bar-Jonah! For flesh and blood has not revealed this to you, but My Father who is in heaven. And I tell you, you are Peter, and on this rock I will build My church, and the gates of hell shall not prevail against it.*" (Matthew 16:13–18)

As we face the 21st century, these words from the Old Testament prophet Isaiah are more than significant for our church in making known Peter's confession of faith, proclaimed for centuries—a changeless Christ for a changing world:

> *Have you not known? Have you not heard? The Lord is the everlasting God, the Creator of the ends of the earth. He does not faint or grow weary; His understanding is unsearchable. He gives power to the faint, and strengthens the powerless. Even youths will faint and be weary, and the young will fall exhausted; but those who wait for the Lord shall renew their strength, they shall mount up with wings like eagles, they shall run and not be weary, they shall walk and not faint.* (Isaiah 40:28–31)

CHAPTER ONE

The Giant Is Born—Where We Came From and How We Got Here—The Identity and Formation of the LCMS

More than 170 years ago, hundreds of Lutheran men, women, and children left their homeland in eastern Germany, boarded five transatlantic ships, and made their way to a new land and a new life. En route, they faced serious challenges and had to overcome numerous difficulties. Many died of cholera or other communicable diseases. One ship was lost at sea, its passengers never heard from again.

They made the journey for various reasons. Many came to preserve their Lutheran doctrine, confessions, and practice. Others ran away from haunting indebtedness. Still others were troublemakers who couldn't get along with their own people in Germany. They all risked life and limb for the sake of seeking new liberty.

These Lutheran immigrants settled in several different parts of North America, including the Northeast, upper Midwest, Texas, and the central United States. They were hardy folks, faced with finding new homes, establishing new churches, learning a new language, developing new livelihoods. They are the ancestors of many of us in The Lutheran Church—Missouri Synod. We are familiar with their history of challenges and difficulties, both in life and in faith.

One group experienced significant conflict but emerged nevertheless as our fathers in the faith. Their journey began as a migration of conservative Lutherans from Saxony in 1839, led by a clergyman named Martin Stephan from Dresden. Two years earlier, Stephan had been removed from office because of allegations of impropriety.

After landing in New Orleans, these Saxon immigrants traveled up the Mississippi River to southeastern Missouri, where they appointed Stephan as their bishop and established a new settlement on about 4,500 acres in Perry County, Missouri. Before the end of their first year in Missouri, Bishop Stephan was again removed from office following accusations of immoral conduct. Without a spiritual leader, the settlers soon succumbed to conflict, particularly between their pastors and lay leaders. This controversy revolved around a theological dispute that threatened their colony and increased the difficulty of their lives.

Dr. Samuel H. Nafzger relates pertinent portions of their story in the May 2004 issue of *The Lutheran Witness*:

> After almost two years of arguing over troublesome questions (of church and ministry), the famous Altenburg debates of April 1841 brought some clarity. Several of the immigrants decided to return to Germany, but a young pastor by the name of C. F. W. Walther convinced the majority that the church was to be found wherever the Gospel was preached and the sacraments administered. Even though they had erred, despite the lack of a bishop, they were still

church, and they could and should get on with the work of the church in this new land.

Six years later, in April 1847, these Saxon immigrants joined with a number of pastors sent to America by Wilhelm Loehe in Bavaria to organize "The German Evangelical Lutheran Synod of Missouri, Ohio, and Other States." They deleted "German" from the name in 1917, and in 1947, on its centennial, the Synod officially shortened its name to "The Lutheran Church—Missouri Synod."

Since its founding in 1847, this church body has experienced ups and downs, highs and lows, growth and decline, conflict and peace. Throughout this time our church has maintained beliefs, teachings, and theological positions based on Holy Scripture, as understood by a group of mainly 16th-century writings collectively known as the Lutheran Confessions. Our Constitution articulates the basis of our theological understandings succinctly:

The Synod, and every member of the Synod, accepts without reservation:

1. The Scriptures of the Old and the New Testament as the written Word of God and the only rule and norm of faith and of practice;
2. All the Symbolical Books of the Evangelical Lutheran Church as a true and unadulterated statement and exposition of the Word of God, to wit: the three Ecumenical Creeds (the Apostles' Creed, the Nicene Creed, the Athanasian Creed), the Unaltered Augsburg Confession, the Apology of the Augsburg Confession, the Smalcald Articles, the Large Catechism of Luther, the Small Catechism of Luther, and the Formula of Concord.

Another document, "The Treatise on the Power and Primacy of the Pope," is not listed in the LCMS Constitution, but is included in the collection of writings known collectively as the Lutheran Confessions.

Sustaining the kind of proactive mission and ministry described in the pages that follow, while also maintaining doctrinal unity, has not been easy in the history of The Lutheran Church—Missouri Synod. Neither is it easy to do so today. At various times issues related to doctrine and practice continue to arise. Nevertheless, as will be addressed in another part of this book, The Lutheran Church—Missouri Synod enjoys a doctrinal unity that is the envy of many Christian churches in the world today.

Regarding mission and ministry, during its history, the LCMS has grown and developed into the 10th largest Protestant body in the United States. In many ways our Synod has been and continues to be a leader:

- **Our commitment to Holy Scripture and the Lutheran Confessions is foundational for mission and ministry.**
- **Our role in missions, theological education, and human care in the larger Lutheran community is a formidable force in worldwide Christian outreach.**
- **LCMS missionaries have been sent "to the ends of the earth" for more than 100 years.**
- **Mission work is currently being conducted in more than 80 countries around the world.**
- **Almost 30 sister or daughter churches have developed in connection with our Synod's mission endeavors.**
- ***The Lutheran Hour* and *This Is the Life* set the pace for religious broadcasting and television programming in America.**
- **Our system of parochial education is the largest among United States Protestant churches.**
- **Our system of higher education is the envy of many Christian church bodies.**

- **Our system of theological education is, in the eyes of many, second to none in Christendom.**
- **Our LCMS Foundation, Lutheran Church Extension Fund, and Concordia Plan Services have been great American success stories.**
- **Concordia Publishing House, which celebrated its 140th anniversary in 2009, continues as one of our nation's leading Christian publishers. Its latest major offering, *The Lutheran Study Bible*, is superb.**
- **The quality and commitment of our lay leaders are outstanding.**
- **Our demonstration of faith active in love through human care and world relief has reached millions of people in times of special need and natural or man-made disaster.**

A succinct overview of our church body by Dr. Samuel H. Nafzger, "An Introduction to The Lutheran Church—Missouri Synod," is included as Appendix A in the back of this book. It provides much basic and important information helpful in understanding the nature and theology of our Synod.

Notwithstanding the achievements and accomplishments of the past and the present, the LCMS faces significant challenges in the future, as do many other mainline American Christian churches. One of our greatest challenges is finding and maintaining the delicate balance between retaining the beliefs, teachings, and confessions with which our church began and to which it still subscribes, while avoiding becoming or even appearing sectarian in a climate and culture radically different from when our church was formed. That's the topic of another chapter.

Before moving in that direction, I need to address one more topic. A discussion of the origin and development of The Lutheran Church—Missouri Synod would not be complete without at least a brief reference to the doctrinal conflict of the 1970s. While many summaries exist, some fairly objective and concise and others described by neither of those words, the one from which I've chosen to share one paragraph (with a longer description in Appendix B) appears in *Heritage in Motion: Readings in the History of The Lutheran Church—Missouri Synod, 1962–1995* (CPH, 1998), edited by August R. Suelflow, former director of the Concordia Historical Institute.

> Crisis for the Synodical Higher Education System from Within: The Seminary-Synodical Conflict
>
> In the late 1960s there was a movement in the Missouri Synod to resist what some saw as liberalizing tendencies. The response of the conservatives was to rally behind the support of Dr. J. A. O. Preus II for President of Synod in 1969. This set the stage for the crisis that prevailed during much of the 1970s as Synod sought to reaffirm its belief in the verbal inspiration and inerrancy of Scripture and to condemn the aberrant use of higher criticism in the interpretation of Scripture. While the theological issues were an issue at other schools, such as the colleges at River Forest and Seward and the seminary at Springfield [Illinois], Concordia Seminary [St. Louis] under Dr. John H. Tietjen became the focal point of the controversy. By the time the dust settled in 1979, Synod had lost three percent of its congregations, and several District and college presidents had resigned. The seminary [in St. Louis], which had been nearly decimated, had rebounded beyond many people's expectations. In fact, one national news organization claimed that this was the first time a major American denomination had successfully reversed its liberalizing drift and returned to its traditional, conservative position.

While much more has elsewhere been said and could also here be added, suffice it to say that the events summarized above have left an indelible mark upon The Lutheran Church—Missouri Synod, both negative and positive. The negative is that congregations, families, and the Synod itself have lived with the pain of separation and division that resulted from the seminary walkout and everything connected with it. Trust at many levels was battered and bruised. Relationships were fractured and forsaken.

The positive is that a major national church body resisted the trend of other major church bodies to drift away from understanding the Holy Scriptures as the inspired, inerrant, infallible Word of God, and the only authoritative rule and norm of faith, life, and practice. We have carefully and intentionally built on a firm foundation—the Holy Scriptures—which are the only rule and norm of faith and practice. We continue to live with the pain of the past and to rejoice in the blessing God has bestowed upon our Synod's faithful honoring of His Holy Word.

CHAPTER TWO

The Giant Grows and Develops—Where We Stand and Why—What We Believe, Teach, and Confess

Many years ago, the church of my forefathers in Serbin, Texas, split. The children from the school at the newly formed St. Peter Lutheran Church, built only a literal "stone's throw away," and the children from the original St. Paul Lutheran Church expressed what they heard at home from their parents by throwing rocks across the cemetery at each other during recess. St. Peter later disbanded and went out of existence, the two churches reunited, and the unified congregation celebrated its 150th anniversary several years ago. Very few people alive today can recall what that controversy was really all about.

Rev. Michael Buchhorn, who at one time served as pastor of the Serbin congregation, recently wrote to me: "At some point, the things which divided them were not as important as what united them. . . . To me, it demonstrates that it is possible by the power of the Spirit (and in some cases the passage of time) to get past the divisiveness so that God-pleasing unity can be restored." This example is illustrative of the fact that, over the years, The Lutheran Church—Missouri Synod has developed a most unfortunate reputation in some circles for infighting and animosity toward one another.

Yet the fact remains that in its history there have been disagreements in the LCMS on significant matters of faith and life. That's because what a church body stands for and builds upon really does matter. Contending for the faith is not always easy and sometimes produces more heat than light.

What the LCMS believes, teaches, and confesses is what makes this church body the giant that it is. Giants are big and strong, able to conquer enemies that threaten their existence and way of life. Our Synod's historic focus on clearly communicating what comes from Holy Scripture and from Scripture alone, has contributed greatly to the foundation on which our congregations, and thus our national church body, are built.

Doctrinal and theological unity and/or division in the LCMS remain very important matters for the future of the Synod. As repeatedly stated, affirmed, and reaffirmed in its constitution, bylaws, doctrinal resolutions, and doctrinal statements, the LCMS believes, teaches, and confesses the following:

- **That there is only one true God, who has revealed Himself in Holy Scripture as the Triune God, Father, Son, and Holy Spirit.**
- **That this God created the world and everything in it in six days.**
- **That Adam and Eve, the first man and first woman, fell into sin by disobeying the command of God not to eat from the fruit of the tree of the knowledge of good and evil in the Garden of Eden.**
- **That since the fall of Adam and Eve into sin, all people are born with original sin and are altogether incapable of pleasing God by their own merits, works, or behavior.**
- **That God promised a Savior to Adam and Eve and, through them, to all people.**

- That this Savior is Jesus Christ, the only Son of God, through whom alone we receive forgiveness of sin, life, and salvation.
- That people who do not have faith in Jesus Christ as Lord and Savior will not spend eternity in heaven, but will experience eternal condemnation in hell.
- That Jesus died for the sins of the whole world.
- That only those who trust in His atoning death on the cross are saved eternally.
- That we are saved by God's grace alone, without any merit or worthiness of our own.
- That we are saved through faith in Christ alone, not by our own efforts, works, or endeavors.
- That the doctrine of justification by grace through faith in Christ is the doctrine on which the Church stands or falls.
- That Christians are called to proclaim to a lost and dying world the doctrine of justification, the good news that God was in Christ, reconciling the world unto Himself, not counting mankind's sins against them.
- That the Scriptures of the Old and the New Testaments are the written Word of God and the only rule and norm of faith and of practice.
- That the Bible is the inspired, inerrant, infallible, written Word of God in all its parts.
- That the Symbolical Books of the Evangelical Lutheran Church (also called the Lutheran Confessions) are a true and unadulterated statement and exposition of the Word of God.
- That all the miraculous accounts recorded in Holy Scripture actually occurred.
- That Jesus was conceived by the Holy Spirit and born of the Virgin Mary.
- That Jesus healed the lame, the deaf, and the blind, and raised the dead back to life.
- That Jesus was crucified, died, and was buried.
- That Jesus rose bodily from the grave and ascended into heaven.

- **That in, with, and under the bread and the wine of Holy Communion, we receive Christ's true body and blood for the forgiveness of sins and the assurance of eternal salvation.**
- **That abortion is not a moral option except as a tragically unavoidable by-product of medical procedures necessary to prevent the death of another human being, the mother.**
- **That homosexual behavior is contrary to the will of God and, therefore, intrinsically sinful.**
- **That marriage is a divine institution which binds one man and one woman together in a one-flesh union not to be broken until death parts them.**
- **That all baptized Christians are members of the priesthood of all believers.**
- **That church fellowship with other church bodies has as its basis complete agreement in doctrine and practice.**
- **That the Scriptures teach that while women are not to hold the pastoral office, they are, like men, to use all of their God-given gifts in service to the Lord and His Church.**
- **That Holy Communion, Holy Baptism, and the Word of God are the means through which God conveys to sinful human beings His grace—His undeserved love and forgiveness—and through which the Holy Spirit calls individuals to faith in Christ.**

While this list is not intended to include every doctrine of the Christian faith, the bullets above embrace the major theological and doctrinal positions of The Lutheran Church—Missouri Synod. These beliefs have made our church the theological giant it has been since its inception. This is what we believe, teach, and confess. With no apology or hesitation, I state here, as I have many times in the past, that this is what I believe, teach, and confess.

What I believe, teach, and confess today is the same as what I first learned at home from my father and mother, what was reinforced by my grandfathers and grandmothers, what I was taught in grade school and in confirmation classes at St. Matthew Lutheran Church in Houston, and what I have learned throughout my life since then, continuing through seminary graduation, as a parish pastor, district, and national Synod leader. My ordination vows, like those of all pastors of our church body, included the promise that, with God's help, I will remain faithful to Holy Scripture and the Lutheran Confessions. I have repeated that promise at each of the three services of installation I have experienced as the 12th president of The Lutheran Church—Missouri Synod. I gladly and freely made those promises, and I continue to pray daily for the strength to keep them faithfully. I believe these teachings and confessions not simply or solely because they are the positions of our Synod, but because I am personally persuaded and convinced that they are the correct teachings of Holy Scripture and are in accord with the Lutheran Confessions.

Our Synod is wonderfully and overwhelmingly united in these beliefs, enjoying a doctrinal unity unequaled in most parts of the Christian Church. Recently I spoke with a retired district president in our church body. He related a conversation he had with a former counterpart from another Christian denomination, who lamented, "In our church we have some people and pastors who still believe in creation, the virgin birth, the resurrection of Christ, and all that [nonsense]!" We in the LCMS simply are not arguing or even debating the major doctrines of the Christian faith so much in contention in other parts of Christendom. We are undeniably blessed with a God-given unity and harmony in confession that is unparalleled among the major denominational church bodies in the world today.

This biblical and confessional commitment has resulted in the growth and development of our Synod throughout much of its history, especially the first 125 years. The Synod has grown from its initial 14 congregations to 6,160 member congregations today. Beginning with the founding of a college and seminary early in its history, the Synod now owns and operates 10 colleges and universities and two seminaries across the nation.

The LCMS also provides many services and resources for its congregations and individual members through Lutheran Church Extension Fund, LCMS Foundation, Concordia Publishing House, Concordia Historical Institute, Concordia University System, and Concordia Plan Services. Many wonderful contributions have been made to the growth and development of the LCMS by the International Lutheran Laymen's League and Lutheran Women's Missionary League, our Synod's two wonderful auxiliaries.

Especially in recent years the LCMS has developed close relationships with a number of church bodies around the world. Known in our circles as "altar and pulpit fellowship," these relationships are determined on the basis of agreement in doctrine and practice. In other words, when, after lengthy and substantive theological dialogue, agreement is confirmed in what our church body and the other in question believe, teach, and confess, our national church convention declares the LCMS to be in church fellowship with the other church body, which declares the same with us. Currently, this relationship exists between the LCMS and 30 other church bodies around the world. Within this relationship, members and pastors of the church bodies in question may commune at the altar of our Lord in each other's congregations and preach in each other's pulpits, respectively.

On an irregular but increasingly frequent basis, relationships with other church bodies—some large and established, others small and emerging—are being explored. These relationships hold the promise of expanding the mission and godly influence of Lutheran

Christianity throughout the world. In countries where the Gospel has not been proclaimed and where churches do not exist, our Synod has a God-given mandate to send missionaries to begin the work. They are faced with barriers of all kinds—financial, cultural, linguistic, governmental, and racial, to name a few. Those barriers are largely nonexistent as the LCMS works with its partner churches in foreign countries, where those concerns are either absent or at least relatively minimal.

In sum, the strength of The Lutheran Church—Missouri Synod is directly connected to its biblical foundation. While sincerely endeavoring to preach and teach the truths of Holy Scripture, informed by the Lutheran Confessions, our Synod is simultaneously engaged in intentional mission work in many parts of the world. This combination of theology and mission is the hallmark of the LCMS. Indeed, over the years of its existence, the giant has grown and developed in remarkable ways! And, at least from my perspective, its most productive period is yet to come! But first the giant has some work to do and problems to solve.

CHAPTER THREE

The Giant Slumbers and Snores—What Has Caused Us to Become Non-Productive—Becoming Our Own Worst Enemy

A few years ago, a pastor friend of mine shared with me these reminders in an e-mail message:

Dear Jerry,

In church Sunday as I heard the words of Jesus' High Priestly prayer I was thinking about all the things that our Synod isn't fighting about and I was truly thankful. We aren't fighting about:

- **Gay Marriage or Gay Rights**
- **The Ordination of Homosexual Pastors**
- **Abortion**
- **The Holy Trinity**
- **The Doctrine of Christ**
- **The Inspiration of Scripture**

- **The Nature of the Gospel**
- **The Real Presence of Christ in the Sacrament**
- **The Historicity or Validity of the Resurrection**
- **The Third Use of the Law**
- **The Doctrine of the Church**
- **Predestination**
- **Creation**
- **Justification**
- **Sanctification**
- **Charismatic Issues**
- **The Descent of Christ into Hell**
- **The Apostles' Creed**
- **The Nicene Creed**
- **The Athanasian Creed**
- **And so much more!!!!!!!! You can add to the list.**

He's right. We have so much more that unites us than divides us! In the years of my service as president of The Lutheran Church—Missouri Synod, I have heard many in the Synod express their joy and thanksgiving to God for the doctrinal and theological unity which in many ways surpasses that of most other Christian Church bodies today. At the same time, I have heard others express their belief that the Synod is deeply divided doctrinally—concerns I do not take lightly.

Through the years, disagreements over matters of doctrine and practice have reared their ugly faces in our presence. It behooves us to acknowledge this reality, both in the past and in the present, thanking God for the resolution of past disagreements while working and praying for the same blessing in the present. Let's explore what causes the giant to sleep, which is not a problem in and of itself. Giants need proper rest. But when they snore, disturb others, awaken in a grouchy mood, are unable to get along with each other or with others, and are distracted from achieving the purpose for which they exist, remedial steps need to be taken. These are very important matters among us.

By virtue of their membership in the Synod, all members of the LCMS have stated their agreement that the writings of the Old and the New Testament are the written Word of God and, therefore, the only rule and norm of faith and practice. All members of the Synod have also publicly agreed that the writings in the Book of Concord are a correct exposition of the Holy Scriptures. The problems result from differing understandings or interpretations of Holy Scripture and/or the Lutheran Confessions.

Many are aware that there are matters about which we in the LCMS disagree. These realities necessarily precipitate questions like the following:

- **How united or divided is the LCMS?**
- **On what matters are we agreed?**
- **Conversely, on what matters do we disagree?**
- **Do the points of disagreement and division in our Synod deal with doctrinal matters or with matters of implementation of doctrinal principles?**
- **Are the divisions or disagreements that exist among us primarily matters of faith and practice, or are they for the most part differences of opinion in matters of *adiaphora*—matters neither commanded nor forbidden by Holy Scripture?**
- **Is the LCMS deeply divided theologically, or are our disagreements primarily related to the fact that for a variety**

of reasons some members of the Synod, prompted by the presence of a pesky political penchant and party spirit, have grown to dislike or distrust one another?

For the sake of fostering continued peace and greater harmony in our Synod, it seems pertinent and appropriate to review some of the most important and most recently discussed theological and practical disagreements in our Synod, matters on which total agreement does not exist among us. It is important that further dialogue about these matters continue to take place among the leaders of our Synod at every level. In the past several years that has been the purpose and focus of the national Synod theological convocations, which have been replicated in the 35 districts (regions) of the Synod. The purpose of these convocations is to promote and maintain unity of doctrine and practice throughout our national church body.

We must recognize the propensity of folks who come from a Germanic Lutheran heritage to be quite concerned about precision in theological formulations and keeping our beliefs from becoming diluted by influence from other Christians with whom we do not agree in theology and practice. In many ways this has been a genuine blessing for our Synod since its inception in 1847. Indeed, a strong concern for remaining true to our beliefs is critical for the future of our church body.

It should also be said that an improper balance between such concern and the necessary implementation of that concern in public proclamation of our beliefs could lead us down a path that ultimately leads to separatism and sectarianism. In addition, the genuine concern for doctrinal purity, together with a lack of clear communication between individuals and groups within our Synod who do not agree on matters theological, has the potential of diluting our focus on mission. In many ways our inward focus has become a preoccupation that has contributed to the sleepyheadedness the LCMS has experienced in the past four decades.

Challenges, struggles, and conflicts have been an integral part of our past, both distant and recent. Congregations and individuals in our Synod have disagreed, argued, and even fought over many issues, resulting in ecclesiastical division and family dissension.

Much of that disharmony has developed from doctrinal difficulties as our Synod has struggled with, among other issues, the important matters of being confessional without becoming sectarian and being in the world without being of the world. Other disagreements have been practical, namely, how our pure doctrine is to be applied in a rapidly changing world. And many of our struggles from yesteryear concern what appear today to be minor issues but which in the past were anything but minor. For example, in the LCMS:

- **It once was considered a lack of faith in God's providence to purchase life insurance.**
- **Membership in the Boy Scouts of America was not allowed.**
- **Lutheran musicians could not play the organ or other musical instruments in non-Lutheran weddings or funerals, and some were even excommunicated for doing so.**
- **Lutherans were not allowed to dance and were often chastised and excommunicated for doing so.**
- **Lutheran pastors and people were not allowed to pray with anyone, anytime, anywhere, outside our own church.**
- **Women were not allowed to sit in church together with men.**
- **Many congregations were in conflict over whether the pastor should continue to preach and teach in German or switch to English.**

Today most in our Synod view these practices from the past, staunchly defended on the basis of Holy Scripture at the time, as matters not specifically commanded or forbidden in Holy Scripture and thus matters of Christian freedom about which there is little, if any, current dissension.

However, serious doctrinal controversies—internal and external—have been instrumental in defining our Synod over the years. It is helpful to review a few of them to remind ourselves that we have always lived as part of the church militant.

- **There was doctrinal debate and controversy before the Synod was even organized. The Saxons who came to this country wrestled with the fundamental question, "Are we church or not?" It was not until the Altenburg Debates that they were able to answer that question, "Yes!" and move forward.**
- **In the early 1840s, there was sharp disagreement about the nature and authority of the pastoral office as it relates to the congregation. Significant schisms resulted.**
- **The Synodical Conference was fractured in 1872 over the doctrine of election. The Predestinarian Controversy resulted in both the Ohio Synod (1881) and the Norwegian Synod (1883) severing their relations with the Synodical Conference.**
- **In the 1940s, the LCMS rejected fellowship with the American Lutheran Church, exposing differences within the Missouri Synod itself. The so-called "Statement of the Forty-Four" raised concerns about the necessary basis for church fellowship and the role and function of extra-confessional doctrinal statements in the life of the church.**

- **Certainly, the most painful internal controversy in the Synod's history focused on the authority of Holy Scripture, polarizing much of the Synod during the 1960s and 1970s. A group of pastors and congregations left the Missouri Synod and formed the Association of Evangelical Lutheran Churches, one of the predecessor bodies of today's Evangelical Lutheran Church in America. This controversy was summarized briefly in chapter 1 of this book.**

These examples from the Synod's history remind us that there have been over the years of our existence theological and doctrinal disputes both inside the Synod and between the Synod and other bodies, generating fervent argument and resulting in bitter divisions and fractured fellowships. While most major considerations regarding these serious doctrinal issues are no longer in contention, we nevertheless continue to experience in our Synod disagreement and divisiveness on several issues. Most such issues have to do with the practical application of our doctrinal principles, notwithstanding the reality that some among us would say that it is impossible to separate doctrine and practice. Here are some matters about which we in the LCMS are not in agreement:

- **The administration of the Sacrament of Holy Communion—mainly the question of who should be allowed, invited, or even encouraged to commune at the altar of our Lord in LCMS congregations.**
- **The service of women—mainly the question of which roles and capacities Scripture allows or commends the participation and involvement of women in the church.**
- **Questions about proper forms of worship—mainly how much uniformity is necessary in the worship life of LCMS**

congregations and how much and what kind of diversity in forms of worship is acceptable.

- **Inter-Christian relationships—mainly the question of how to remain a biblical, confessional, evangelical, Lutheran, Christian church body boldly confessing the truth in love, while recognizing and relating to other Christians and Christian churches who are part of the Holy Christian Church, honoring our covenants of love to avoid unionism and syncretism.**
- **The respective roles of and relationships between clergy and laity.**

Congregations of our Synod in different places and at different times wrestle with one or more of these issues, which can become divisive, both within a congregation and in the broader church context. In the years ahead, our Synod will need to continue to work under Holy Scripture and the Lutheran Confessions to achieve similar solidarity in these matters on which we do not yet agree. Where Scripture speaks plainly and clearly to the question at hand, the matter is resolved. Where Scripture does not speak plainly, clearly, or at all to the question at hand, it behooves us as a group of rational, reasonable, mature, Christian people to come to a godly and common-sense conclusion regarding how to proceed with mutual respect and non-offensive conduct.

In the meantime, I believe it is prudent and appropriate for me as president of The Lutheran Church—Missouri Synod to address these concerns in this book. I will focus my comments about these matters primarily to the realm of reminding the reader what our Synod has said regarding them, referencing scriptural and confessional support, adding a few thoughts and suggestions of my own.

Admission to Holy Communion

One of the issues causing the greatest amount of disunity and division in The Lutheran Church—Missouri Synod concerns questions of admission to Holy Communion in our congregations.

There is little if any disagreement among us on our doctrinal articulation of the Lord's Supper as a sacramental gift of God's grace for repentant Christians wherein the body and blood of our Lord are truly present in, with, and under the bread and wine for the forgiveness of sin and assurance of life eternal. But there is in our midst a significant disagreement regarding policies of admission to Holy Communion, namely, who should be allowed, invited, or even encouraged to receive the Sacrament at the Altar in our LCMS congregations, campus ministries, and military chaplaincies.

This disagreement has resulted in no small amount of conflict and strife. At one end of the spectrum are those who hold that only "card-carrying members" of the LCMS should commune in our congregations. At the other end of the spectrum are those who allow and encourage to commune all who are baptized Christians, penitent sinners, believe in the real presence of the body and blood of Christ in the sacrament, and promise to amend their sinful lives—regardless of their church membership.

To illustrate this variety of approaches, I share here a few examples of Communion announcements that have come to my attention:

- **The Lord's Supper:**

In joyful obedience to the teaching of our Lord Jesus in Holy Scripture, it is the practice of the Evangelical Lutheran Church that Holy Communion be distributed only to members in good standing of The Lutheran Church—Missouri Synod or to those whose church is in full doctrinal unity with us. Visitors who for the above reasons are unable to attend, yet interested in one day partaking of the Holy Sacrament with us, are encouraged to talk to the pastor about instruction class. The body may be received by having the wafer placed directly in your mouth by the pastor or placed in your hand. The blood may be received from the individual cup or the common cup.

- **Communion Statement**

Today we celebrate the Sacrament of Holy Communion. Here our Heavenly Father promises anew His unconditional love, renews His pledge of forgiveness in Christ, and offers His Holy Spirit as strength for daily faith and life. You are invited to commune with us. However, since God reminds us that thoughtless or faithless reception of the Sacrament can incur His judgment (1 Corinthians 11:27–32), the Scriptures call those who commune to personally examine themselves and in their communing publicly confess:

- **I am a baptized Christian and I trust in Jesus Christ as my Lord and Savior.**
- **I am a sinner in need of God's forgiveness.**
- **I believe that Christ is truly present with His body and blood under bread and wine offering me forgiveness of sins, life, and salvation.**
- **I will live in the strength of the Holy Spirit to God's glory, in ministry with His people, in mission to His world.**

We trust that your communion with Christ and His people will strengthen your faith, increase your love, and empower your witness to Father, Son, and Holy Spirit. If you have questions about your communing, please speak with the Pastor. Children are invited to accompany parents to the altar for the blessing.

- **Holy Communion**

The Apostle Paul wrote, "A man ought to examine himself before he eats of the bread and drinks of the cup" (1 Corinthians 11:28 [NIV]). In order to examine yourself before attending the Lord's Supper, ask yourself the following questions:

1. Do I believe in the Triune God: Father, Son, and Holy Spirit?
2. Do I believe that I am a sinner, and am I sorry for my sins?
3. Do I believe that Jesus Christ, by His death, offers me forgiveness for all my sins?
4. Do I believe that I receive the body and blood of Christ in and with the bread and wine (not merely symbolically present)?
5. Do I desire to turn from my sinful ways?

If you are unable to answer "yes" to any of the above questions or feel as if further instruction is needed, please talk to a pastor or elder before communing, as participating without a proper understanding of Holy Communion can be spiritually harmful (see 1 Corinthians 11:27–29).

If you can answer "yes" to all of the above questions, then come with a repentant heart and join us in the reception of the Lord's Supper. Children who have not yet taken part in Communion instruction classes are invited to come forward for a blessing.

Bible Reference Passages to the Above Questions

1. Matthew 3:16–17; Matthew 28:19; John 1:1–14; Acts 5:3–4
2. Proverbs 28:13; Romans 3:23; 1 John 1:8–9
3. Romans 5:8; Colossians 2:13; Hebrews 9:28; 1 John 1:7
4. Matthew 26:26–28; 1 Corinthians 10:16; 1 Corinthians 11:24–25
5. Isaiah 1:16; John 8:11; Romans 6:12

Some of these announcements include a confession of the nature of the Sacrament itself and are generally consistent in describing the proper attitude toward the Sacrament and the beliefs required (notably that of a baptized, penitent believer in Christ who believes the body and blood of Christ are truly present in the Sacrament for the forgiveness of sins) for receiving the Sacrament. There is also in these Communion statements a certain inconsistency in the requirements and expectations of those who would approach the altar of the Lord, especially with regard to church membership and whether or not the prospective communicant has received instruction prior to communing. One of them would be considered by some in our Synod as being too inclusive regarding who is allowed to commune. Another one might be considered by others in our Synod as being too restrictive.

Let's look at what the LCMS in convention has said on this matter, based on the Synod's understanding of Scripture and the Lutheran Confessions.

In 1967, the Synod, affirming that "the celebration and reception of Holy Communion not only implies but is a confession of the unity of faith," summarized its historic position regarding "close Communion" by stating, "That pastors and congregations of The Lutheran Church—Missouri Synod, except in situations of emergency and in special cases of pastoral care, commune individuals of only those synods which are now in fellowship with us" (1967 Res. 2-19).

In Res. 3-01 of the 1981 convention, the Synod severed altar and pulpit fellowship with the American Lutheran Church (ALC), which was declared in 1969. This resolution states, in part:

> Whereas, the LCMS has long encouraged its congregations and pastors in extraordinary circumstances to provide responsible

> pastoral care, including the administration of Holy Communion to Christians who are members of denominations not in fellowship with the LCMS; therefore be it Resolved, That the LCMS recognize that its congregations and pastors, as circumstances warrant, may provide responsible pastoral care to individuals of the ALC.

The Synod's long-standing position has been reaffirmed on numerous occasions in recent decades. At its 1986 convention, for example, the Synod again declared, "That the pastors and congregations of The Lutheran Church—Missouri Synod continue to abide by the practice of close communion, which includes the necessity of exercising responsible pastoral care in extraordinary situations and circumstances" (Res. 3-08). Please note the word "necessity," which clearly indicates that "exercising responsible pastoral care in extraordinary situations and circumstances" is not an option, but a necessary responsibility.

At its 1995 convention, in Res. 3-08, the Synod affirmed this position, while adding that the pastors and congregations of the LCMS "beseech one another in love to remember that situations of emergency and special cases of pastoral care or extraordinary situations and circumstances are, by their nature, relatively rare."

In its 1999 report on "Admission to the Lord's Supper," the Synod's Commission on Theology and Church Relations reminds us on the basis of Scripture that admission to the Lord's Supper has a vertical dimension (relationship of the communicant and the Lord) and a horizontal dimension (relationship between and among communicants). Admission to the Sacrament involves not only worthy reception by the individual (vertical dimension), but also a unity in confession (horizontal dimension). Thus the Synod stated in 1986 that, in keeping with the principle of Christian love, "The practice of close communion seeks to prevent both harmful reception of the

Sacrament as well as a profession of unity in confession in faith where this unity does not exist" (Res. 3-08).

Unfortunately, issues of admittance to the Sacrament continue to be a point of tension among us, mainly due to differing interpretations of the phrases "responsible pastoral care" and "extraordinary situations and circumstances."

This wide variation in understanding what constitutes "extraordinary situations and circumstances," including the question of whether such situations ever occur, and what truly constitutes "responsible pastoral care" are major contributing factors to the dissension among us. The perspective often articulated in such discussions is that since the Sacrament is not necessary for salvation, what circumstance would constitute an "extraordinary situation"? Is it extraordinary or a "situation of emergency" when a visiting son or daughter who was confirmed in but is no longer a member of an LCMS congregation desires to commune with his or her mother at the mother's home congregation on Mother's Day, Christmas, or Easter? And, similarly, is it truly "responsible pastoral care" for a pastor to commune such a visitor?

Some pastors in our Synod will not administer Communion to such visitors, even when the visitors were baptized and confirmed in the congregation where they now desire to commune or are members of the pastor's own family, but are not currently members of an LCMS congregation. Other LCMS pastors and people view such a decision as unbiblical, unnecessary, unthinkable, offensive, or all of the above. At the same time, some pastors in our Synod interpret the terms "responsible pastoral care," "situations of emergency and special cases of pastoral care," and "extraordinary situations and circumstances" in a manner that might appear to be too broad or too generous.

Responsible practice of admission to the Sacrament avoids the two extremes, which are equally incorrect: opening LCMS altars to anyone who wants to commune, regardless of what that person believes, teaches, or confesses ("open communion"), or, conversely, closing LCMS altars to prospective communicants (including LCMS members) who are not members of the host congregation or who may be non-LCMS Christians in either an "extraordinary" or an "emergency" situation requiring the exercise of "responsible pastoral care."

The real challenge exists in the realm of pastoral or congregational decisions regarding admission to the Lord's Supper in circumstances that lie somewhere between these two extremes. The fact is that one cannot nail down or clearly categorize every possible occasion that calls for a "responsible pastoral care" decision or every instance that constitutes an "extraordinary" situation or circumstance. The Synod's position recognizes this, but some in our midst do not. Herein lies one source of friction, along with that generated at the opposite extremes of this matter as noted above.

I submit that the primary responsibility of the host pastor and congregation is to communicate to worshipers and prospective communicants in every way possible, teaching and instructing verbally and in written format the biblical truth concerning what Scripture says about who Jesus is, what He has done, and what is occurring at the altar of the Lord and the Communion rail of the church. This should include the clearly stated (1 Corinthians 11: 28) responsibility of the prospective communicant to examine himself or herself, thus placing the principal burden of this decision upon the prospective communicant—while, of course, not removing or discounting the serious responsibility that pastors, as "stewards of the mysteries of Christ," bear in this regard.

There is a continuing need for consistency in practice in the Synod in keeping with our declared commitments to Holy Scripture and the Lutheran Confessions and in accord with our Synod's declaration that "the contemporary application of our historic position necessitates continued practical guidance for the faithful administration of the Sacrament" (2007 Res. 3-09). This has implications for the spiritual life and health of those to whom Jesus is speaking in these words: *"Come to Me, all who labor and are heavy laden, and I will give you rest. Take My yoke upon you, and learn from Me, for I am gentle and lowly in heart, and you will find rest for your souls. For My yoke is easy, and My burden is light"* (Matthew 11:28–30) and *"I am the bread of life; whoever comes to Me shall not hunger, and whoever believes in Me shall never thirst. But I said to you that you have seen Me and yet do not believe. All that the Father gives Me will come to Me, and whoever comes to Me I will never cast out"* (John 6:35–37).

My brothers and sisters in Christ, we must be very careful in the administration of this Holy Sacrament. We certainly must not "cast pearls before swine" (Matthew 7:6 NKJV). We must also constantly consider and always recognize that it is a means of God's grace in the lives of repentant sinners, not a reward to be given or withheld for reasons that go beyond the clear teaching of Holy Scripture. We believe, teach, and confess that the Spirit works, whenever and wherever He chooses, through the means of grace. Our task ultimately is not to keep people away from the means of grace, but to connect people to those means, faithfully bringing people into contact with God's Word and Sacraments.

As a starting point for the kind of serious study and prayerful reflection necessary for godly consensus on this matter, I humbly and respectfully recommend that we begin our conversation on the basis of 1995 Convention Resolution 3-08:

> Resolved, That the Communion Card statement of the Commission on Theology and Church Relations be recommended to the member congregations of Synod for guidance:
>
> "The Lord's Supper is celebrated at this congregation in the confession and glad confidence that, as He says, our Lord gives into our mouths not only bread and wine but His very body and blood to eat and to drink for the forgiveness of sins and to strengthen our union with Him and with one another. Our Lord invites to His table those who trust in His words, repent of all sin, and set aside any refusal to forgive and love as He forgives and loves us, that they may show forth His death until He comes.
>
> Because those who eat and drink our Lord's body and blood unworthily do so to their great harm and because Holy Communion is a confession of the faith which is confessed at this altar, any who are not yet instructed, in doubt, or who hold a confession differing from that of this congregation and The Lutheran Church—Missouri Synod, and yet desire to receive the Sacrament, are asked first to speak with the Pastor or an usher. For further study, see Matt. 5:23, ff.; 10:32ff; 18:15–35; 26:26–29; 1 Cor. 11:17–34.

For a collection of selected pertinent references to the Sacrament of Holy Communion from the Lutheran Confessions, please see Appendix C.

The Service of Women in the Church

Another matter on which agreement in our Synod has not yet been achieved is the role of women in the church. This disagreement is manifested in numerous ways. Some pastors and congregations believe the Scriptures do not allow women to vote in congregational assemblies or serve in any capacity other than as a worship service participant or one who performs acts of love and kindness (mostly culinary in nature) at times of congregational gatherings, bereavements, weddings, and anniversaries.

Other pastors and congregations believe the Scriptures do not specifically address and thus do not forbid women's involvement in offices or functions of the congregation, since there is no mention in Scripture of a voters' assembly or congregational offices other than deacon, elder, and overseer. There also are some cases—not a large number—of congregations and pastors who believe women should be allowed to occupy the pastoral office. This perspective is based on their contention that there is an absence of clear passages in Scripture that address that topic unequivocally. This argument is offered notwithstanding numerous references from Holy Scripture that our Synod has long understood to forbid women from holding the pastoral office.

Since 1969, our Synod has expressed its collective belief on the teaching of Holy Scripture, allowing women to vote and hold congregational offices, but not to occupy the pastoral office. Still, some in our Synod would severely restrict the involvement of women in the church at many levels, while others would favor no restrictions at all. Let's take a look at what the Synod said in 1969, and since then, in its official resolutions regarding the role and service of women in the church.

- **Woman Suffrage**

In 1969 Res. 2-17 "To Grant Woman Suffrage and Board Membership" the Synod first declared:

> Those statements of Scripture which direct women to keep silent in the church and which prohibit them to teach and to exercise authority over men, we understand to mean that women ought not

> to hold the pastoral office or serve in any other capacity involving the distinctive functions of this office.

The Synod further declared: "We hold [likewise] that Scripture does not prohibit women from exercising the franchise."

At subsequent conventions of the Synod this position has been repeatedly affirmed, including at the 1995 convention in Res. 3-05, in which it is noted that woman suffrage lies in the realm of Christian freedom. That is, congregations are free to adopt, or not adopt, the practice.

Recognizing the sensitivity of the issue of woman suffrage in the Synod, the Synod urged in 1969 "that in the implementation of any changes in this area of women's ministry in the church . . . cautious and deliberate action in the spirit of Christian love" should be exercised. The Synod has also recognized that though woman suffrage is in the realm of Christian liberty, congregations may disagree regarding the expediency of the practice in their situation. It has urged mutual respect, "so that our walk together may continue in harmony and that we 'maintain the unity of the Spirit in the bond of peace' (Eph. 4:3)" (1986 Res. 3-09).

For a brief discussion on woman suffrage, see the CTCR's 1985 report *Women in the Church: Scriptural Principles and Ecclesial Practice* (Section III, C), in which the Commission reaffirmed the Synod's position.

- **Utilization of the Gifts of Women in the Church**

Recognizing that God has bestowed unique gifts "upon both men and women of the church, the priesthood of believers," and that "the Synod has not yet utilized the service of women to the fullest extent in the life and work of the church," the Synod in 1989 adopted Res. 3-04A, "To Encourage Services of Women," which states in part: "That the Synod recognize with thanksgiving all of God's gifts to His church, in particular the gift of people" and "That the Synod encourage Districts and congregations to make full appropriate use of the ministry and service of women."

In two additional resolutions the Synod has expressly affirmed that women and men are equally members of the priesthood of all believers by faith in Jesus Christ. Yet, the Synod also has recognized that "women have not always been accorded the opportunity to give full expression to their privileges and responsibilities as members of the priesthood of all believers" (1992 Res. 3-04).

The Synod has recommended specific actions to encourage greater use of women's gifts. For example, the 1989 convention encouraged every district "to establish a Commission on Women or provide other vehicles for the purpose of (1) sharing resources for the ministry of women; (2) encouraging women to recognize and accept their responsibility for what the church teaches; (3) identifying existing and further ministries ready for their qualified and joyful service; and (4) calling attention to the eagerness and desire of the women of the church to share their gifts" (Res. 3-04A).

The CTCR's 1994 report on *The Service of Women in Congregational and Synodical Offices*—whose conclusions have been affirmed by the 2004 Synod convention—begins as follows:

> The Scriptures without qualification affirm that all believing Christians, both men and women, are priests of God (1 Peter 2:9; Rev. 1:6). Through Baptism God has made them all, equally and without distinctions of importance or value, members of the one body of Christ (1 Cor. 12:12–13; Gal. 3:27–28; Rom. 12:5). No one is baptized to be either man or woman. To the members of the "royal priesthood" (1 Peter 2:9) of believers belong all of the rights, privileges and responsibilities which Christ has given

to His church on earth (1 Cor. 3:21, 22; Matt. 16:13–19; 18:17–20; John 20:22, 23; Matt. 28:18–20; 1 Cor. 11:23–25; Treatise 23). (7)

These are important affirmations of the joyful and capable service that women are able to contribute to God's Church on earth, all to His glory.

- **Ordination of Women**

As stated above, the 1969 decision of the Synod to grant woman suffrage also summarized the Synod's historic position on the ordination of women, that "Those statements of Scripture which direct women to keep silent in the church and which prohibit them to teach and to exercise authority over men, we understand to mean that women ought not to hold the pastoral office or serve in any other capacity involving the distinctive functions of this office."

With specific reference to this statement, the Synod has reaffirmed its position on this issue at five of its conventions:

- **1971 Res. 2-04: "To Withhold Ordination of Women to the Pastoral Office"**
- **1977 Res. 3-15: "To Reaffirm the Synod's Position on Women with Reference to the Pastoral Office"**
- **1986 Res. 3-09: "To Reaffirm Position of LCMS on Service of Women in the Church"**
- **1986 Res. 3-10: "To Reaffirm Position of Synod on Ordination of Women"**
- **1989 Res. 3-13A: "To Study and Clarify Services of Women in Congregational and Synodical Offices"**
- **1998 Res. 3-25A: "To Affirm Position of Synod That Only Men May Hold the Pastoral Office"**

In *A Statement of Scriptural and Confessional Principles*, adopted as an official doctrinal statement of the Synod in 1973, the Synod referred to the issue of women's ordination (IV. Holy Scripture, C. The Gospel and Holy Scripture). The Synod rejected as a distortion of the relationship between the Gospel and the Bible the following:

> That the Gospel rather than Scripture, is the norm for appraising and judging all doctrines and teachers (as, for example, when a decision on the permissibility of ordaining women into the pastoral office is made on the basis of the "Gospel" rather than on the teaching of Scripture as such).

With respect to the role of women in general, the Synod in that same document (IV. Holy Scripture, F. The Infallibility of Scripture) rejected the following view:

> That the Biblical authors accommodated themselves to using and repeating as true the erroneous notions of their day (for example, the claim that Paul's statements on the role of women in the church are not binding today because they are the culturally conditioned result of the apostle's sharing the views of contemporary Judaism as a child of his time).

- **The Service of Women in Congregational and Synodical Offices**

At its 1989 convention the Synod asked the CTCR, in consultation with the Council of Presidents, to prepare "a study on the eligibility of women for service in all offices of the congregation, including that of chairman, vice-chairman, and elder, and District and synodical boards and commissions" (Res. 3-13A). In 1994, the CTCR completed a study titled "The Service of Women in Congregational and Synodical Offices." At its 2004 convention the Synod adopted Res. 3-08A "To Affirm the Conclusions of the 1994 Report: The Service of Women in Congregational and Synodical Offices." The Synod's position is summarized in this "Resolved":

> That the Synod affirm that women on the basis of the clear teaching of Scripture may not serve in the office of pastor* nor exercise any of its distinctive functions, and that women may serve in humanly established offices in the church as long as the functions of these offices do not make them eligible to carry out "official functions [that] would involve public accountability for the function of the pastoral office."
>
> *The Synod holds that the office of pastor is a divinely instituted office.

Other resolutions of significance regarding this matter include:

- **1989 Res. 3-13A: "To Study and Clarify Services of Women in Congregational and Synodical Offices"**
- **1992 Res. 3-05: "To Urge Completion of Study on Service of Women in All Congregational Offices"**
- **1995 Res. 3-06A: "To Continue to Study The Service of Women in Congregational and Synodical Offices in Light of "Dissenting Report" and Other Ongoing Studies by the CTCR on the Role of Women in the Church"**
- **2004 Res. 3-08A: "To Affirm the Conclusions of the 1994 Report: The Service of Women in Congregational and Synodical Offices."**

Following the 2004 convention action (Res. 3-08A), discussion has taken place regarding the Synod's position on the service of women, particularly in congregational offices. Some in the Synod have argued that what Scripture teaches regarding the order of creation prohibits women from holding any and all offices in the church involving the exercising of authority over a man. In its 2006 report titled Response to Expressions of Dissent (2004–2006) the CTCR offered the following clarifying statement:

> If the position descriptions for [humanly instituted offices] call upon women to carry out distinctive pastoral functions, then . . . women may not serve in such offices—because this is what Scripture clearly teaches about the implications of the order of creation for such service. Underlying the Synod's position is not only an affirmation of the order of creation, but a deliberate effort to say no more and no less than what Scripture alone says regarding the implications of the order of creation for the service of women in the church.

For the full discussion regarding this statement, see the CTCR's 1994 report and accompanying "Guidelines for Congregations" prepared by a Task Force appointed by the president of the Synod.

- **Women Serving Holy Communion**

Noting that "there is divergence of opinion in the Synod concerning women serving as assistants in the distribution of Holy Communion," the Synod in 1989 Res. 3-10 "To Address Practice of Women Serving Holy Communion" called attention to the following counsel given by the Commission on Theology and Church Relations in its 1983 report *Theology and Practice of the Lord's Supper* (p. 30) and reaffirmed in its 1985 report *Women in the Church*:

> the commission strongly recommends that to avoid confusion regarding the office of the public ministry and to avoid giving offense to the church, such assistance be limited to men. (p. 47)

The Synod then resolved: "That the pastors and congregations of the Synod be urged to conform their practices to this counsel."

The CTCR's 1985 report on *Women in the Church*, when discussing "practical applications" regarding the role of women in the church, contains the reminder that in applying biblical principles regarding the service of women "one must bear in mind that the New Testament presents no ceremonial law regulating the details of public worship," and this is true specifically also of the distribution of the Sacrament. No New Testament text addresses details regarding the distribution of the Sacrament. The Scriptures do speak about the divinely instituted office of the public ministry, however, and require the church to honor and uphold this unique office. In light of these considerations, the CTCR's counsel (quoted above) refrains from citing a clear biblical prohibition against women assisting in the distribution. But because the public administration of the Sacrament is regarded as a specific function of the pastoral office, the CTCR advises that assistance in the distribution be limited to men to avoid giving offense to the church in this area. See the CTCR's two reports *Theology and Practice of the Lord's Supper* and *Admission to the Lord's Supper*.

- **Summary of the Service of Women in the Church**

On the basis of my observation and experience, the women in the LCMS are wonderful Christian people who love the Lord deeply and care for His Church sincerely. Most LCMS women do not desire to be pastors. Some who have felt strongly about doing so have left the LCMS and joined other church bodies where they could become pastors. LCMS women do have a strong desire and need to serve in capacities beyond the very important services of providing meals for congregational members in need or grief, or of being members and leaders of a local, regional, or national women's organization.

The real concern I have observed is that there are instances where women are treated with disrespect and have not been allowed to serve in roles that utilize their God-given gifts in meaningful ways. For example, most regrettably, it has been reported to me that some women have been told by their pastors that they may not enter the chancel area of their church building, even to prepare the elements of Holy Communion. Some women are not even allowed as members of the altar guild to touch the elements of the Sacrament. In some congregations women are not permitted to teach a Bible class when men are present. And the list goes on.

While I truly hope and believe that such examples are exceptions rather than the rule, they demonstrate the presence, at least in some places, of an unhealthy attitude toward women and an improper understanding of the positions of our Synod regarding the service of women in the church. The Synod in convention has taken the steps necessary to honor the gifts of women and to encourage those gifts to be used in appropriate ways. You or I may not fully agree with the decisions made by the delegates to these conventions. Nevertheless, unless and until the official positions of the Synod regarding the service of women in the church are amended or rescinded, these positions are to be honored and upheld.

I thank God for the women of The Lutheran Church—Missouri Synod and pray that their godly service will continue to be a blessing to our Synod and to the world we are called to reach with the Gospel of Christ.

Questions about Proper Forms of Worship

Throughout the years of service to the church at large, my wife, Terry, and I have attended worship services in many congregations of our Synod. Some of the forms of worship employed are highly liturgical, frequently described as services with "smells and bells." These "traditional" or "liturgical" services may well include liturgy from one of the hymnals produced by the LCMS, chanting by the pastor or other worship leader, classical music provided by organ and a variety of other musical instruments, and special liturgical vestments, including chasuble, worn by the clergy, and even the use of incense.

Liturgical worship is the form of worship I was raised in and which I employed throughout my years of parish ministry. I have never worn a miter, carried a crosier, or swung an incense pot. Yet I have great respect for formal, liturgical, traditional worship. I have also experienced some very spiritual, biblical, and Christocentric worship services that could only be characterized as non-traditional or contemporary in style. Unfortunately, I have also attended some services, both traditional and non-traditional, that have left much to be desired in content and conduct.

Many congregations in the LCMS offer a variety of worship experiences, including especially those with multiple worship opportunities each week. In quite a few of these cases, the "blended" or "contemporary" services may vary widely. Most involve musicians who play guitar, drums, violin, keyboard, and other instruments, along with a "praise team" of congregational members who lead the congregation in contemporary songs of worship. The pastor might or might not be robed and leads an order of worship consisting primarily of singing, Scripture reading, homily, and prayer. The Sacrament of Holy Communion is sometimes, but not always, offered. The confession and absolution, ecumenical creed, and Lord's Prayer are often, but not always, a part of the service. Casual, even informal attire is often worn by worshipers, who include people of all ages.

Many pastors have testified that members of their congregations are much more likely to invite non-churched friends and family members to the more informal services rather than the traditional services. When asked why this is so, they reply that the non-traditional services generally tend to be more informal, thus providing natural opportunity for visitors to feel more comfortable than is often the case in a formal, more liturgical service. They also indicate that the overwhelming majority of new members are first introduced to the congregation through the informal, blended, or contemporary services rather than through the traditional, formal services of worship.

Disagreement exists in our Synod on whether certain contemporary worship expressions employ doctrinally pure resources faithfully and whether certain traditional worship expressions do so meaningfully and effectively. Some pastors and congregations believe that congregations of our Synod should use nothing other than worship forms and hymns contained in one of the hymnals produced and published under the auspices of our Synod. Others believe that doctrinally pure material and formats for worship and singing are contained in other worship resources and may be properly used in services of worship in LCMS congregations.

One of the conditions of membership in the Synod is "Exclusive use of doctrinally pure agenda, hymnbooks, and catechisms in church and school" (LCMS Constitution, Article VI). Strictly speaking, this means simply but significantly that congregations and ministers of the Gospel who are members of the Synod should not use agendas, hymnbooks, and catechisms that are not doctrinally pure. Again, strictly speaking, this condition of membership does not limit members and congregations of the Synod to use only materials published by or under the auspices of the Synod, since materials published by other sources might also very well be doctrinally pure; for example, songs or hymns consisting exclusively of direct quotations from Holy Scripture.

Our Synod has encouraged its congregations to give their "worship life . . . the highest priority" and has urged that "all worship (liturgies, sermons, songs, prayers, etc.) conducted within the Synod . . .

1. be Christ-centered and not human-centered;
2. distinguish properly between Law and Gospel;
3. emphasize the Gospel of Christ's forgiveness; and
4. be faithful to the Word of God and in harmony with our Lutheran Confessions" (1992 Res. 2-02).

Other resolutions adopted by the Synod in convention refer to an "Objective" of the Synod listed in its Constitution that deals with worship practice: "Encourage congregations to strive for uniformity in church practice, but also to develop an appreciation of a variety of responsible practices and customs which are in harmony with our common profession of faith" (LCMS Constitution, Article III). Within all these parameters, pastors and other worship leaders do well to approach their task with great care that those who gather in worship are cognizant of God's presence among them in Word and Sacrament, and that the elements of the worship service result in the strengthening of faith and assurance of forgiveness, life, and salvation through the merits of Jesus Christ, our Lord and Savior.

From 2007 to 2009 the Synod's Council of Presidents studied the theology and practice of worship in our congregations and expressed its conclusions and counsel in a document titled "Theses of Worship." The reader may find this work helpful.

It is important to note that the Synod in convention in 2004 adopted Res. 2-04:

> To Affirm Responsible Use of Freedom in Worship
>
> WHEREAS, God is extravagantly rich in His grace (SA III, 4) and through His means of grace grants His gifts of forgiveness, life, and salvation; and
>
> WHEREAS, God has granted us freedom in the Gospel; and
>
> WHEREAS, Our Lutheran Confessions recognize that human rites and ceremonies are not necessary for salvation and yet at the same time acknowledge the usefulness of these rites, especially insofar as they promote good order and tranquility in the church (AC VII, 2-3; XXVIII, 55–56; AP VII/VIII, 33; XV, 51; FC SD X 5–9); and

WHEREAS, Our Synod's Constitution recognizes these twin poles of freedom and responsibility and encourages "congregations to strive for uniformity in church practice, but also to develop an appreciation of a variety of responsible practices and customs which are in harmony with our common profession of faith" (Art. III, 7); and

WHEREAS, There are diverse viewpoints in our Synod concerning what is appropriate and salutary in corporate worship; therefore be it

Resolved, That the Synod, in convention, affirm respect for diversity in worship practices as we build greater understanding of our theology of worship and foster further discussion of worship practices that are consistent with that theology; and be it further

Resolved, That we encourage pastors, musicians, and worship leaders to exercise this freedom responsibly, using resources such as *Text, Music, Context: A Resource for Reviewing Worship Materials* to assess worship materials; and be it finally

Resolved, That the Commission on Worship initiate a process leading toward the development of diverse worship resources for use in The Lutheran Church—Missouri Synod.

Finally, Holy Scripture is quite clear about this matter, at least regarding the use of a variety of musical instruments in worship, in passages such as Psalm 150:

> Praise the Lord! Praise God in His sanctuary; praise Him in His mighty heavens!
>
> Praise Him for his mighty deeds; praise Him according to His excellent greatness!
>
> Praise Him with trumpet sound; praise Him with lute and harp!

Praise Him with tambourine and dance; praise Him with strings and pipe!

Praise Him with sounding cymbals; praise Him with loud clashing cymbals!

Let everything that has breath praise the LORD! Praise the LORD!

INTER-CHRISTIAN RELATIONSHIPS

In our Synod we have differing understandings of how to relate to Christians in other church bodies who, though members of the Holy Christian Church, hold beliefs different from our own. A very important question is how our Synod can remain a confessional, evangelical, Lutheran church while recognizing that we are not the only members of the Body of Christ.

Quite vivid is my recollection of a meeting my wife, Terry, and I attended in Arizona, shortly after my assuming the office of president of the Synod. The meeting involved leaders and representatives of the three largest Lutheran bodies in the United States. At the opening banquet, after introducing the elected leaders of the three church bodies and their spouses and outlining the program for the evening, the master of ceremonies said, "Before our meal we will now observe a moment of silence."

At the time, I was aware of the reticence of one of the church bodies in question to pray with people from church bodies with whom that particular church body was (and still is) not in altar and pulpit fellowship. Nevertheless, I thought it odd that "a moment of silence" would be called for, rather than at least a moment of silent prayer.

The moment was even more remarkably incongruent in light of the fact that another of the church bodies represented at the banquet had already established full church body fellowship with a number of churches beyond the realm of Lutheranism *per se.* So in the midst of this wide, even gigantic chasm between the two church bodies just now described, those of us from the LCMS observed not only a moment of silence but also a moment of silent prayer.

This vignette demonstrates at least some of the challenges we face in the LCMS regarding how we relate to other Christians. On the one hand, we confess in the Apostles' Creed: "I believe in the Holy Christian Church, the communion of saints . . . " We also confess in the Nicene Creed: "I believe in one, holy, Christian, and apostolic church . . . " In both creedal statements we acknowledge the existence of Christians in other expressions of the Body of Christ than our own. The Augsburg Confession states that the church is "the assembly of all believers among whom the gospel is purely preached and the holy sacraments are administered according to the gospel" (VII, 1). Above all, St. Paul writes in his letter to the Ephesians: *"There is one body and one Spirit—just as you were called to the one hope that belongs to your call—one Lord, one faith, one baptism, one God and Father of all, who is over all and through all and in all"* (Ephesians 4:4–6).

Despite all the external divisions in contemporary Christendom, we Lutheran Christians believe that there is, properly speaking, only one Church in heaven and on earth. Yet there remain significant differences in the whole body of doctrine believed, taught, and confessed by individual church bodies within the Body of Christ. As confessing Christians whose body of doctrine we believe to be in accord with Holy Scripture as interpreted by the Lutheran Confessions, we dare not remain silent regarding matters of doctrinal difference with other Christian churches. At the same time, we have an obligation to "speak the truth in love" regarding these differences. The main questions are how, when, where, and under what circumstances dare we speak that truth in love. Conversely, under what circumstances do we decide not to speak at all, primarily by not participating in any way with those we consider "heterodox"?

Historically, the LCMS has said that membership in our Synod requires "renunciation of unionism and syncretism of every description, such as serving congregations of mixed confession, as such, by ministers of the church; taking part in the services and sacramental rites of heterodox congregations or of congregations of mixed confession; and participating in heterodox tract and missionary activities" (LCMS Constitution, Article VI, Conditions of Membership). In certain cases, interpreting and applying these requirements can be somewhat challenging.

To some, these requirements have the appearance of sectarianism and communicate the wrong message to Christians from other denominations. To others, participating in any way, shape, or form with non-LCMS Christians communicates to the observer that there is no difference between us and them and thus constitutes a denial of what we believe, teach, and confess about matters of doctrine and practice on which we disagree with the church body in question.

This is nothing new. Dr. Samuel H. Nafzger, in his article "Syncretism and Unionism" in the July 2003 issue of *Concordia Journal*, recounts a portion of our Synod's early history that indicates the way our church's founders dealt with this very topic and how we face these same challenges today:

> When Walther and the Saxons came to America, they did not encounter Germany's territorial churches, though the kinds of people they met were not much different. Their primary church-relations encounters were with Reformed Christians and with American revivalists. It is interesting to read how the Saxons related to the Reformed congregations in their area, suggesting

that in the absence of a Lutheran pastor, the members of their congregation in St. Louis might ask Pastor Wall, the pastor of the Union Church, to perform their Baptisms.

But the field of inter-Christian relationships has become considerably more complex for the typical Missouri Synod pastor at the beginning of the twenty-first century. Not only has there been a proliferation of religious groups, both Christian and non-Christian, but this has been accompanied by incredible changes in the culture and society in which we live, brought on by increased mobility, intermarrying, and the advent of the Internet and the Information Age. Syncretism and its inevitable result—relativism—are in the very air we breathe.

Though our fathers and grandfathers could advise their members to avoid the sectarians, such advice is no longer possible today. Today we are drowning in information, and as a result, many people have retreated into a sound-byte/bumper-sticker approach to things metaphysical.

The end result of these developments is a galloping individualism, an impatience with "abstract" concepts such as the corporate nature of the church, a retreat into a reliance on subjective experience, a loss of loyalty to institutions (a desire to be "believers" but not "belongers" mentality), and a pick-and-choose approach to what one believes about things religious, a phenomenon sometimes referred to as "Cafeteria Catholicism." Is it any wonder that our people and our pastors often find it difficult to understand the LCMS's position on closed communion and church fellowship, positions that our society regards at best as unfriendly and aloof, and at worst as incredibly sectarian and unchristian?

A number of years ago when I served as president of the Texas District of The Lutheran Church—Missouri Synod, I participated in a pastors' conference in the west Texas town of Midland. One of the speakers was the pastor of the Nazarene Church in Big Spring, 40 miles northeast of Midland. In the course of his presentation, this pastor told the story of a severe drought in that part of Texas a few years earlier. The local ministerial alliance had decided to hold a service of prayer for rain, to which all Christians in the community would be invited. Our local LCMS pastor in Big Spring, aware of the constitutional conditions of membership referenced above and of other articulations of this position in various resolutions of the Synod, respectfully and regretfully declined to participate in the service of prayer for rain and advised the members of his congregation not to attend the event.

When the Nazarene pastor concluded his story, one of the LCMS pastors in attendance at the conference asked the question, "What did your people think was the reason our LCMS pastor and his people did not participate in the service of prayer for rain?" The Nazarene pastor replied, "My people and I thought the reason they did not participate was because they didn't give a damn about the drought or its impact on our community!" When our local LCMS pastor heard that answer, he was crushed. He had lived in the Big Spring community for 25 years and was a very visible and active community leader who cared very much for his community. To hear the perception that he and his people did not care about the impact of a drought on the community and its citizens was a devastating experience.

Another illustration in my experience as president of the Texas District occurred when an ordained member of my staff came to me a few months prior to the high school graduation of one of his children. Knowing that he was a Lutheran pastor and the father of one of their classmates, the high school graduating class had invited him to deliver the sermon at the baccalaureate service. He came to my office one day to seek my counsel in the process of deciding whether to accept this invitation.

Aware of the position of our Synod against "taking part in the services and sacramental rites of heterodox congregations or of congregations of mixed confession" and desiring not to cause possible or perhaps even inevitable problems for me, his ecclesiastical supervisor, were he to participate, he decided not to do so. After he shared with me his decision, I reflected to him my fervent thoughts and deep regrets, primarily for two major reasons. I regretted that the members of his child's high school graduation class would be deprived of hearing a message that I knew would have been an uncompromising, unapologetic, clear, faithful articulation of the truth of God's love in Christ and the assurance of forgiveness of sin through the blood of Christ on the cross, who died for all. I further regretted that it was entirely possible if not quite probable that the message the students would actually hear that day from whoever would subsequently accept the invitation to deliver a message at the baccalaureate service would be one that was likely to confuse Law and Gospel (if these two chief doctrines of the Christian faith would even be mentioned) and would not clearly present the biblical truth about sin and grace.

These two true stories are illustrative of the dilemmas faced by pastors in the LCMS who sincerely desire to be faithful to the positions of our church body. At the same time, most LCMS pastors also realize that the culture in the United States today is one that no longer understands, if it ever did, that our non-participation in a service, wedding, baccalaureate, funeral, or other event with non-LCMS Christian participants is intended to communicate our doctrinal disagreement with the sponsoring church or churches. In fact, such non-participation actually communicates a mixed message to those who know that the LCMS pastor has chosen not to participate. Instead of presenting a faithful witness to the truth of the Gospel, in many cases the message communicated by non-participation is one of exclusivity or aloofness, telegraphing a false spirit of being "holier than thou."

Over the years our Synod has repeatedly addressed such matters. One can find actions and convention resolutions dealing with church fellowship and inter-Christian issues throughout the annals of The Lutheran Church—Missouri Synod. Following are highlights of a few:

In 1932, our Synod in convention adopted a document titled "A Brief Statement of the Doctrinal Position of the Missouri Synod on Church Fellowship." As is the case with other fellowship resolutions of ours, this one, reflecting the first objective from Article III of our Constitution, carried a dual message. On the one hand, it stressed the importance, based on Matthew 15, of always discriminating between orthodox and heterodox church bodies. We do not have church fellowship with unorthodox churches.

On the other hand, it reminded us that the Church, with a capital "C," is not just The Lutheran Church—Missouri Synod, but rather the invisible communion of all believers. This Church, the document said, "is to be found not only in those external church communions which teach the Word of God purely in every part, but also where, along with error, so much of the Word of God still remains that men may be brought to the knowledge of their sins and to faith in the forgiveness of sins, which Christ has gained for all men."

This document, then, called for us to repudiate unionism—fellowship with the adherents of false doctrine—while at the same time not labeling as unchristian those who, on every point, are not in total agreement with the Missouri Synod.

In 1965, our Synod adopted a resolution banning our participation in joint worship services—that is, services with those with whom we have not established altar and pulpit fellowship. Yet, it was also decreed that, should a pastor resolve in his mind that participating in such a service is somehow acceptable under the circumstances, or that the service really didn't amount to joint worship in the first place, no judgment should be voiced against this pastor or his congregation without personal, fraternal discussion and the ascertaining of all the facts involved.

Thus, while this resolution "laid down the law" about joint worship, it also promised to give any alleged offender, if not the benefit of the doubt, then at least his day in court, so to speak. Our church would "toe the line" on issues relating to fellowship and joint worship, but we would also first listen to those who appeared to have crossed the line before declaring them guilty of a grievous sin.

That same year, 1965, the Synod's Commission on Theology and Church Relations prepared a document called *Theology of Fellowship*. This important work, adopted by the 1967 convention, was then and still is the only CTCR document adopted in convention as the official position of the Synod, demonstrating the significance of this document for the doctrinal unity and harmony of our Synod.

The fellowship guidelines put forth in this document were, like the "Brief Statement" of 1932, somewhat double-edged. That is, they again sounded a warning for the church to avoid the danger of unionism, but they also sounded a warning for the church to avoid the twin danger of unnecessary separatism. The church must strive, the guidelines said, to work *zealously* for the extension of its fellowship where this can be done without compromising sound doctrine.

When ecclesiastical practice is in harmony with Scripture and the Lutheran Confessions, the guidelines said, the church is edified. On the other hand, when ecclesiastical practice constitutes a demonstrable denial of the Gospel, the work of the church is undermined. However, the guidelines added, and this is important, "Christians ought not apply this principle legalistically or employ doubtful logic and labored conclusions to prove that a certain practice is against the Gospel." In other words, sectarianism, taken too far, can be a sin.

The point I'm trying to make by reviewing these resolutions is that our Synod has always held firmly to the importance of proper fellowship practices, to the need to avoid syncretism, unionism, inappropriate joint worship, and the like. At the same time, this firmness has always been accompanied by a note of compassion, by an attempt to understand difficult situations on a case-by-case basis, by a willingness not to rush to judgment, and by granting that there are circumstances in which avoiding the danger of separatism, without compromising sound doctrine, might include participation in a service or *ad hoc* gathering of Christian people that includes participants who are not members of the LCMS.

Furthermore, it is one of our Synod's objectives that the LCMS should "work through its official structure toward fellowship with other Christian church bodies . . . " (LCMS Constitution, Article III). Over the years of its history, the LCMS has actually and officially declared altar and pulpit fellowship with 31 other Lutheran church bodies. After rescinding such fellowship with the former American Lutheran Church in 1981, the Synod today remains in formal church body fellowship with 30 other Lutheran church bodies, only one of which is in the United States. Declaring such fellowship is not a simple process and is taken quite seriously among us.

A growing concern in this regard is the reality that a number of church bodies with whom our Synod currently enjoys altar and pulpit fellowship have relationships with other church bodies with whom our Synod is not in such fellowship. How are we to relate to such non-related church bodies with which we have no formal declaration of oneness in doctrine and practice, but with which our partner churches are freely engaged in manifestations of altar and pulpit fellowship? Or how are we to relate to embryonic church bodies that have not yet matured and developed to the point that our process of determining unity in doctrine and practice should be implemented? In those cases, that fully developed, intricate, and complex process which ultimately leads to the declaration of altar and pulpit fellowship is simply premature.

We have numerous opportunities to develop working relationships with other church bodies throughout the world with whom we have not yet discovered and declared altar and pulpit fellowship. Many of them are coming to our Synod, looking to us for leadership and partnership in proclaiming the Gospel in situations and circumstances in dire need of the human, fiscal, and theological resources we have been blessed by God to be able to provide. We need to continue to develop and exercise proper biblical ways and means of relating to other Christian church bodies and organizations, both nationally and internationally, even in ways and means that are short of altar and pulpit fellowship, in a manner that in no way compromises our confession of faith. This is especially important in our national and world culture where increasingly people are indifferent or even hostile toward the Christian faith and where atheism, Mormonism, and Islam continue to make inroads in our country and in the world.

This is the basic question I asked our Synod's Commission on Theology and Church Relations to address a few years ago, which resulted in a document titled *Church Relations in the 21st Century.* This document was reviewed and considered by the LCMS Council of Presidents and seminary faculties and was unanimously approved by the CTCR in 2009. Here is the concluding statement of this document:

> Christians who share a common confession express that confession nowhere more clearly or visibly than when they kneel at the same altar to receive the body and blood of Christ and when they share a common pulpit. The process and protocols leading to a formal declaration of church fellowship by the Synod in convention have served us well when declaring with established church bodies with whom we have shared something of a common history. As we move into more fluid situations in the 21st century, we need additional ways to identify and acknowledge agreement in confession that are appropriate to the history and nature of ecclesial communities that are emerging in various parts of the world but who do not share the same kind of institutional habits and identities. In these ways we seek to manifest our agreement and so confess our unity at the altar and pulpit in a manner that is faithful to our theology of the church.

The CTCR is also in the process of finalizing a document requested by the 1981 Synod convention on the subject of inter-Christian relationships. I believe these documents and their use throughout the Synod will be most helpful as we face continual challenges and opportunities in being a confessional Lutheran church in a pluralistic culture.

For years, especially in more recent times, the subjects of unionism, syncretism, and participation in services with other Christians or events with non-Christians, have been a source of concern and challenge for the LCMS. In previous writings I have quoted Dr. J. A. O. Preus, who served from 1969 to 1981 as the eighth president of The Lutheran Church—Missouri Synod during the tumultuous years of our church's doctrinal controversy over the authority of Holy Scripture. In his report to the 1981 Convention of the Synod, Dr. Preus addressed this very topic, expressing disappointment and frustration at the lack of progress in achieving his hopes regarding these important matters:

> We also have a whole series of overtures dealing in one way or another with the subject of interchurch relations and unionism and separatism. I have been in the ministry for over 35 years and have been involved in discussions of unionism and related matters for all of these years. I have hoped that during my years in office some greater clarity could be developed among us as to what really is unionism and what must be dealt with in a disciplinary way, as over against things that might appear to some to be a compromise of the Word of God but to others are not such at all and no intent at compromise is intended. I hope that the Synod will try to develop rubrics and guidelines for a church of 3 million members in the 1980s and 90s, rather than always relying on definitions which are a century old, which deal basically with a European situation and are not particularly helpful for our modern time. I believe our fathers were eminently sincere and totally correct in what they did, but I think we have to rethink our own position on these matters so as to make their position our own or so as to make their position something that is workable and feasible and acceptable in our own midst. We can all agree that we want to avoid a total separatism on the one hand and a wild, irresponsible ecumenism on the other. The difficulty is to find a

middle path which will avoid both of these extremes and which can work in all situations in our church.

(Dr. Jacob A. O. Preus, President's Address, 1981 LCMS Convention Proceedings, pp. 65–66)

Interestingly, only several months earlier, Dr. Preus participated in "A Pilgrimage for Life" in St. Louis, sponsored by the Archdiocesan Pro-Life Committee and Clergy for Life. Participants were:

- **A Roman Catholic priest who served as the Coordinator of the Archdiocesan Pro-Life Committee, who gave the welcome;**
- **Dr. Preus, president of Clergy for Life, who gave the "Declaration of Purpose";**
- **A Jewish rabbi, who read the Old Testament lesson;**
- **A United States astronaut, who gave a personal witness;**
- **A Baptist pastor, vice-president of Clergy for Life, who read a New Testament lesson;**
- **Dr. Jean Garton, LCMS laywoman and president of Lutherans For Life, who gave a personal witness;**
- **A Greek Orthodox pastor, treasurer of Clergy for Life, who read the Gospel lesson;**
- **A coordinator for Lutheran Outreach Ministry, who gave a personal witness;**
- **The Catholic Archbishop of St. Louis, who gave the benediction.**

Obviously Dr. Preus believed his participation in an event like this was appropriate. I assure you that in the LCMS today not a small number of pastors and others would disagree.

Almost three decades later, we still are working to find the "middle path" to which Dr. Preus referred in 1981. Indeed, this is not a new topic, having been the subject of the writings of church leaders for many years.

For example, in its report *Theology of Fellowship,* officially adopted by the Synod in 1967 (Res. 2-13), the CTCR states that Christians "not only *may* but *should* join in fervent prayer" with those whom they engage in doctrinal discussions "with a view to achieving doctrinal unity." In this report the Commission goes on to state:

> Our Synod should clearly recognize that, in the case of necessary work on the local, national, or international level, where the faith and confession of the church are not compromised, and where it appears essential that the churches of various denominations should cooperate or at least not work at cross-purposes, our churches ought to cooperate willingly to the extent that the Word of God and conscience will allow.

This document also offers guidance for situations that are not altogether clear. It continues:

> In the many cases [that] do not seem to fall readily under the guidelines enunciated above (e.g., prayers at all kinds of meetings), every Christian should for his own person observe the apostle's injunction, "Let everyone be fully convinced in his own mind" (Rom. 14:5). With regard to his brother, whose conscience may not judge in all matters as does his own, let every Christian observe the instruction of the same apostle, "Why do you pass judgment on your brother? Or, why do you despise your brother? For we shall all stand before the judgment seat of God. . . . So each of us shall give account of himself to God" (Rom. 14:10, 12).

In short, while there is considerable agreement in the Synod regarding the Lutheran understanding of church fellowship, there is also widespread disagreement regarding precisely which joint activities with other Christians and Christian churches belong to the practices of church fellowship or inter-Christian relationships and which activities do not.

It is important and instructive to note that in the writings of our church fathers on the topic of pulpit fellowship, which would certainly include the concept of inter-Christian relationships, there is found a strong confessional willingness to proclaim the truth *even in the pulpits of other denominations so long as the conditions under which and the manner in which this is done are not objectionable.* At the 1870 Convention of the Central District, Dr. C. F. W. Walther, Dr. F. C. D. Wyneken, and Dr. H. C. Schwann, (the first three presidents of our Synod who collectively served for the first 52 years of our Synod's existence) took part. The convention specified that a Lutheran pastor who agrees to speak in the pulpit of "a strange church" must take care not to give his own congregation reason for suspicion that he agrees with preachers of other denominations in their doctrine and that he must have the strength and fortitude to confess the truth also in "a strange pulpit."

The 1870 convention unanimously concluded:

> If it is asked, accordingly, whether it is contrary to the conscience of a Lutheran minister upon invitation to preach in a strange church the answer is: No. Christ has preached in the synagogues, the apostles in the temples of idols, and we should be glad to preach in the pope's palace if given permission. It would be a sin to reject offhand an offer that we preach the gospel also to others. (*Funfzehnter Synodal Bericht des Mittleren Districts der Deutschen*

Evangelisches Lutherische Synode von Missouri, Ohio, und andern Staaten, Cleveland, Ohio, 1870, p. 43)

Furthermore, the August 1868 issue of *Lehre und Wehre* (*"Doctrine and Defense"*) asserts:

> It need hardly be said that an orthodox teacher certainly may preach the Word of God in its clearness and truth also to the congregation of a heterodox teacher without sinning against the will and Word of God and without violating his office as a servant of the orthodox church—if only he has been properly invited by those who have a right to do so. . . . If Christ has a full right also to rule among His enemies, why shall not His servant render testimony in God's name for the truth, bearing witness with a free, courageous spirit, announcing the truth as it lives and moves in his heart, and do this without circumlocutions or cowardly reticence—so long as he does not speak uninvited into the flock of another and so long as he clearly sets forth his position as one definitely committed to the truth of God, and enemy of all false doctrine and unionism. (p. 253)

Essentially, the question of inter-Christian relationships, namely, how we in the LCMS should relate to other Christians and the church bodies to which they belong, forces us to discern carefully what it means to be a biblical, confessional, evangelical, Christian church body, especially in a culture that is at best indifferent and at worst downright hostile to the Christian faith. In the past and even to a certain extent in the present, the LCMS has approached this question largely by avoiding contact with such church bodies and, for the most part, its members.

In the present and into the future, the LCMS must rethink its position in this regard. For if our church fathers in the 19th century were bold, courageous, and confident enough to preach "in a strange church" or "to the congregation of a heterodox teacher *without sinning against the will and Word of God and without violating his office as a servant of the orthodox church," why should we be fearful, timid, or ashamed to do so unapologetically, uncompromisingly, boldly, courageously, and faithfully?* For if we are to be a confessional church, our confession must be heard!

The Respective Roles of and Relationships between Clergy and Laity

Despite our theological clarity on the subject of church and ministry, there exists in some corners of our Synod a lack of agreement, both in theory and in practice, regarding the role, responsibility, authority, and accountability of the office of pastor and the laity or priesthood of all believers (1 Peter 2:9) in the church. Such lack of agreement can result in misunderstanding and conflict between laity and clergy, with a corresponding negative impact on the life, ministry, and mission of their congregations.

Concerned that conflict between pastors and congregations is causing harm to the body of Christ and hindering the church's proclamation of the Gospel, the Synod has officially addressed the issue of pastor/congregation relationships, adopting fairly recent resolutions on the subject. In 1992 Res. 3-06A the Synod stated that the church is harmed when either the pastor or the congregation "attempts to exercise unscriptural authority over the other" and further stated:

> Resolved, That the Synod reaffirm the scriptural position of the church and its ministry as taught in the Lutheran Confessions that God has instituted the office of the pastoral ministry and that the one who holds this office carries it out on behalf of and with accountability to God and those through whom God has called him

and

> That the Synod guard against all distortions of the scriptural position.

In 1998 Res. 3-07—referring to biblical texts such as 1 Timothy 3:2–4; 1 Peter 5:2; 1 Corinthians 9:14; 1 Thessalonians 5:12–13; and Hebrew 13:17—the Synod urged in its final "Resolved":

> That pastor and people conduct themselves toward each other with the love and tenderness of Jesus Christ our Savior by whose death we are forgiven and live.

The Synod in 1998 Res. 3-07 made three specific suggestions for the increase of harmony between pastors and congregations:

- **Mutual study of the Word of God and the Table of Duties in Luther's Small Catechism.**
- **When conflict begins, congregations and pastors need to "seek early help . . . by inviting their District President to bring the good services of his office to their assistance."**
- **Offering prayers in weekly worship services "that the Word of God may have free course and not be hindered by the Old Adam and the sinful flesh of either pastor or people."**

The 2001 convention of the Synod affirmed the Synod's official position on the doctrine of church and ministry as set forth in Dr. C. F. W. Walther's 1851 *Theses on Church and Ministry* (declared to be the Synod's official position in 1851). Noting that the Synod "has experienced during its history confusion with regard to the doctrine of church and ministry," the convention "Resolved" (Res. 7-17A):

> That The Lutheran Church—Missouri Synod meeting in convention in the year of our Lord 2001 affirm the above referenced writings of C. F. W. Walther (*The Voice of Our Church on the*

> *Question of Church and Ministry* [published in 1852 and containing Dr. Walther's above-mentioned Theses]) as the definitive statement under Holy Scripture and the Lutheran Confessions of the Synod's understanding on the subject of church and ministry.

Dr. Walther's Theses on the Ministry are appended to the CTCR's 1981 report on *The Ministry: Offices, Procedures, and Nomenclature.* The CTCR explained that Walther's theses were attached to the report "not merely as a matter of historical interest, but as a testimony to the theological and practical consistency of The Lutheran Church—Missouri Synod in its view of the ministry." The CTCR's report has been commended to the Synod "for study that the Synod might open dialog and come to a clearer understanding of the Doctrine of the Ministry" (1998 Res. 7-14A "To Address Nomenclature of Church Workers").

Other Causes of Division

In addition to matters of doctrine and practice, which include the implementation of what we believe, teach, and confess, there are other causes of division in our Synod. While perhaps not specifically a matter of doctrinal disagreement, there exists a sometimes subtle, sometimes not-so-subtle sense of pietism, pride, and party spirit among us. Often articulated in theological terminology, this spirit is discernible in numerous ways, notably in Internet and other mass communications, in fractured circuits of our Synod, and also at district and Synod conventions. I humbly, pastorally, and respectfully encourage all who read these words, including the one who writes them, to search their heart for genuine repentance and a plea for forgiveness.

That concern, while far from universally present or even prevalent in our Synod, is demonstrative of the presence of a different spirit than that to which the Holy Spirit's words in Holy Scripture direct us:

> But I say, walk by the Spirit, and you will not gratify the desires of the flesh. For the desires of the flesh are against the Spirit, and the desires of the Spirit are against the flesh, for these are opposed to each other, to keep you from doing the things you want to do. But if you are led by the Spirit, you are not under the law. Now the works of the flesh are evident: sexual immorality, impurity, sensuality, idolatry, sorcery, enmity, strife, jealousy, fits of anger, rivalries, dissensions, divisions, envy, drunkenness, orgies, and things like these. I warn you, as I warned you before, that those who do such things will not inherit the kingdom of God. But the fruit of the Spirit is love, joy, peace, patience, kindness, goodness, faithfulness, gentleness, self-control; against such things there is no law. And those who belong to Christ Jesus have crucified the flesh with its passions and desires. If we live by the Spirit, let us also walk by the Spirit. Let us not become conceited, provoking one another, envying one another. (Galatians 5:16–26)

While these words are intended for all Christians, they are particularly appropriate for those who serve in the pastoral ministry, pastors to whom Christ has given the responsibility to watch over the souls of those entrusted to our care, "*as those who will have to give account*" (Hebrews 13:17a). Indeed, the office of the pastoral ministry and those who serve therein are integral to vital and healthy congregations.

Dear brothers and sisters in Christ, even in the very important matter of defending the faith, it behooves us as children of the heavenly Father to follow the example of the humility of Christ our Lord. Paul writes to the Philippians:

> Do nothing from rivalry or conceit, but in humility count others more significant than yourselves. Let each of you look not only to his own interests, but also to the interests of others. Have this mind among yourselves, which is yours in Christ Jesus, who, though He was in the form of God, did not count equality with God a thing to be grasped, but made Himself nothing, taking the form of a servant. (Philippians 2:3–7)

Finally, some causes of division are directly or indirectly related to disagreements regarding administrative decisions, official opinions, or adjudicatory judgments of panels, boards, committees, commissions, employees, or officers of the Synod. Some division is caused by dislike for or distrust of individual human beings. This is not hugely surprising, given the propensity of human beings, perhaps particularly German Lutheran human beings, to be critical of anyone who makes decisions not in total agreement with what we believe to be right. Such disagreements, properly expressed and discussed, are indeed appropriate.

Elected and appointed leaders are always accountable for their decisions and actions. However, we must always be aware of and on our guard against our sinful propensity to participate in rumor or unfairly judgmental criticisms without being certain we know all the facts and without first speaking to the person in question, respectfully and fraternally attempting to understand and perhaps persuade. In the process, it behooves us to refrain from exercising the freedoms of speech and of the press in expressing our opinions in a manner that contributes to a spirit of distrust and division.

It is important that we encourage those who disagree with actions or decisions of those appointed or elected to positions of responsibility in our congregations, districts, and national Synod to express such disagreement in a manner that honors the 8th commandment and the words of St. Paul:

> We ask you, brothers, to respect those who labor among you and are over you in the Lord and admonish you, and to esteem them very highly in love because of their work. Be at peace among yourselves. (1 Thessalonians 5:12–13)

With all these matters in mind, the 2007 Convention of our Synod addressed the matter of harmony in our Synod in Resolution 4-01A:

> WHEREAS, God's Word calls us to "unity in the Spirit through the bond of peace" (Eph. 4:3); and
>
> WHEREAS, Synod structure provides the manner through which differences might be settled; and
>
> WHEREAS, Though agreed procedures have been followed, personal opinions and differences regarding practical application of clearly stated doctrine have made for continued discord; and
>
> WHEREAS, Such discord has and is hindering the mission and is disheartening to God's people to the point of withholding their support "for the common good"; therefore be it
>
> Resolved, That the Council of Presidents and Board of Directors as elected leaders of the Synod be given the responsibility to initiate a specific plan for the sake of the whole church to restore harmony in our Synod.

Please note the words "Though agreed procedures have been followed, personal opinions and differences regarding practical application of clearly stated doctrine have made for continued discord." These "personal opinions and differences regarding practical application of clearly stated doctrine" require our careful and prayerful attention, as do the plans currently in process under the leadership of the Council of Presidents and Board of Directors "to initiate a specific plan for the sake of the whole church to restore harmony in our Synod."

Before leaving the topic of theological unity and division, it is important to remind ourselves that witnessing to the pure Gospel in a pluralistic America brings challenges and difficulties. In order to face and overcome them, it is imperative that we speak with one voice, in Christian love.

Regarding this necessity, Dr. Walther said at the first convention of the Iowa District in an essay titled "Duties of an Evangelical Lutheran Synod":

> My dear brothers, let us be on our guard! Satan is sly. Right now we are brothers, living together in peace and love. But Satan will lay for us snares by which he hopes to destroy the sweet, brotherly love we now have in our hearts. We dare never think that it is enough if we just remain united in our faith and our doctrine. . . . It is frightening what harm can result when members of a church organization do not vigilantly guard their fraternal love. (*Essays for the Church* by C. F. W. Walther, Vol. II, p. 56, CPH, 1992)

Again, regarding the vital importance of purity of doctrine communicated in peace and unity, Dr. Walther states:

> A fifth major duty is that it (the Synod) strive for peace and unity in the truth in its midst. He quotes Luther: "Where there is no love, there doctrine cannot remain pure!" Then Walther says, "We dare never think it is enough if we just remain united in our faith and doctrine." (*Essays for the Church*, Vol. II)

We in the LCMS are wonderfully blessed with doctrinal purity. Yet, internal struggles and sharp disputes cause us to become our own worst enemy. At some times more so than at others, the giant sleeps and snores, its peaceful slumber disturbed by its inability at times to get along with itself. As a result, our witness to the Gospel is diluted and diverted, as we are preoccupied with matters we all believe are important and cry out for resolution among us.

Out of a deep and abiding concern for the health and vitality of our Synod, I remind the reader that while we certainly have had and continue to have an abundance of difficulties and disagreements, we are undeniably blessed with God-given unity and harmony in many, many ways. Whether the giant sleeps or wakes up in a grouchy mood or is disagreeable or non-productive or even downright cantankerous, the giant comprises a group of individual Christians who are sinful human beings. Purely by the grace of God, we sinful human beings are one people—forgiven and united by God's love in Christ.

Jesus prayed, "[A]lso for those who will believe in Me through their [the disciples'] word, that they may all be one, just as You, Father, are in Me, and I in You . . . that they may be one even as We are one . . . that they may become perfectly one, so that the world may know that You sent Me and have loved them even as You loved Me" (John 17:20–23). May God place His gracious hand of blessing upon our Synod, granting ever-increasing unity and harmony among us, now and in the future, for the sake of the mission of Christ!

CHAPTER FOUR

The Giant Awakens and Arises—What Roads We Take and What Roadblocks We Encounter—Fixing and Funding the Mission

As part of our family's celebration of the birth of our Lord Jesus, my wife, Terry, and I had the privilege on Christmas Eve 2008 to worship with our family at Faith Lutheran Church in Georgetown, Texas. Nearly 27 years earlier, I had been called by the Mission Board of The Lutheran Church—Missouri Synod's Texas District to develop this congregation as a new mission. There was nothing there when we arrived with our two children, then in the 4th and 6th grades, not even a paper clip.

Today this parish is a thriving, vibrant community of Lutheran Christians involved in a multimillion dollar construction project that will result in a new sanctuary designed to seat 600 people. Much has changed at Faith Lutheran, but all the important things remain the same.

We arrived at church early that night, in plenty of time to find a place where all of us could sit together. As we awaited the beginning of the service, I noticed a little girl walking down the aisle all by herself. She was about three years of age, all dressed up in a frilly Christmas dress that had either been sewn or purchased by someone in the family for this very special occasion—Christmas Eve worship!

With no apparent family members in sight, she approached the general direction of our pew. I grew concerned that perhaps she had become separated from her family and gotten lost. So I approached her, gently, kneeling down in order to be able to look at and speak with her face-to-face. I asked, "May I help you find someone or something?"

In a sweet, soft voice, she replied, "I'm looking for a place to sit for church tonight."

About that time I looked up and saw a young woman who appeared to be her mother and a few other people, probably also family members, approaching the place where we were talking. I greeted the mother and the rest of her family, commented on what a sweet young daughter she had, and said good-bye and "Merry Christmas" to the little girl.

Later that night, throughout the next day, and to this very moment, I have a picture of that little girl in my mind. As I reflect on her simple statement that she was just looking for a place to sit for church that night, I thought about our own children, then 35 and 38 years of age, and about our grandchildren, then 13 and 14 years of age. I also thought about my parents. Dad has been in heaven since New Year's Day 1983. Mom is 93 years old as this book is published, still very much alive and going strong! And I remembered with fondness my grandparents, all of whom have been in heaven for more than 30 years. While my initial thought was about how much the world has changed since our children were three years old and how very much the world has changed since I was that age, the reality of change really sank in when I reflected on how much has changed since my parents, and especially my grandparents, were three years old. In the case of my eldest grandfather, that would have been 1884!

When reflecting upon the vast changes that have occurred in the world and in our own country in the past 125 years, I've also contemplated the changes that have occurred in the church during that period of time. On occasion, I've observed that in many ways the church of today is different from my grandfather's church. Let me unpack and explain that a bit.

My paternal grandfather lived most of his life in south Texas. While there were Hispanic people living in his town at the time, the area was predominantly Anglo. Most of the people who lived there were Roman Catholic. The Lutheran church to which my grandfather belonged was small but healthy, at least from the perspective of a grandson whose primary knowledge of congregational matters was restricted to every Sunday attendance at worship and Sunday school, Vacation Bible School, confirmation class, and Walther League youth group meetings.

My grandfather spent much of his adult life serving on church boards and committees and as an officer of his congregation, which was entirely Anglo. To my recollection, there were no Hispanics in his church. As for the community, there were no Muslims. There was not one Hindu. And if any resident of that south Texas community was an atheist, he or she did not have the courage to say so.

My parents and aunts and uncles were raised in traditional, conservative, Lutheran Christian homes. In the communities where they grew up there were no drug problems. Few couples were known to have children out of wedlock. If a young man and young woman decided to live together without being married, they quickly learned that this was simply not acceptable.

Most folks back then had never flown in an airplane. Needless to say, there were no cell phones, personal computers, or e-mail. The mention of terms that are commonly understood today, such as Facebook, YouTube, and Twitter, would have produced blank stares on the faces of my grandparents, their friends, peers, and other folks who lived among and around them.

A major task of the church in those days was to keep up with all the children being born to Lutheran parents. Running the church and caring for those in the congregation, most of whom were born into it, was a main focus. For example, my grandfather was one of eight children. He had 63 first cousins. And in those days, the size of his family was more nearly the rule than the exception.

Contrast this with the challenges faced by Lutheran congregations today. In many rural areas of our country, "Mom and Pop" farming enterprises are increasingly being purchased by corporate conglomerates, resulting in a significant decrease in the numbers of farms that have been in a family for generations, even centuries. Accordingly, family farms now no longer constitute the primary motivating factor for families to live in rural or small-town communities. In other cases, the family farm continues to exist until the current generation retires or passes away. In those situations, as families move out or die out, the farm and farmhouse are offered for sale, an offer more and more likely to be made and consummated by the corporate conglomerates referenced above.

In many of these cases, the young people who were born and raised on the farm leave home for college and often never come back, choosing instead to move to urban and suburban areas, lured by the possibility of more promising job opportunities or offers. In increasing number, independent school districts in rural areas are merging with neighboring districts and even some of the consolidated districts are turning out the lights. Businesses in small towns and rural communities often cannot survive, with the result that once vibrant, thriving Main Streets now more nearly resemble emerging ghost towns.

Meanwhile, in urban areas of our land, our churches are surrounded by people of different cultures and often different languages. Many architecturally beautiful, Gothic sanctuaries built in the late 19th or early 20th centuries still stand, monuments to what were once upon a time healthy, thriving congregations of hundreds, if not thousands, of people actively involved in congregational life and ministry. Today many of those congregations struggle for survival as most of their former members have either passed from this life into eternity or have moved from the communities surrounding the church buildings in question to outlying suburbs, motivated to do so by concern, anxiety, or fear regarding declining real estate values and changing communities more and more populated by people whose looks and language are strange, foreign, or frightening. Today most of these congregations do not consist of hundreds of people, and certainly not thousands. The pews in their spacious sanctuaries are mostly empty, the precious few worshipers facing onerous financial challenges foreshadowing an uncertain future.

Whether in urban, suburban, rural, or small-town environments, pastors tell me that many if not most young men and women who come to get married these days are already living together and that, in the vast majority of cases, even those who are not doing so have engaged in pre-marital sexual relations. Many families are touched by divorce, drug abuse, abortion, and homosexuality. Many communities in the nation, especially larger ones, have or are not far from Muslim mosques or temples for Mormons, Hindus, and

Buddhists. And what community doesn't have atheists or people critical of or even hostile to the Christian faith?

These are only some of the challenges and opportunities facing the 21st-century church. How are we to be the church in these circumstances? Consider these questions:

- **How does our historic identity as a 19th-century German American church impact our calling and challenge to be a 21st-century American church reaching out to people of many nationalities, cultures, and creeds?**
- **How are we to carry out God's mission of reaching lost people for Christ—the ONE Mission that is an integral part of our Synod's vision?**
- **How can we remain faithful to God and His Gospel in the face of these challenging times and circumstances, while responding to the need for ministry that is aware of, sensitive toward, and responsive to today's culture—a culture vastly different from that in which our Synod was formed more than 162 years ago? How do we share the Gospel with youngsters who are plugged into their iPods or who spend most of their waking hours texting or, much worse, "sexting" their friends?**
- **How do we communicate with immigrants from Croatia, China, Ghana, Nigeria, Bolivia, Mexico, and so many other countries?**
- **How do we bring the Gospel to a rural community that is losing its young people and about to turn out the lights?**
- **How do we respond to media saturation that bombards us with information and images diametrically opposed to our Christian values and beliefs?**

- **How do we touch the lives and hearts of people—young, middle-aged, or chronologically advanced—who have not been raised in the church? Many of them are biblically illiterate, some having never set foot in a Christian church. Many cannot recite from memory the Lord's Prayer and have no familiarity with the Apostles', Nicene, or Athanasian creeds. (Even "spell check" on my computer just now did not recognize, much less know how to spell, "Athanasian"!)**

The answer is to use every means available, without compromising or apologizing for who we are or what we believe, clearly communicating the Good News of God's love in Jesus Christ, who alone is the way to eternal salvation. Our task and privilege is telling "the old, old story of Jesus and His love" in ways that address the deepest spiritual needs of people whose life experience differs greatly from our own and most certainly from that of our parents and grandparents. It means being faithful in the process of putting "new wine" into "new wineskins" (Luke 5:38 NIV).

The apostle Paul writes,

> To the Jews I became as a Jew, in order to win Jews. To those under the law I became as one under the law (though not being myself under the law) that I might win those under the law. To those outside the law I became as one outside the law (not being outside the law of God but under the law of Christ) that I might win those outside the law. To the weak I became weak, that I might win the weak. I have become all things to all people, that by all means I might save some. I do it all for the sake of the gospel, that I may share with them in its blessings. (1 Corinthians 9:20–23)

The culture in which the church exists today more than ever requires listening to and discerning the hopes, dreams, cries, and pains of the people in our communities. We need to translate what Scripture tells us about God's grace into the everyday language of people for whom Scriptural concepts are not part of everyday conversation. In many cases, this means venturing into unknown and unfamiliar territory. It includes the necessity of exercising careful, sensitive discernment of the deeply felt but often camouflaged spiritual needs of people who may not even be aware that those needs exist.

My grandfather was a faithful Christian, a godly man who loved the Lord and loved his church. I am convinced that were he alive today, he would be seeking answers to these questions and would not be afraid to take appropriate risks for the sake of the Gospel—risks that today are quite different from what he faced in his lifetime.

The church is not immune to changes in culture and in the world around it. With regard to matters neither commanded nor forbidden in Holy Scripture, the church sometimes changes intentionally. That's not all bad. Not many American churches today still conduct worship services in languages originally spoken by our immigrant forefathers, but rarely still spoken today in our country. (The founder of our Synod, Dr. C. F. W. Walther, fought unsuccessfully to make irrevocable the article in his congregation's constitution mandating the use of the German language in worship.) And indoor plumbing is a vast improvement over the outhouses of the past! But in addition to intentional change in response to the changing culture around it, the church also changes unintentionally, gradually, reluctantly, even unknowingly, because people change. And the church is comprised of people.

Some of those changes are good and result in a more effective and far-reaching witness to the Gospel. Communication and transportation advances have enabled the church to impact with the Gospel parts of the world previously impossible to reach. Missionaries can use Skype to stay in touch with family members and church leaders back home, communicating across the globe in seconds rather than weeks. Getting missionaries to the foreign field now takes hours rather than the months required years ago. Pastors, educators, and other church leaders have access to virtually unlimited theological, homiletical, exegetical, and many other resources, available at the click of a mouse. These same church leaders can communicate electronically and cost effectively with most of the people they serve.

Others of those changes present significant challenges. The deterioration of the family in American culture has resulted in broken relationships and fractured families who bring to church a host of relational, psychological, and spiritual issues crying out for attention. The proliferation of atheism, Islam, Mormonism, and other non-Christian religions or philosophies has contributed to a greater confusion on the part of people in the church regarding the truth and authority of Holy Scripture. Not everyone in the Christian Church today actually believes that saving faith in Christ is the only way to eternal salvation. A multitude of ethical, moral, and biological developments present theological challenges today that were unknown to the church a century or even a half century ago. Competing forces and multiple choices in society have resulted in the church not being the only option for people's attention on Sunday morning. Declining denominational loyalty and increased mobility in society have contributed to a steady decline in church membership in most Christian denominations. And the list goes on.

Indeed, in many respects, the church of our grandfathers is quite different from that of our grandchildren because the world in which our grandfathers lived is markedly different from the world in which our grandchildren live. In many ways the church of the 21st century is a challenged church, seeking to discover how best to respond to the changes going on all around it and even inside it and how to seize the opportunities accompanying such changes. We are living in this time of transition from the church of our parents and grandparents to the church of our children and grandchildren. In so doing, we must never forget this truth: "Jesus Christ is the same yesterday and today and forever" (Hebrews 13:8).

It behooves us in the Christian Church of today to ensure that our communication of the truths of Holy Scripture and the articulation of the Gospel of our Lord Jesus Christ do not change, even though the values of the world and even the methods of communicating the whole counsel of God are changing all around us. As the church of our parents and grandparents becomes the church of our children and grandchildren, the heritage we have received must be passed on to the generations that follow. We are merely vessels God uses for that purpose, expressed in the words of Paul to the church in Corinth:

> For what we proclaim is not ourselves, but Jesus Christ as Lord, with ourselves as your servants for Jesus' sake. For God, who said, "Let light shine out of darkness," has shone in our hearts to give the light of the knowledge of the glory of God in the face of Jesus Christ. But we have this treasure in jars of clay, to show that the surpassing power belongs to God and not to us. (2 Corinthians 4:5–7)

As a national church body leader, I am faced every day with decisions and challenges about how to remain faithful to the truths of God's Word, accepted and espoused by my parents and grandparents, while also knowing full well that today's post-Christian culture has produced an atmosphere of disinterest in, disrespect for, and even disgust with the church in America and beyond, challenges that impact the church of my children and grandchildren. The attitude of society toward the church has changed dramatically. And the self identity of the church has changed as well.

For instance, in the early stages and throughout much of its history, our national church body primarily defined itself as an orthodox, confessional, evangelical, Lutheran Christian church body in the context of a country populated by people who were almost entirely connected with some other kind of Christian Church.

When one of our congregations with which I am familiar was begun 125 years ago, at a time when my grandparents were being born, the founding pastor said to the group of almost entirely German Lutherans who had gathered, "The greatest enemy our church must face is German Methodism." That movement was a serious threat, largely because the German Methodist Church in those days was wrestling with the vicarious atonement of Christ and other significant doctrinal issues. In addition and not insignificantly, there were no atheists in that small central Texas community. And even if there were, they were not making themselves known. Nor was there any evident existence of Muslims or Mormons within hundreds, if not thousands of miles from that community.

For those early and faithful pioneers of our church, their identity was mostly a matter of orthodoxy (right teaching) versus heterodoxy (other teaching). And in Lutheran circles, we clearly and proudly, sometimes even to the point of sinfulness, identified ourselves with the former and considered all other Christians to be the latter.

Today our national church body is faced with quite different challenges. The church of my children and grandchildren exists in the midst of many people for whom Christianity is neither meaningful nor respected. The kinds of people who were not present when that church in central Texas was begun 125 years ago are now virtually everywhere. As a result, the church today is challenged with defining itself as an orthodox, confessional, evangelical, Lutheran Christian church body in the context not only of orthodoxy versus heterodoxy, but also and primarily in the face of a culture that is at best indifferent to Christianity and at worst harshly antagonistic to the Christian faith.

Recently I was driving through the small town of Rice, Minnesota, when I noticed a highway sign that said, "This stretch of highway is maintained by Minnesota Atheists." Now most of us are aware that there are many Lutheran people and a not-so-small number of other Christian folks who live in that great state. But that highway sign was placed to let it be known that not everyone in that community belongs to a Christian church or professes the Christian faith. There are also atheists who are downright proud to be so! My grandparents never faced that phenomenon. My grandchildren are living it.

The challenge facing the church in this context includes accomplishing our God-given mission of making known the love of Christ proactively, non-judgmentally, winsomely, non-apologetically, and faithfully, even though our doing so might not be well-received by all who see and hear what we in the Christian Church are doing and saying. In a nutshell, this challenge is essentially that of proclaiming a changeless Christ in a changing world.

Those who came before us, including my dear grandfather, were faithful to that mission. May those who come after us find us faithful as well.

Preparation of Professional Church Workers

In order to assist the church in its present and future mission, faithful and proficient church workers and leaders are required. These must be men and women who love the Lord Jesus and understand and cherish the Gospel. They must be people who discern the challenges faced in the world today of "making known the love of Christ by word and deed within our churches, communities, and the world."

Accordingly, a word is in order regarding the preparation of professional church workers. Our Synod is wonderfully blessed with the Concordia University System, comprised of ten colleges and universities, and with our two seminaries. In many ways, our system of higher education is second to none and is the envy of many Christian church bodies.

Originally designed primarily or even exclusively for the preparation of pastors and teachers for the LCMS, our ten Concordias now provide collegiate and university education for a variety of professional endeavors. The schools of the Concordia University System offer a wide variety of programs. Some 157 undergraduate programs and more than 50 graduate programs are available.

Preparation of future workers for the church usually begins in the home, where godly and faithful parents instill in their children a love for the Lord and His Church. Grandparents and other family members are also influential in this process. Both parents and grandparents can play a vital role in the suggestion and even encouragement for their children and grandchildren to consider becoming a pastor or commissioned minister of the Gospel in the LCMS.

In my own case, my parents (my grandparents never really said much about the topic until after I became a pastor, at which time they were very supportive, even delighted) were not particularly keen on the idea of my entering the church work profession. My father's education ended at high school, resulting in a life spent in an honorable vocation as a meat cutter and, eventually, as vice-president in charge of the meat departments in a chain of more than 30 food stores in Houston. But he always wanted "something more" for his children.

It is understandable, therefore, that when I broached the idea of professional church work as a possible career, his loving response was that he had hoped I would choose a professional career which would enable me to achieve what he in his life had been unable to do. Based on his family's perception and the conventional wisdom of his generation, those who decided to become pastors were typically the young men in the family who were not strong enough to stay on the farm and assume responsibility for the manual labor connected with the family's agricultural endeavors or not smart enough to become doctors, lawyers, or engineers. So he encouraged me to do something else, to choose a career in which he thought I could, in his words, "make something of yourself."

While my father has been in heaven for nearly three decades, he knew me as a pastor and mission developer. He died before I became involved in ministry at the district and Synod level. But his godly and fatherly influence as a lay leader in a congregation of men and women who, humanly speaking, were in a socioeconomic class above that which he and my mother experienced, has left an indelible mark on my life and professional church work career. He loved life. He loved the Lord and the church. He loved his wife and children. He was a faithful steward who taught me most of what I know about Christian stewardship and first-fruit giving. He knew how to lead. He knew no fear. And he had deep respect for the office of the pastoral ministry, notwithstanding his differing hopes and dreams for his own son. I'd love to be able to tell him some day about my experiences in the pastoral ministry and the realm of church leadership.

The process of preparing professional church workers continues in the local congregation, where godly and faithful pastors and other professional church workers demonstrate through the joy of their ministry the meaningful and fulfilling calling in which they serve.

Many such professional church workers also proactively encourage the young people in their congregations who seem to have the God-given abilities and gifts necessary for full-time church work careers to consider prayerfully whether God is calling them to such service. Indeed, a high percentage of first-year students at our seminaries indicate that the example and encouragement of their parish pastors, teachers, and other church professionals provided significant influence in their decision to pursue a career as a professional church worker.

Again, that was not my experience, at least not with the pastor or other church workers at my home congregation. I received affirmation and encouragement to become a pastor from people in the congregation of my childhood and teenage years, including friends of my parents, but not from my pastor or, to my recollection, from my parochial school teachers. I did receive such encouragement and affirmation from other pastors at whose feet I sat later in my young life—my campus pastor at Texas A&M, pastoral counselors of Gamma Delta (the national Lutheran student organization in which I was active during my collegiate years), and a number of district presidents with whom I came into contact over the years. And I subsequently received wonderful affirmation from three of my parochial school teachers after entering the pastoral ministry.

With or without encouragement from parents, grandparents, pastors, teachers, directors of Christian education, or deaconesses, those called by God to professional church work careers receive professional preparation to do so in centers of higher education at the church's colleges, universities, or seminaries. Increasingly, those institutions are becoming deployed centers of learning, including new technology, courses offered online, even seminary courses taught over iTunes U.

The 2007 issue of "Pastoral Education" said this about new technology: "God's Word remains. That is for sure. God's truth is timeless. But God gives gifts and more gifts by which to teach. Many tools for learning continue to surface. The seminaries use technologies and creative resources to teach students to serve God's people as pastors. Some HOT new things are Podcasts and Web sites. iTunes are available. Distance education is expanding. In-service preparation, contextual education, modules and mentors are HOT." Advancements of many kinds are reshaping professional church worker education.

Trends show that the number of professional church workers needed in the LCMS in the years ahead presents a unique challenge. The number of retirees is increasing while the number of people entering church work professions is declining. The actuarial folks who provide assistance to our Concordia Plan Services say that more than half the pastors currently serving in our Synod are over 50 years of age. The postponement of retirement or willingness of pastors to serve smaller congregations in semi-retirement has reduced the number of congregations seeking to call a pastor, thus making the number of calling congregations appear much smaller than would be the case without the continued service of pastors at or beyond retirement age.

The members of the Synod's Council of Presidents regularly report the number of congregations calling a pastor (usually in the range of 350 to 400). In addition, 350 to 400 congregations have no permanent pastor, are not in the process of calling one, and are being served by a retired pastor, a DELTO (Distance Education Leading To Ordination) student, a Specific Ministry Pastor vicar, or some other form of Synod-approved provider of pastoral ministry. So, essentially, at any given time, between 12–15 percent of the Synod's 6,160 congregations are without the services of a permanent pastor.

We need men and women to serve as church work professionals in the future to provide pastoral care, Christian education, and leadership in mission and ministry. The value of proactively encouraging the young people of our church to consider church professions cannot be overemphasized.

Like their ordained brethren, commissioned ministers of the Gospel also play a crucial role in the health and vitality of LCMS congregations. Included in this category are commissioned professors, teachers, principals, directors of Christian education, directors of Christian outreach, directors of family life ministry, directors of parish music, deaconesses, parish assistants, and certified lay ministers. Most of these are in increasingly high demand and short supply. This is especially true in the case of male elementary school teachers. Serving in that capacity as a contract teacher prior to enrollment at the seminary was a wonderful experience in my young post-baccalaureate life. I highly recommend that experience!

Most professional church workers receive their basic educational preparation at one of our Concordia colleges or universities. Others, as was true in my case, matriculate at another private or public university. Some later become rostered ministers of the Gospel through our Synod's colloquy process. Still others enroll at one of our seminaries.

Since the inception of the Concordia University System in 1992, enrollment at our Concordia colleges and universities has increased from 10,000 to 23,318 students—13,138 undergraduate and 10,180 graduate students in the fall of 2008. The number of undergraduate students has remained almost constant over the past three years, while the number of graduate students has increased dramatically.

The number of reported LCMS students is 4,000 to 5,000, while total Lutheran student enrollment at the 10 institutions approximates 6,000.

This trend coincides with the number of high-school-aged students in our church body—a number that continues to decline. For example, the number of high school students (15–19 year olds) in the LCMS in 1980 was 220,000. Today, there are approximately 100,000 students in the LCMS ages 14–19. Today in our Synod we have fewer than 50 percent of the high-school-aged students we had 30 years ago.

Another startling statistic is that in 1994, LCMS congregations reported baptizing 47,763 babies. Thirteen years later, assuming that confirmation happens at about that age, LCMS churches reported junior confirmations of 20,673—only 43 percent of the children we baptized 13 years earlier. That's a loss of 27,000 children somewhere. Frankly, we in the LCMS are doing poorly in fulfilling the injunction of Proverbs 22:6: *"Train up a child in the way he should go; even when he is old he will not depart from it."*

The number of LCMS seminary students has fluctuated over the years. The combined graduating classes from our two seminaries during the Seminex crisis in the mid-1970s decreased overnight and then gradually increased over the years, reaching a post-Seminex high of 229 in 2007. Since then, the number of residential students has again decreased, slowly but surely. Meanwhile, alternate routes to the pastoral ministry have attracted non-traditional students, including those involved in the newly approved Specific Ministry Pastor program. What the future holds for pastoral formation remains to be seen, especially as that future is bound to be affected by an exponential increase in distance learning and other electronic or Web-based instructional technologies.

Besides a decrease in seminary students, a continued decline in the number of students preparing for church work careers in general raises legitimate concern about the future supply of professional church workers in our Synod. While this trend mirrors the decline in the number of college-aged students in our nation, it may reflect other factors as well. In our nation's present economic downturn, the cost of education must be a contributing factor.

This trend also reflects the growing competition potential church work students face from other professional careers offering more attractive scholarship support during the collegiate years and greater financial rewards after graduation. These and other factors combine to increase the likelihood that parents and other influential people are less likely than in previous decades to encourage young people to consider lives of service in professional ministry. *"Pray to the Lord of the harvest that He will send workers into the harvest fields."*

Following is the 2008–09 school year full-time-equivalent enrollment at our 10 CUS institutions:

Ann Arbor 852
Austin 2,269
Bronxville 734
Irvine 2,453
Mequon 6,549
Portland 1,709
River Forest 4,185
Selma 579
St. Paul 2,644
Seward 1,344

The CUS Web site says:

The Concordia University System office and the 10 Concordia campuses continue to promote the mission and ministry of

> Lutheran, Christ-centered higher education with recruitment efforts throughout the country, beginning with a personal letter to eighth-grade students whose names and addresses are shared by their congregations with the Board for University Education office in St. Louis. Annually an appeal is made to LCMS congregations to celebrate Concordia Sunday as an approach to tell the story of Lutheran higher education.

The Lutheran Church—Missouri Synod is only as strong as its congregations. By the same token, its congregations are only as strong as their pastors, other professional church workers, and lay leaders. All serve together, in harmony and mutual respect, to the glory of God and the building up of His Church here on earth and of His kingdom hereafter in eternity.

FOCUSING ON THE MISSION

Since its inception, The Lutheran Church—Missouri Synod has been a mission-minded church body. From its original organizers of 12 pastors and 14 congregations, the Synod has grown to more than 6,000 congregations, with current mission endeavors in some 80 countries (see Appendix D for a summary of the Synod's mission activity throughout its history). Our headquarters building in St. Louis is called the International Center of The Lutheran Church—Missouri Synod. While the local or regional flavor of the name of our church body (Missouri) is confusing to people on the national and international scene, the fact is, the LCMS is a national church body with international relationships.

The table in Appendix D presents an amazing picture of how intensively and extensively the LCMS has been and continues to be involved in mission efforts around the world. What the table cannot communicate is the progression of mission strategy and the development of missiological principles that have come about since the LCMS first began foreign mission work in the late 19th century. Let's explore briefly some of those changes.

Initially, the work of foreign missionaries was extremely challenging. A missionary, along with his family if he were married, was identified, called, trained, and sent to foreign soil with the expectation that he would establish a presence and begin a mission in the village or community where he resided. In many cases, the missionary essentially became pastor to the mission he established.

In those early years, missionaries sent to India, various African countries, and other developing nations encountered many obstacles. Transportation was available mostly by oceangoing vessels, which took as long as three months to transport missionary families to their destination. Communication was poor, if not nonexistent, resulting in long periods of silence between missionary families and their loved ones and mission partners back home. Furloughs were few and far between, meaning family contact occurred only after, in many cases, a separation of years. School-aged children of missionaries more often than not were sent to missionary boarding schools, in many cases so far away from their families that parents and children saw each other only a few days or weeks a year.

Often, fatal diseases with no immunizations available took their toll. In Obot Idim, Nigeria, a cemetery is dedicated and reserved entirely for LCMS missionaries, their spouses, and children who lost their lives for the sake of the Gospel. Visiting that cemetery and seeing the grave markers of those heroes of the faith who responded to the calling of God and of our Synod to go where no one representing our church had ever gone has left an indelible mark on my life and faith. That mark grew even deeper when I saw a number of graves bearing the names of infant and toddler missionary children.

Today missionaries travel on commercial airlines, arriving at their destinations in hours rather than weeks or months. Cell phones, Skype video connections, home schooling or the availability of international schools, and in most cases vastly improved living conditions have wrought many positive changes in the lives of missionaries and their families. On the mission field today, the focus is primarily on planting multiple missions, identifying and training local men with the requisite gifts and respect to serve as pastors in the missions established. The focus is less and less on our expatriate LCMS missionary becoming the sole pastor of one or more mission congregations. Notwithstanding these changes in mission strategy and improvements in communications and overall living conditions, our missionaries remain heroes of our church meriting great respect and generous support.

Not surprisingly, mission focus and strategy are not the same in every country of the world. Local demographics, political circumstances, and other factors are considered by the Board for Mission Services in determining how best to do mission work in each country.

Here's what the LCMS World Mission Web site says about international work. Note especially the "priority platforms" in the four regions of the world in which we are at work:

> LCMS World Mission has more than 110 years of experience in foreign mission fields. The LCMS commissioned its first overseas missionary in the 1890s to India.
>
> Today, LCMS World Mission works with partner church bodies and emerging church bodies worldwide. We have active work or mission relationships in approximately 85 countries. For administrative and strategy purposes, international fields are divided into four regions, including Africa, Asia, Eurasia, and Latin America.

> In each region, LCMS World Mission has identified "priority platforms" through which our work to proclaim the Gospel, plant churches, develop leaders, and direct resources are connected:
>
> - **Africa—Reaching people through human care ministries**
> - **Asia—Reaching people through education ministries**
> - **Eurasia—Reconnecting people to their Christian heritage**
> - **Latin America—Training national missionaries**
>
> In countries where a national church body is well established, LCMS World Mission seeks to lend its partnership to build the capacity of the national church, its leaders and members to enable it to be a missionary church itself. This may take the form of offering personnel to train leaders, or consulting services in areas of outreach or development where the national church has identified a need, or offering financial assistance to complete projects which contribute to building a healthy, self-sustaining national church.
>
> In places where there is no established church or the number of unreached people is relatively high, LCMS World Mission offers career and volunteer personnel, financial, and other resources to establish Lutheran communities of faith, and to train national leaders, who will in turn evangelize new communities and train new leaders.

In addition to international mission endeavors, the LCMS is heavily involved in a national mission focus. Here's what the LCMS World Mission Web site says about our national mission work:

> Today, as the ethnic diversity of the United States increases, so does the diversity of mission outreach to these different cultures. The Lutheran—Church Missouri Synod declared the United States to be a "world mission field" in 1992 at its Synod convention. In 1998, the Synod adopted Pentecost 2000 as a special initiative to start 1,000 new cross-cultural ministries in the United States by the year

> 2000. Since in 2001, that goal was still not met, the Synod convention again voted to extend the mission effort as Pentecost 2000+ until 2004, at which time the goal had been exceeded. A registry of these ministries may still be viewed at www.pentecost2000.org.
>
> LCMS World Mission efforts in the United States continue to build on the foundation laid by Pentecost 2000 in partnership with LCMS districts, congregations, and mission societies. Under the global Lutheran mission movement—called *Ablaze!*—the LCMS in its 2004 convention voted to share the Gospel with 50 million unreached or uncommitted people in the United States as part of the 100 million global effort. In addition, goals include planting 2,000 new congregations by 2017 and training thousands of new workers and laity to address the mission efforts required in the United States. Work will be focused in the most strategic areas that can be identified. In addition, LCMS World Mission has set a goal for revitalizing 2,000 LCMS congregations.
>
> National mission efforts are extensive and diverse, not only among Caucasian people, but also among ethnic and various immigrant groups, and special needs groups, such as the Deaf and Blind. LCMS World Mission also gives leadership to seminary programs to train missionaries for church-planting among these groups in the United States and to congregations that desire to grow in their missional approach to their communities by offering resources, seminars, and other kinds of training.

In both international and national mission work, a growing trend is developing, producing both great excitement and significant challenge. Interestingly this "new" trend actually began almost a century ago. C. S. Meyer, in *Moving Frontiers* (pp. 306–7, citing Professor E. L. Arndt in his *Missionsbriefe I*, February 1912, pp. 19–23), writes:

> This pattern of decentralization was no more evident than in mission work, both in the United States and overseas. Professor E. L. Arndt in 1912 could hardly contain his chagrin with the Synod over the opening of a China mission. He wanted to initiate the work, but Synod argued that it should take the lead. Arndt complained: "The history of our Synod . . . glitters with enterprises that were first begun in smaller circles and then taken over by Synod. . . . Practically all progress we can record has first been planned and begun in smaller circles. . . . Why should we not rather permit even individual congregations to send out missionaries to the heathen?" Synodical officials gave in and, grudgingly, allowed Arndt to do his work in China.

The trend that Professor Arndt envisioned so long ago and which recently reemerged is that of personal involvement in mission. For many years our Synod conducted its mission work, primarily on foreign soil, by receiving financial support from congregations and individuals, who by themselves were not directly involved in doing the mission. The role of congregations and individuals in that paradigm was, simply but significantly, to "pay and pray." The actual work of bringing the Gospel to foreign lands was accomplished by the mission board and staff, who identified, trained, sent, supported, and supervised the work.

Today, largely as a result of the shrinking global community, relatively inexpensive worldwide transportation, advances in technology and communication, and the development of personal relationships around the world, mission work is actually being done by individuals, families, congregations, organizations, institutions, and societies. Much of this work is accomplished through short-term mission events or experiences, many lasting just one or two weeks. Some of the work is accomplished by long-term volunteers, people who commit to living on a foreign mission field for as long as two years—or even longer. Some of this longer-term work is coordinated with LCMS World Mission. Unfortunately, much of it is done unilaterally, in many cases without contact between the mission provider and LCMS World Mission or the LCMS partner church body, where such exists, in the country where the mission work is being done. And some such work is being done in partnership with church bodies other than the LCMS.

This lack of coordination is not good. In countries where LCMS partner churches are present, it is not uncommon for me to receive word from the presidents or bishops of those churches expressing concern at best, frustration and other emotions at worst, at their lack of awareness of the work being done in their country. Often such work occurs in places and among groups of people where and with whom the partner church would not recommend or approve such work.

In addition, work on foreign soil that is begun but not completed by individuals or groups, sometimes even those who are a part of the Synod structure, has resulted in foreign churches and church bodies coming to the president of the Synod with questions, disappointments, frustrations, and unmet expectations. When someone or some group with a connection to the LCMS develops relationships and begins work of any kind in a foreign land, those who receive the benefit of that work naturally but incorrectly assume that the work is being done with the awareness, blessing, and support of the Synod itself. In many instances this is not the case. While assumed to be well-intentioned and spiritually motivated, such uncoordinated efforts and incomplete projects often are ill advised and even counterproductive.

As a result of these changes and challenges, LCMS World Mission is in a period of transition. Where once its primary focus, as indicated above, was to do the work by direct involvement—calling, sending, supervising, and supporting missionaries, underwritten by the gifts and prayers of people and congregations of the LCMS—its primary role now is providing coordination, communication, collaboration, and compliance. All this is done in a spirit of genuine partnership with those desiring the hands-on experience of doing mission work themselves. The sincere desire of LCMS World Mission is to accomplish the Synod's mission objective "vigorously to make known the love of Christ by word and deed within our churches, communities, and the world" in a manner that implements the best practices, soundest missiological principles, and most helpful church relations sensitivities possible.

One emerging model of this new mission direction is "Congregation Connect," which originated as a result of a congregation's unhappy experience several years ago. The congregation called the Synod's mission department in St. Louis, seeking a meaningful way for its people to get involved personally with mission work on a foreign field. The answer given was, essentially, that the congregation should just send money to St. Louis and pray for the work that the Synod would accomplish on behalf of the congregation. Neither satisfied nor motivated by that reply, the congregation decided to go out on its own to discover a mission field in which its members could become personally involved. For several years thereafter, the congregation did its mission work, supported by hundreds of thousands of dollars of contributions from members of the congregation, with no contact or collaboration between the congregation and the Synod's mission department.

Then, a few years ago, informal conversations began between this congregation's pastor and another representative from the Synod's mission department. Those conversations ultimately led to what is now called Congregation Connect (CC), which has become a model of cooperation between congregations and LCMS World Mission. The mission statement of CC is:

> Congregation Connect will connect congregations to long-term mission partnerships focused on the sending of short-term mission teams that will share the gospel and meet the needs of mission hosts." Its vision is: "To connect LCMS congregations and their members to mission fields through long-term relationships."

Parishes involved with Congregation Connect share the hope we have in Christ with those being served, providing human resources to meet the goals and objectives of partner churches and missionaries, while giving their members the opportunity to serve overseas under the auspices of LCMS World Mission. All concerned understand and share the philosophy that short-term mission work needs to be done in the context of long-term projects. To accomplish these objectives, congregations partner directly with the mission fields for a predetermined amount of time, focusing on sending short-term teams and offering prayer, financial support, and other means of helping the mission field accomplish its goals.

Some congregations have volunteered, with World Mission approval, to mentor other congregations in this process. Congregations involved in Congregation Connect select leaders to be trained in managing teams; working cross-culturally; developing sound mission practices, policies and procedures; and working with LCMS World Mission. One hopes and prays that all of this will result in heightened awareness of mission work around the world, long-term relationships built by congregations centered on Gospel proclamation, the use of resources in responsible ways, and increased funding for mission work across the globe.

This is certainly not to say that all mission work can or should be done by short- or long-term volunteers. Career missionaries are still very much a part of the strategic plan of our Synod's mission department. As a matter of fact, one of the specific objectives of the *Ablaze!* movement is to increase by 50 percent the number of career missionaries on foreign fields. Without such long-term commitments on the part of men and women gifted, called, and willing to commit a significant portion of their lives and ministries to the foreign mission field, the work we have been given by God to accomplish would suffer greatly.

FUNDING THE MISSION

This chapter would not be complete without a discussion of how the mission work of our Synod is funded. Financial resources for the mission and ministry of The Lutheran Church—Missouri Synod come primarily from two sources—designated support and undesignated support.

Undesignated or unrestricted support simply refers to the dollars that come from congregations through the Synod's 35 districts to support the work headquartered at the International Center of our Synod in St. Louis. Here's how that support is received.

All 6,160 congregations of the LCMS receive offerings from their members, the annual total of which amounts to approximately $1.4 billion. Each congregation, normally through its voters' assembly or church council, freely and independently decides how much, if any, of its annual offerings to forward to its district office for mission and ministry at the district and national Synod level. In some cases, congregations are quite generous, contributing significant percentages of their offerings—running into the tens or even hundreds of thousands of dollars—to district and national Synod work. In other cases, for whatever reason, congregations send a very small percentage of their offerings and, in all too many cases, congregations send absolutely nothing. Such congregations receive and enjoy all the rights and privileges of membership in the Synod but do not participate in the duties and responsibilities of such membership, which include supporting mission and ministry beyond the congregation. If such is the case with your congregation, respectfully and evangelically I encourage you to ask your congregation to reevaluate its commitment to support the national and international mission and ministry of your church body.

The total annual amount sent from congregations to the districts, through which their membership in the Synod is held, is about $70 million, or roughly 5 percent of total congregational offerings. The remaining 95 percent, on average, is expended by individual congregations for local mission and ministry expenses, including salaries, employee benefits, mortgage payments, insurance, program costs, and so forth. Some congregations support mission endeavors that may or may not be related to the LCMS. Others include in their budgets allocations for one or both of our seminaries, our colleges and universities, our Recognized Service Organizations, or other mission and ministry enterprises.

Each of the 35 districts, normally through its board of directors, freely and independently decides how much of the offerings it receives from district congregations will be forwarded to the national Synod. In recent years, the total amount remitted by the 35 districts to the national Synod has been between $19 and $20 million, an amount less than 1.5 percent of the total annual congregational offerings of $1.4 billion. In other words, the national Synod currently receives in undesignated support less than 1½ pennies of every dollar contributed in the offering plates of the 6,160 LCMS congregations.

The sum total of offerings received by national Synod from congregations through their districts has been slowly but surely declining over the past three-and-a-half decades. For the sake of comparison, in 1973, total offerings given at the congregational level amounted to $285 million. About $24 million of that (or 8 percent) was forwarded on to district and Synod ministries. Thirty-five years later, in 2007, the amount forwarded on to district and Synod was $19.5 million, or about 5 percent of total congregational offerings. Adjusted for inflation, the buying power of $19.5 million today would be equivalent to about $5 million (a far cry from $23.7 million!) 35 years ago.

In many cases, the amount submitted by a district to the national Synod is a fixed percentage of receipts received by the district from its congregations, while in other cases the amount is simply a certain sum as determined by the district board of directors. Here's how those numbers look for the past 35 years:

- **In 1973, the percentages of offerings received by districts and subsequently remitted by the districts to national Synod ranged from 5.94 percent (the low) to 79.02 percent (the high), with 56.69 percent being the average.**
- **In 1973, the amounts remitted by districts to national Synod ranged from $25,000 (the low) to $2.4 million (the high), the average being $677,180.**
- **In 2007, the percentages remitted by districts to national Synod ranged from 9.13 percent to 51.97 percent, for an average of 28.8 percent. That average percentage is only half of what it was in 1973.**
- **In 2007, the amounts remitted by districts to national Synod ranged from $61,490 to $2.76 million, the average**

being $552,645. That amounts to an average remittance per district of $124,535 less than the average remittance per district in 1973.

- **In the 35-year period from 1973 to 2007, 22 districts reduced their remittance to national Synod by a total of $7,022,640 per year, while 13 districts increased their remittance to national Synod by a total of $2,750,155 per year, resulting in a net decrease from 1973 to 2007 of $4,272,485 per year.**

The composite report of receipts by districts from congregations and remittances of districts to national Synod for calendar year 2007 and 1973 is included as Appendix E.

In the face of this gradual but steady decline in undesignated contributions flowing from congregations to their districts to the national Synod, the national Synod and many of its organizations and institutions more than three decades ago began seeking additional funding to accomplish ever-increasing mission and ministry challenges and opportunities. So it is today that you and I and many others receive requests for direct contributions to district and Synod ministries of many kinds, to our Concordia University System institutions, to our two seminaries, to social ministry providers, Recognized Service Organizations, and so on.

The monies from individuals, congregations, foundations, bequests, and so forth, received by and earmarked specifically for ministries connected with the LCMS, Inc., are categorized as designated or restricted support. In 2008, designated or restricted gifts amounted to more than $60 million. Together with undesignated, unrestricted support of about $20 million, the total LCMS budget for the 2008–2009 fiscal year was $84 million.

In 2005, I appointed the Blue Ribbon Task Force on Funding the Mission, which submitted its report to the 2007 convention of the Synod. Its "Brief Summary" reports the following:

> For 30 years a trend away from the predominantly "unified budget" approach to funding the work of our congregations, districts and Synod has evolved into a predominantly "direct giving" system. This shift has been a blessing by not only increasing the number of dollars given to the work of the Lord, but also connecting individuals, congregations and districts more directly to the work they have decided to support. But the shift has brought a greater and greater burden on the scope of work that can be done with the shrinking pool of unrestricted (unified budget) dollars.
>
> Congregations are affected by individual direct giving . . . districts are compoundedly affected by congregational direct giving . . . and as the last one in the unrestricted feeding (funding) chain, Synod has reached a crisis as a result of individual, congregational and district direct giving. Resolution 4-06 of the Synod's 2004 convention called for this Task Force to present a "funding system" to our church one year prior to the 2007 convention of the Synod. The attached report offers 11 recommendations that make up the funding system that is here summarized:
>
> - **We must work to resolve the dysfunctional behavior in our church body so that our resources (time, energy and funds) are expended to achieve the work we need to do for the expansion of the Lord's kingdom.**
> - **We encourage the Blue Ribbon Task Force on Synodical Structure and Governance to address some fundamental inefficiency in the LCMS so that we can focus on being good stewards of the funds entrusted to us.**

- **We must begin the educational reforms necessary to provide congregations, districts, church workers and other entities a better understanding of the "business (mission) of the LCMS" as a national church body.**
- **We must initiate a STEWARDSHIP RENAISSANCE within the church for the good of the church and to the benefit of those who would otherwise be lost for all eternity.**
- **We must promote the concept that "walking together" means more than wearing an LCMS lapel pin. We need our people and our leaders to understand not only the blessings of Synodical membership but also the responsibility of such voluntary membership.**
- **We need to impose upon those organizations that benefit from membership in the LCMS a reasonable expectation of support for the work the Synod has agreed to do together.**
- **We need to continue efforts to find efficiencies in our operations at every level so as to insure that waste is not a part of our Biblical stewardship principles.**

The 11 recommendations of this Task Force call us to step back for a moment from the trend toward restricted giving that has developed in our church and bring some order out of the present distribution of funds chaos. The recommendations call us first of all to prayer and the study of God's Holy Word. The result of such a spiritual foundation has led the Task Force to believe that the two areas of congregational service that have been nearly destroyed by the distribution shifts in funding must be restored: STEWARDSHIP AND EVANGELISM. If we were an outwardly and inwardly growing church many of the distribution of fund inequities would be compensated for by spiritual and numeric growth.

We also acknowledge in our report that the divisions in our church over the last 30 years have hampered our effectiveness no less than the factions in Corinth emptied that first century church of the power available to them. Add to that the fact that our structure has been created piecemeal over the last 100 years and needs to be addressed for maximum efficiency of the Lord's resources. To that end, we are grateful for the study being done by the Blue Ribbon Task Force on Synodical Structure and Governance. However until any changes are made to our structure we must celebrate the blessing of 35 districts and 600 circuits and see in them the path for improving good relational communication that leads to wise distribution choices at every level. We are making several recommendations that begin at the Synodical level to more effectively disseminate information to inform the "person in the pew."

The chain of that information process must be relational. We have to build trust. The Synod should interact more with district staffs and boards and provide them the material they in turn will provide to the congregations to inform the "person in the pew." To challenge each level of the church in their distribution decisions the Synod will expect from districts the minimum amount of unrestricted dollars necessary to operate the synod's "common good" ministries. Districts in turn will be given new ways to increase a trusting relationship and helpful communication with congregations pointing out to them the many blessings received by their being a part of district and Synod and eventually challenging them with a "fair share" amount that they should consider BEFORE they make their other decisions about direct giving. Congregations are already pretty good at doing this very thing with their members.

This new way of "operating together" will not happen overnight. And some investment will have to be made in improving the

> process "up front." For that reason we are suggesting some new funding be expected at the Synodical level from organizations and entities who draw benefit from being connected to the Missouri Synod, but at this time do not regularly support the "common good" activities of the Synod.
>
> We have a Great God . . . who has left us wanting for nothing. But we are challenged: "To whom much is given, much is required." When it comes to our stewardship decisions, the Lord deserves our best. In the spirit of moving this great church body in that direction we commend to you our report.
>
> —Blue Ribbon Task Force for Funding the Mission, July 2006

There is no doubt in my mind that the people of The Lutheran Church—Missouri Synod have sufficient resources to provide for the mission and ministry challenges and opportunities we face. And when our people know about those challenges and opportunities, they will respond.

At the time this book is written, our Synod is involved in a $100 million campaign to support the mission and ministry objectives of the *Ablaze!* movement that require financial support. Even in the midst of a national and worldwide financial crisis, our people and congregations to date have responded with more than half that amount—$52 million! I have every confidence that, by God's grace, the people of our Synod will continue to provide the resources necessary to accomplish the mission of reaching those who are lost in sin and without the hope of eternal life in Christ our Lord.

St. Paul says it well in his letter to the Corinthians regarding the gifts to be gathered by the Corinthian Christians for the churches in Macedonia:

> So I thought it necessary to urge the brothers to go on ahead to you and arrange in advance for the gift you have promised, so that it may be ready as a willing gift, not as an exaction. The point is this: whoever sows sparingly will also reap sparingly, and whoever sows bountifully will also reap bountifully. Each one must give as he has decided in his heart, not reluctantly or under compulsion, for God loves a cheerful giver. And God is able to make all grace abound to you, so that having all sufficiency in all things at all times, you may abound in every good work. As it is written, "He has distributed freely, He has given to the poor; His righteousness endures forever." He who supplies seed to the sower and bread for food will supply and multiply your seed for sowing and increase the harvest of your righteousness. You will be enriched in every way to be generous in every way, which through us will produce thanksgiving to God. For the ministry of this service is not only supplying the needs of the saints but is also overflowing in many thanksgivings to God. By their approval of this service, they will glorify God because of your submission flowing from your confession of the gospel of Christ, and the generosity of your contribution for them and for all others, while they long for you and pray for you, because of the surpassing grace of God upon you. Thanks be to God for His inexpressible gift! (2 Corinthians 9:5–15)

May that encouragement stir our hearts to respond in like manner for the sake of God's mission entrusted to our care, both nationally and internationally. As the giant awakens and arises, may God grant clarity of vision in focusing and funding the mission the giant is to accomplish.

CHAPTER FIVE

The Giant Encounters Other Giants—The Witness of Our Church in a Post-Church Culture—In the World But Not of the World

The cover of a recent national news magazine carried these words, arranged in the shape of a cross: "The Decline and Fall of Christian America." Inside, an article focused on the end of Christian America as we know it and what that change means for us as a nation.

The article cited portions of a 24-page summary of the 2009 American Religious Identification Survey, which found that 15 percent of Americans claim no religious affiliation (up from 8 percent in 1990). The article went on to state that while traditionally the Pacific Northwest had been the home to most of these unaffiliated types, in 2008, the Northeast is the area with the highest number of Americans claiming no religious affiliation.

Consider for a moment these other findings of the survey:

- **In 1990, 86 percent of Americans identified themselves as Christians; today that has fallen to 76 percent.**
- **In 1990, 1 million people identified themselves as atheists or agnostics; today that number is 3.6 million.**

- **Today 1.2 percent of the population is Jewish; 0.6 percent of Americans are Muslim.**

While these numbers in themselves fall far short of describing America as a country no longer comprised of a majority of citizens claiming to be Christian, the main point of the article is this: America today is less Christian than just a few years ago and is becoming less Christian all the time.

To illustrate graphically that point, opposite the first page of the article is a full-page photo of a wall on which hangs a crucifix. In the foreground is a speaker's podium with a flexible, goose-necked microphone stand, with the microphone noticeably missing. The obvious point proposed by the picture is that religion is losing influence in American society.

While that point may be arguable, in many cases it is obviously true. As I think back over my life, I recall clearly the days when church and church-related activities were pretty much the center of our family's life and activities. When our church had worship services, we were there. When our church had a picnic, we were there. When our church youth group had a meeting, I was there. As a matter of fact, in my adolescent and teen years the so-called Sunday Blue Law was in effect, meaning that it was illegal for almost any business in the community to be open on Sunday. The church had a virtual monopoly on the time and attention of people on "the Lord's Day."

All that began to change when the Blue Law was repealed. Stores that once were closed on Sunday were now wide open. Athletic events once "verboten" on Sunday were now scheduled any day of the week the coach or anyone else in authority decided they should be held. Gradually but definitely the church and its activities were no longer "the only game in town."

Today, for many people, Sunday is just another day of the week, except that it falls on a weekend, which for many people simply and only means time away from work. The tradition, pattern, and routine that our family and many other families in America used to observe on Sunday morning was getting out of bed, eating breakfast, getting dressed in clothing none of us wore on other days of the week, getting in the family car, and driving to church (usually, at least in our case, arriving a few moments late), then driving back home after Sunday school and Bible class were over. Today many Americans, including Christians and even Missouri Synod Lutherans, stay home, sleep late, go to the beach or ballgame or children's athletic tournament, or spend the day shopping for whatever might strike their fiscal fancy that day.

The bottom line is that the church and church activities are in competition with many other choices that people have the freedom to make every day of the week, including Sunday. And since statistics from different parts of our country indicate that only 3 percent of people on the West Coast to about 30 percent elsewhere in the nation attend church on any given Sunday, the other choices, at least for the time being, are winning the numerical battle.

Add to that phenomenon of freedom of choice the reality of waves of immigrants who have come to our shores in the past half century. Like the ancestors of most of us in the Lutheran church, whose forebearers brought with them the faith of their fathers and mothers, namely, the Christian faith in general and the Lutheran Christian faith in particular, those who have recently come to America from faraway lands also bring with them the faith of their forefathers and foremothers.

However, those who have come most recently have brought with them a variety of beliefs quite different from Lutheran Christianity. Accordingly, you and I might very well have living next door to us not Baptists or Methodists or Catholics or Presbyterians or Episcopalians or other Lutherans, but very possibly and perhaps even very likely

Muslims or Hindus or Buddhists or Shintos or Baha'is. Or, if the survey summarized in the article referenced above is accurate, your next-door neighbors might simply but significantly be folks who claim no religious affiliation whatsoever.

These new realities beg the question, "How will the witness of our church to people in a post-churched culture be accomplished?" Much about that question has been and continues to be written and spoken by Christian leaders in America, including leaders in the LCMS. Most notably, Dr. Robert Newton, president of the LCMS California-Nevada-Hawaii District, has spoken widely across the Synod about the pre-church, churched, and post-church cultures or mission contexts extant in America and in other places around the world. Here is a very brief synopsis of his thesis:

- **In a pre-church culture, the unchurched—those who have no connection with the church—are the insiders. The missionaries—those connected with the church who are sent to bring the Gospel to the unchurched—are the outsiders. The task of missionaries/outsiders in a pre-church context is to communicate the Gospel to the cultural insiders, namely, the unchurched.**
- **In a churched culture, where belonging to the church is widely accepted and possibly even expected, the churched—those who are connected to the church—are the insiders. The unchurched—those who have no connection to the church—are the outsiders. Pastors, particularly, are insiders. In a churched culture, the church and its pastors have credibility in the community. To be a part of the church is desirable. Non-Christians come to the church to hear the Good News of Christ, which, in many ways, makes the mission of the church more doable than it is in a pre-church culture.**

- **In a post-church culture, the community around the church is increasingly unchurched—not connected to the church—but the church continues to operate as if it were living in a churched society. The insiders—namely, those who are not connected to the church—become harder for the outsiders—those who are connected to the church—to identify and to win for Christ.**

Many realities, including the statistics referenced in the magazine article described above, indicate that we are living today in this post-church society. This means we Christians need to sharpen our focus on and conquer our fears regarding ways and means of communicating the Gospel to people who may have absolutely no connection with or awareness of the church. One way to do so is to increase the localization of our mission outreach, focusing on the unchurched with the specific intention of addressing their everyday needs with the power and peace of the Gospel of Christ.

Since stereotypical generalizations are often inaccurate, and because differing conditions exist in different parts of our country and world, it behooves Christian leaders around the world to discern the context—pre-church, churched, post-church?—in which their church exists. Only by doing so can they determine the intentional and strategic plans necessary for accomplishing the mission of Christ. These insights are most helpful for pastors and other leaders in congregations of our Synod as we address how best to provide a faithful witness to Christ in a post-church culture.

Congregations are being challenged with understanding what is happening both inside and outside the church. In a post-church culture, it is not enough for congregations to think about how best to serve the people who already are a part of the church. Rather, congregations must also examine, evaluate, and refocus their mission and ministry at every level to learn how best to address the needs, touch the lives, and reach the hearts of those who live in the darkness of sin—those who are not at all a part of the Christian Church and faith we profess.

In this process, many LCMS congregations are thinking, planning, staffing, and budgeting creatively, no longer assuming that patterns of the past will work in the present or future. Holistic ministry and mission efforts with a view toward identifying and responding to the needs of unchurched people in the community surrounding the church are emerging in congregations whose leaders understand the post-church culture.

So, for example, congregations in metropolitan areas and small towns alike are opening and operating health clinics or providing parish nurses in an effort to reach people with medical needs and no access to proper health care. Similar outreach-oriented ministries, with slightly or perhaps significantly different focus, are being initiated by congregations across our Synod. Congregations are reaching out, intentionally and strategically, to homeless people, single parents, civil servants, people affected by divorce, victims of abuse, people trapped by addiction, individuals grieving the death of spouse or child, newly arrived immigrants, and others. People in such circumstances, without contact and care from church-related ministries, might otherwise never come into contact with the Gospel of Christ.

In all these cases, the motivation for ministry is that articulated by St. Paul to the church in Corinth:

> For the love of Christ controls us, because we have concluded this: that one has died for all, therefore all have died; and He died for all, that those who live might no longer live for themselves but for Him who for their sake died and was raised. (2 Corinthians 5:14–15)

The kinds of ministries described above have to do with one-on-one relationships that can be developed only by individual-focused ministries of pastor and people in Christian congregations. On a broader scope, the church at large has both the opportunity and responsibility to witness to Christ in a post-church culture. How best can that occur? Quality Christian education and unapologetic Christian witness play key roles.

Since its inception, The Lutheran Church—Missouri Synod has emphasized the value of Christian education at every level. Today, centers of education—from preschool to kindergarten to elementary to junior high and high school to colleges and universities to seminary and post-graduate—are sponsored and supported by individual congregations, clusters or associations of congregations, districts and national Synod. Solid Christian education, biblically and confessionally based, is a major strength and hallmark of the LCMS.

These educational ministries provide great opportunity for witness to the Gospel, especially since in many, if not most cases, a significant percentage of students in our Lutheran elementary, high school, and university classrooms are not baptized and come from homes where the love of Christ is virtually unknown. What a tremendous opportunity we have in our Lutheran schools to share clearly and convincingly the truths of God's love for mankind in the person of Jesus Christ. Just think about it. Families and individuals actually pay our agencies of Christian education for the privilege we have of teaching their children not only how to spend their lives in a professional or vocational calling, but also how to live their lives under the Word of God, which brings into their lives the blessings of health, healing, and hope through the Gospel!

Educational endeavors in our Synod are not without challenges. Increased competition from public schools supported by public funding and private or other faith-based enterprises with much larger endowments than the LCMS has been able to muster to date, has placed a significant financial burden on many of our educational institutions. Yet, as stated elsewhere in this book, Christian education looms large on the horizon of opportunities for Gospel witness and proclamation, especially in a post-church culture.

Additionally and importantly, the LCMS has many laymen and laywomen engaged in the public and private educational arena. While their freedom to share the Gospel of Christ is tethered significantly by federal and state law, their very presence, modeling of Christian values, and demonstration of Christian principles have a formidable impact on the lives of those who sit at their feet. I thank God for all Christian teachers, professors, administrators, and support staff involved in the educational enterprise, at every level, in a vast variety of educational settings, for their Christian influence in the lives of learners of every race, color, and creed.

Unapologetic Christian witness in the public arena presents great opportunity for sharing the Gospel of Christ in a post-church culture. As previously noted, people in our country are not flocking to the church today to the same degree they did in previous years. Nevertheless, there are many indications that people in our country and around the world have a very real hunger and thirst for things spiritual, often seeking at great personal or financial expense a deeper understanding of life and its ultimate destination.

Yet the topic of what has been called "witness in the public square" is a matter of some debate among us. Indeed, the giant encounters other giants, and this is one that casts a large shadow in our midst and, without our resolve, will dampen our public witness and public perception as a church.

The basic question revolves around the biblical appropriateness of a Lutheran Christian, especially a pastor, speaking, praying, or in any other way publicly representing the Christian faith as someone connected with The Lutheran Church—Missouri Synod, particularly when people of different faiths are present. While our Synod does not prohibit and even encourages public witness in general, the debate in our circles focuses most specifically on whether such witness is appropriate in places and at occasions where public worship, especially public prayer, is involved.

The wording of our Synod's Constitution that is at the center of this debate is this:

> Article VI Conditions of Membership
>
> Conditions for acquiring and holding membership in the Synod are the following:
>
> 1. Acceptance of the confessional basis of Article II.
> 2. Renunciation of unionism and syncretism of every description, such as:
>   a. Serving congregations of mixed confession, as such, by ministers of the church;
>   b. Taking part in the services and sacramental rites of heterodox congregations or of congregations of mixed confession;
>   c. Participating in heterodox tract and missionary activities.

The key words are "Renunciation of unionism and syncretism of every description." Hardly household words in America, "unionism" and "syncretism" have had and continue to have significant meaning in the LCMS. Let's explore their definitions.

Dr. Samuel Nafzger, in his article "Syncretism and Unionism" in the July 2003 *Concordia Journal*, offers the following observations regarding these two terms:

> 1. The terms *syncretism* and *unionism* are not found in the Scriptures or in The Book of Concord.
> 2. Since the time of the Reformation, *syncretism* has been a term used by Lutheran theologians to refer to the "mixing of religions"

without the resolution of the doctrinal differences that divide them.

3. In The Lutheran Church—Missouri Synod, the term *unionism*, which came into usage as a result of the state-forced union of the Lutheran and Reformed churches in Prussia in 1817, was originally used synonymously with the term *syncretism*. These are terms that connote the compromise of the Gospel through the relativizing of its doctrinal articles.
4. The Constitution of the Missouri Synod gives as examples (not definitions) of syncretism or unionism "the serving" of congregations of mixed confession by its member pastors and their "taking part in the services and sacramental rites of heterodox congregations of mixed confession." This provision was not understood as necessarily prohibiting joint prayers with Christians belonging to heterodox or erring churches.
5. The Constitution of the Missouri Synod, by giving as the first reason for the formation of the Synod the objective of working for fellowship with other Christian church bodies, indicates that the renunciation of all forms of syncretism does not mean that the members of the Synod should have nothing to do with other Christian churches. The Synod's Constitution rejects not only syncretism but also sectarianism and schism, i.e., separatism. The CTCR states: "It is evident that the concepts of unionism and separatism are intimately related. Unionism is attempted union when separation is in order, and separatism is separation when union is in order."
6. The most concise definition of *syncretism* or *unionism* is that given in Francis Pieper's *Brief Statement*, adopted officially by the Synod in 1932, which states: "We repudiate unionism, that is, church fellowship with the adherents of false doctrine."

7. As the term *unionism* came to be more frequently used to refer to the mixing together of religions by coming together in church fellowship with erring Christian denominations before the resolution of doctrinal differences, the term *syncretism* was increasingly understood as the mingling together of the Christian religion with non-Christian faiths.

Dr. Nafzger's article continues:

An overview of the contemporary religious situation as seen through the lens of the Scriptural and Confessional principles presented in the Lutheran Confessions provides the basis for the following observations:

1. By definition, syncretism and unionism compromise and relativize the objective and exclusive truth claims of the doctrine of the Gospel.
2. The dangers of syncretism and unionism as defined above are more real and more prevalent today than perhaps ever before since we live in an age that prizes these very qualities as necessary for living in an increasingly pluralistic society.
3. The subject of inter-Christian relationships is not exhausted by a discussion of church fellowship. (The terms *church fellowship*, *inter-church relations*, and *inter-Christian relationships* are not synonymous terms.)

The matters of interchurch relations, unionism, separatism, syncretism, participating in events or services involving non-LCMS participants, etc., have been and continue to be addressed in our Synod. These are not easy topics, as noted above. They cry out for biblically based resolution among us. This topic was explored in greater detail earlier in this book.

In this regard, our Synod's Commission on Theology and Church Relations, in its document titled *The Lutheran Understanding of Church Fellowship*, has presented helpful, biblical, and confessional observations and recommendations on this topic. This document, which includes guidelines for participating in civic events, was commended and approved by the 2001 LCMS Convention "for continued use and guidance" in Res. 3-07A. In addition, the Synod has asked the Commission on Theology and Church Relations for further guidance, including appropriate ways of relating to other Christians belonging to churches not in church fellowship with our Synod.

Many of the concerns identified in this chapter have found expression in the paragraphs included in the *Response Report to The Lutheran Understanding of Church Fellowship*. The response to the fellowship document has been discussed at length, particularly in recent years, in large part because the section called "Cases of Discretion" has such a contemporary application in the so-called Yankee Stadium event.

The Yankee Stadium event illustrates the opportunity for public witness and the "giant" faced by such witness both within the LCMS—through the parochial perception of its members—and outside the Synod—through the public perception of the community-at-large, including other religious circles and society in general. Here is a summary of that event:

- **As we all know, terrorists destroyed the World Trade Center Towers in New York City, September 11, 2001, killing 3,000 people, including LCMS members and friends and relatives of LCMS members. That traumatic event occurred just three days after I was installed as the 12th president of The Lutheran Church—Missouri Synod. Our nation and the world have been radically affected by the events of that day.**
- **Atlantic District President Dr. David Benke was invited by the office of the Mayor of New York City to participate**

in "A Prayer for America" in Yankee Stadium, September 23, 2001. Before accepting the invitation, President Benke sought the counsel of his ecclesiastical supervisor, the president of the Synod. On the basis of my careful study and clear understanding of the collective will of the Synod, I provided counsel to Dr. Benke that his participation appeared to be permissible and appropriate.

- During its meeting that same weekend, on September 26, 2001, the LCMS Council of Presidents adopted a resolution that read, "In light of the tragic events of September 11th . . . a pastoral letter should be sent to all pastors and church workers. . . . The draft prepared by committee was revised a number of times by the members of the whole Council. A motion was unanimously passed to adopt the letter as amended and revised, bearing the signature of the President of Synod, all the Vice-Presidents of Synod, and all the District Presidents." While not specifically referencing the Yankee Stadium event in the letter itself, strong expressions of support and affirmation regarding President Benke's involvement in that event were offered orally by members of the Council, including some who were later critical of his participation.

The letter itself states, in part: "We commend President Kieschnick and District President Benke for the strong leadership they have given at this time. We commend them, and others like them, for the compassion and the encouragement they have given to the caregivers. We are especially grateful for the many pastors and church leaders who seize the opportunity to bring a clear testimony of hope in Christ to people everywhere."

- **Nevertheless, some pastors filed formal charges to have me removed from membership in the Synod for the counsel I provided to Dr. Benke. Those charges were followed by an official opinion of the Commission on Constitutional Matters that the president of the Synod is accountable only to the convention of the Synod. I was and still am quite well aware and fully accepting of the fact that the president of the Synod is accountable to the convention of the Synod, which is ultimately my "boss."**
- **Formal charges were also brought by individuals and congregations against Dr. Benke, seeking to have him expelled from membership in the Synod. Those charges were formally resolved. Dr. Benke was initially suspended from the clergy roster of the Synod by a Synod vice-president assigned by majority vote of the Praesidium of the Synod to handle this case. Subsequently, Dr. Benke's appeal to the duly constituted and conducted Dispute Resolution Panel resulted in the final decision that he should not be expelled from the Synod. He was and still is fully reinstated to his office as district president.**

A few additional comments are in order. In the days and weeks following September 11, people in our Lutheran congregations throughout the Synod, particularly in the Atlantic, New England, New Jersey, Eastern, and Southeastern districts, were grieving and in a state of shock following this terrible and traumatic act of terrorism.

- **Children in our Lutheran schools were struggling with questions of life and death, many of them directly affected by the deaths of parents, siblings, loved ones, and friends.**
- **How does one tell a child that his or her father or mother or anyone else near and dear to that child**

    - was not only burned beyond recognition but also cremated beyond existence in the unfathomable intensity of the heat, smoke, and flames of the explosion; or
    - made a literal life-and-death (actually, death-and-death), split-second decision to jump from the window of a 110-story tower rather than face the kind of death just described; or
    - in one way or another has quite literally disappeared and will never again be heard from or seen?
- Pastors, teachers, and social workers experienced depression and exhaustion as a result of working almost around the clock trying to answer such questions—questions posed not only by others but also by themselves—while at the same time providing spiritual care and comfort to the people in their congregations, schools, and communities.
- Life still has not returned to normality in our country, especially in those communities most directly affected by a handful of terrorists on that now historic day.

Just the day before President Benke sought my counsel on his invitation from the office of Mayor Giuliani to come to Yankee Stadium, he and I, together with counterparts from the Evangelical Lutheran Church in America, had toured Ground Zero.

- We smelled the stench of death and burning flesh.
- We saw the looks of shock and horror on the faces of police officers, firemen, and volunteers.
- We did what we knew how to do. We prayed. We cried. We grieved. We prayed some more.
- We demonstrated tangible care to survivors and relatives of victims in any way we knew how.

That's the context in which President Benke made a pastoral decision to participate in the Yankee Stadium event, doing so with my counsel as his ecclesiastical supervisor. Some have vehemently disagreed with his decision and with my counsel to him. Many others have expressed strong support for both, thankful for his presence and prayer at a time of crisis and trauma.

My counsel to President Benke was based primarily on the Synod's collective understanding of the teaching of Holy Scripture, expressed in Resolution 3-07A of the 2001 Synod Convention, referenced earlier in this chapter. Pertinent quotes from the unanimously adopted report of the Commission on Theology and Church Relations, commended by that resolution "for continued use and guidance in the Synod," include:

- **"Pastors . . . are often asked to participate in activities outside of their own and other LCMS congregations. Some of these are civic events. Offering prayers, speaking, and reading Scripture at events sponsored by governments, public schools and volunteer organizations would be a problem if the organization in charge restricted a Christian witness. For instance, if an invitation requires a pastor to pray to God without mentioning Jesus, he cannot in good conscience accept. Without such a restriction, a Lutheran pastor may for valid and good reason participate in civic affairs such as an inauguration, graduation or a right-to-life activity. These occasions may provide opportunity to witness to the Gospel. Pastors may have honest differences of opinion about whether or to what extent it is appropriate or helpful to participate in these or similar civic events. In these cases charity must prevail.**
- **"There are also 'once-in-a-life-time' situations. It is virtually impossible to anticipate all such situations or to establish**

> **rules in advance. Specific answers cannot be given to cover every type of situation pastors and congregations face. These situations can be evaluated only on a case-by-case basis and may evoke different responses from different pastors who may be equally committed to LCMS fellowship principles. The LCMS has always recognized this."**

Subsequently, a few members of the Commission serving in 2001, having been asked, have indicated that they never anticipated an event such as Yankee Stadium when approving this report. I submit that few, if any of us, anticipated an event such as the one that occurred on September 11, 2001.

Others have suggested that the Synod's constitution, bylaws, and convention resolutions should not be used to address the propriety of actions of members of the Synod. Rather, such actions should be judged only by specific passages of Scripture. In fact, our synodical covenants of love are based on the premise that our Synod's constitution, bylaws, and resolutions are in accord with, or at least not contrary to, Holy Scripture, as the Synod in convention collectively determines what we understand the Bible to teach concerning specific matters of faith and life. If an individual member or officer of the Synod believes there is a conflict between our Synod's governing documents and the Scriptures, he or she has both the opportunity and the obligation to persuade the Synod that such is the case, in accord with our agreed upon process.

The bottom line is that, when faced with the necessity of providing pastoral counsel to a district president of the Synod who needed to make a pastoral decision in a time of public trauma and deep spiritual need, I found in the CTCR report guidelines that sounded eerily as though they had been written for just such a circumstance—guidelines that were "commended for continued use and guidance" in the Synod.

I said to the delegates at the 2004 Convention of the Synod:

If this 2004 Convention of the Synod should decide that it does not agree with that resolution (3-07A) adopted by the 2001 Convention, or with my interpretation of it, then this Convention has the responsibility to express the position of the Synod in a different way. Unless and until such action is taken, I have no choice but to stand by my oath of office as President of this Synod, to fulfill my constitutional duty and God-given responsibility to uphold and abide by the Synod's collective will, regardless of any individual understanding or opinion that may be expressed otherwise.

Further, as indicated in Part I of my Report to the Synod, I agree with and uphold the position of the LCMS that pastors of our Synod should have the freedom, tempered with the accompanying responsibility, of "offering prayers, speaking, and reading Scripture at events sponsored by governments . . . " if the organization in charge does not restrict a Christian witness, and if this can be done without any compromise of our Scriptural, Confessional and constitutional commitments.

Along with this decision-making freedom there must be a climate of trust in the Synod, especially among our pastors. For The Lutheran Church—Missouri Synod to be functional and healthy, we must trust that our pastors can and will make God-pleasing decisions in day-to-day circumstances, as well as in exceptional situations. I truly pray and trust, especially in extraordinarily difficult and gut-wrenching times of pastoral decision making, that our pastors will seek to follow the Lord's will and that in circumstances where disagreements surround another's decisions, charity will prevail.

Our pastors must be allowed to be pastors, without fear of backlash or formal charges around every decision-making corner. This kind of trust, resulting from Scriptural faithfulness and Christian charity, will enable a healthy, faithful and bold public witness to the Gospel of our Lord Jesus Christ.

One more word needs to be said on this subject. As previously reported to the Synod, I believe Dr. Benke's prayer could and should have been a stronger articulation of the truth of Holy Scripture regarding the absolute necessity of faith in Jesus Christ as the only way to eternal life. Here is what I said on two occasions, in my memos to the Synod of February 11, 2002, and January 22, 2004:

> Some from among both those who agree and those who disagree with Dr. Benke's Yankee Stadium participation have expressed the view that his prayer was lacking in clarity and did not provide as clear a witness to the Gospel as it might have. I have spoken with Dr. Benke about this matter. It should be noted that he has expressed his own agreement with the view that his prayer could and should have been more complete in its expression of faith in Jesus Christ as the only way to salvation. In his response to the charges against him he has admitted this deficiency and has asked for the Synod's forgiveness.

Here are the exact words of Dr. Benke himself, originally posted on January 4, 2002, online and in print since that date, and referenced in my memos to the Synod, noted above:

> I made a pledge very early on to take seriously those who differed with me. So in the area of specific wording, to whoever has had problems and criticisms, I am sorry that I didn't get the words out more clearly or accurately or completely. Although it was never intentional, I know that my words have offended some in my denomination, and for that offense I apologize, sincerely, and ask for forgiveness.
>
> David H. Benke

> January 4, 2002
>
> As your ecclesiastical supervisor, Dr. Benke, I assure you again, as I have in the past, of the forgiveness you have requested, by the grace of God, through Jesus Christ our Lord.
>
> Beyond these words, and any that I may share in response to questions submitted during the Q & A portion of this report, I believe it is time to put this matter behind us and get on with the mission our Lord has given.
>
> In the meantime, I am pleased to report that the assignment I gave to the Synod's Commission on Theology and Church Relations almost immediately following the events of September 2001 has been completed and distributed to the Synod in the form of a document titled *Guidelines for Participation in Civic Events.* I publicly thank the Commission for its excellent work in preparing this document, adopted by a vote of 14-2. It is scheduled to come before this convention for consideration and commendation.
>
> In addition, our Convention theme, **One Mission:** *Ablaze!* is enhanced by a resource titled "*Witness & Worship in Pluralistic America*" (Concordia Seminary, St. Louis, 2004). This document provides both proper caution and evangelical encouragement in our endeavor to reach people around the world with the Gospel of Christ. One example will suffice: "The Great Commission obligates the church to be **in** the world without becoming **of** the world in order to witness **to** the world."

This is only one example of how the vital matter of witnessing to the pure Gospel in a pluralistic America, even and perhaps especially in the presence of those who do not acknowledge or believe in the only true God, Father, Son, and Holy Spirit, brings along with it many challenges and difficulties. In order to face and overcome this giant, it is imperative that we speak clearly, sensitively, and humbly, yet boldly, courageously, and uncompromisingly, in Christian love, supported by the power of God's love.

Each time I recall the "Yankee Stadium" experience, I'm reminded of the way the prophet Elijah responded to the opportunity he faced, in the presence of the prophets of Baal, a foreign idol. His story is related in 1 Kings 18 in this exciting narrative:

> So Ahab sent to all the people of Israel and gathered the prophets together at Mount Carmel. And Elijah came near to all the people and said, "How long will you go limping between two different opinions? If the LORD is God, follow Him; but if Baal, then follow him." And the people did not answer him a word. Then Elijah said to the people, "I, even I only, am left a prophet of the LORD, but Baal's prophets are 450 men. Let two bulls be given to us, and let them choose one bull for themselves and cut it in pieces and lay it on the wood, but put no fire to it. And I will prepare the other bull and lay it on the wood and put no fire to it. And you call upon the name of your god, and I will call upon the name of the LORD, and the God who answers by fire, He is God." And all the people answered, "It is well spoken."
>
> Then Elijah said to the prophets of Baal, "Choose for yourselves one bull and prepare it first, for you are many, and call upon the name of your god, but put no fire to it." And they took the bull that was given them, and they prepared it and called upon the name of Baal from morning until noon, saying, "O Baal, answer us!" But there was no voice, and no one answered. And they limped around the altar that they had made. And at noon Elijah mocked them, saying, "Cry aloud, for he is a god. Either he is musing, or he is relieving himself, or he is on a journey, or perhaps he is asleep and must be awakened." And they cried aloud and cut themselves

after their custom with swords and lances, until the blood gushed out upon them. And as midday passed, they raved on until the time of the offering of the oblation, but there was no voice. No one answered; no one paid attention.

Then Elijah said to all the people, "Come near to me." And all the people came near to him. And he repaired the altar of the Lord that had been thrown down. Elijah took twelve stones, according to the number of the tribes of the sons of Jacob, to whom the word of the Lord came, saying, "Israel shall be your name," and with the stones he built an altar in the name of the Lord. And he made a trench about the altar, as great as would contain two seahs of seed. And he put the wood in order and cut the bull in pieces and laid it on the wood. And he said, "Fill four jars with water and pour it on the burnt offering and on the wood." And he said, "Do it a second time." And they did it a second time. And he said, "Do it a third time." And they did it a third time. And the water ran around the altar and filled the trench also with water.

And at the time of the offering of the oblation, Elijah the prophet came near and said, "O Lord, God of Abraham, Isaac, and Israel, let it be known this day that You are God in Israel, and that I am Your servant, and that I have done all these things at Your word. Answer me, O Lord, answer me, that this people may know that You, O Lord, are God, and that You have turned their hearts back."

Then the fire of the Lord fell and consumed the burnt offering and the wood and the stones and the dust, and licked up the water that was in the trench. And when all the people saw it, they fell on their faces and said, "The Lord, He is God; the Lord, He is God." And Elijah said to them, "Seize the prophets of Baal; let not one of them escape." And they seized them. And Elijah brought them down to the brook Kishon and slaughtered them there. (1 Kings 18:20–40)

While it would be neither prudent nor lawful in today's America to dispatch and dispose of those who follow false gods in the same way Elijah and his people did the prophets of Baal, I find in this story great encouragement and strength for witnessing to non-Christians in our post-church culture. And while the task today of persuading non-Christian people that there is only one true God does not involve a sacrificial altar, properly prepared bull, and all-consuming fire from that true God, it should be done with equal fearlessness and clarity.

With conviction and confidence, we say to those who honor false gods: How long will you go limping between two different opinions? If the Lord is God, follow Him; but if Baal, then follow Him. And whether the method God chooses to reveal Himself is one that displays His miraculous might, as in the story of Elijah and the prophets of Baal, or one that reveals Him in "a low whisper" (1 Kings 19:12), we await the response of the people whose hearts He moves to say, "The Lord, He is God; the Lord, He is God."

As the giant awakens and encounters other giants, he does so with the full confidence that "the Lord your God is God of gods and Lord of lords, the great, the mighty, and the awesome God!" (Deuteronomy 10:17).

CHAPTER SIX

The Giant Chooses a Fork in the Road—Where We Are Going and How We Get There—Vision and Mission of an American Church in the 21st Century

In the 1968 U.S. presidential campaign, Robert F. Kennedy often uttered these lines: "There are those who look at things the way they are and ask, 'Why?' . . . I dream of things that never were and ask, 'Why not?' "

When I was a young pastor serving my first parish at Lutheran Church of the Good Shepherd in Biloxi, Mississippi, an elected leader of the congregation approached me one day and asked what my vision was for the future of the congregation. I had been taught in seminary that the job of a pastor, besides preaching, teaching, and administering the sacraments, was to equip the people of God for ministry. But I think I must have been daydreaming the day the professor covered the topic of vision for the future. So I responded to the question rather inadequately; I had no clue at that time in my life what a congregation's vision for the future might look like.

An almost identical question was asked by the staff of the Texas district of the LCMS shortly after I was first elected district president in 1991. The question was, "What's your vision for the Texas district?" At the time the question was asked, I was trying to figure out how to identify gifted and qualified men to be considered by congregations I was assisting in calling a pastor. So my answer to the vision question was something quite profound: "My vision for the Texas district is to find the most gifted and qualified pastors for the congregations of this district."

That answer hardly satisfied the men who had posed the question. But here again, I don't recall receiving any seminary or other training on developing a vision for the second largest geographical district in our national church body. Ultimately, the question was quite helpful, as it led to a process of collaborative conversation among the leaders of the district. This conversation resulted in the development of a vision and mission statement for the district's mission-and-ministry partnership with its 350 congregations: "Reach the lost, disciple the saved, and care for people—locally and globally."

Often I'm asked what I think about the future of The Lutheran Church—Missouri Synod, a question that begs a visionary reply. Behind this question I sometimes sense a spirit of pessimism regarding the sustainability of our church body. This is particularly so when those who ask the question are aware of the apathy or scarcity of denominational loyalty emanating from many congregations and church leaders when the topic concerns anything beyond the boundaries of their own parishes.

During my extensive travels across the nation during the years of my service as a national church body leader, I have observed and listened to many pastors, educators, congregational members, district staff, and district presidents. On the basis of these observations and conversations, I perceive the following realities:

- **The LCMS is a graying, declining church body, but I believe that Christian educational endeavors, compassionate human-care efforts, and intentional mission outreach provide unlimited opportunities, through the power of the Holy Spirit, for transforming the LCMS into a vibrant, vital gathering of Christians in mission to the world.**
- **The LCMS has been fractured by a party spirit that has, to a great degree, obscured the mission zeal it may have once possessed, but there are many, many exceptions that give me great hope for the future of the Synod.**
- **The LCMS is held together by the grace of God, the theological confession of that grace at work in the world, and the passion of many to communicate this confession through Word and deed to both the saved and unsaved.**

Before going further with the topic of vision and mission in an American church in the 21st century, let me share a few words about tradition. Jaroslav Pelikan said, "Tradition is the living faith of those now dead. Traditionalism is the dead faith of those still living."

Greg Morris of Leadership Dynamics makes these observations about tradition:

> The musical *Fiddler on the Roof* takes place in Anatevka, a . . . village in czarist Russia in 1905. Tevye, the hardworking Jewish dairyman, tells us that everyone's lives in their community are governed by tradition. Tevye states: "Our traditions tell us what to wear, what to eat. Our traditions tell us to wear prayer cloths. Our traditions tell us what to believe. 'Where do you get your traditions?' you may ask. I'll tell you! . . . I don't know!"

Most of us find security within the friendly confines of our traditions. The familiar is comfortable and well-known and so we tend to gravitate toward our usual way of doing things. Tradition is our history, our heritage and our legacy. While there is nothing wrong with tradition, we must be constantly aware that tradition does not degenerate into traditionalism.

Traditionalism speaks a language that outsiders cannot understand. It is filled with jargon, terminology, and activities that are meaningless to the "uneducated." What once began as a clear-cut mission or vision slowly drifts off course. What was motivated by purpose and direction now has become mechanical and routine and in the process has lost its vitality and effectiveness. The church or ministry organization that loves the status quo soon becomes irrelevant to this generation while maintaining their past traditions. Perhaps that is why some of Christ's harshest words were spoken against traditionalism when He rebuked the Pharisees with, "You nullify the word of God by your traditions!" (Mark 7:13)

Mark Twain observed that "The only thing that likes change is a wet baby." Traditions die hard because change is uncomfortable. Change requires us to adopt new behaviors based on new paradigms. Change requires us to sail further from shore as we leave the placid waters of the familiar and venture into the turbulent unknown. But if we are unwilling to change or modify the way we do things, there can never be any progress or improvement.

If our purpose is increased ministry effectiveness, then:

1. We don't have the privilege to be provincial. Our message of redemptive and transforming grace is timeless. But the methodology of communicating the gospel to a 21st century audience needs to be current.

2. We don't have the privilege to be protective. In an effort to maintain our traditions and administrative regularity, we often become "gatekeepers" rather than "trailblazers." Growth can be uncomfortable, but it is the only evidence of life.
3. We don't have the privilege to be perpetual. Is our goal simply to perpetuate the past? As Eddy Ketchursid said, "If your horse is dead, for goodness sake, dismount."

> The Apostle Paul reminds us, "For if a man is in Christ he becomes a new person altogether—the past is finished and gone, everything has become fresh and new" (2 Corinthians 5:17, Phillips). Change is at the very heart of the Christian life and because of that we're in the transformation business.
>
> Remember, where you're going is more important than where you've been!

I do not totally agree with that final statement. In The Lutheran Church—Missouri Synod, the past is very important. We cherish our heritage and history. (A tour through the splendid new Concordia Historical Institute Museum at our International Center in St. Louis drives this point home very well.) We also learn from what has happened in the past in order to prepare to face the future. So how do we in the LCMS envision what lies ahead? What role do challenge and change play in the future? Let's take a look.

Re-Envisioning Mission in the New Century

As the Christian Church addresses the challenges and opportunities it faces in the 21st century, how does the future look? The church of our grandchildren is different from that of our grandfathers because the world of our grandchildren is different from that of our grandfathers. I believe that to be true. I also believe that the mission to be accomplished, reaching lost people for Christ, and the message by which that mission is accomplished, a changeless Christ for a changing world, must remain the same for our grandchildren as it was for our grandfathers. So, how will it be possible with the vast and fast-moving changes all around us to get a clear picture of the future ways and means by which the 21st century Christian Church's mission will be accomplished and its vision fulfilled?

"Vision" is defined by the thesaurus in a number of ways: "dream, hallucination, apparition, idea, mental picture, image, visualization, revelation, prophecy, farsightedness, imagination, forethought, prediction, sight, ability to see." Each of these synonyms (with the possible exception of "hallucination" and "apparition") contributes to what constitutes a leader's vision for the future of the people or organization he or she is both blessed and burdened to lead.

In the case of The Lutheran Church—Missouri Synod, our church body's national convention in 2004 resolved to "endorse and respond enthusiastically to" the vision articulated as "One Mission, One Message, One People." Those six simple words deserve significant comment.

Holy Scripture is replete with biblical references regarding the Vision of ONE, especially our oneness in Christ:

- "And He made known to us the mystery of His will according to His good pleasure . . . to bring all things in heaven and on earth together under one head, even Christ" (Ephesians 1:9–10).
- "Make every effort to keep the unity of the Spirit through the bond of peace. There is one body and one Spirit—just as you were called to one hope when you were called—one Lord, one faith, one baptism; one God and Father of all, who is over all and through all and in all" (Ephesians 4:3–6).

- "Live a life worthy of the calling you have received. Be completely humble and gentle; be patient, bearing with one another in love. Make every effort to keep the unity of the Spirit through the bond of peace" (Ephesians 4:1–3).
- "I appeal to you, brothers, in the name of our Lord Jesus Christ, that all of you agree with one another so that there may be no divisions among you" (1 Corinthians 1:10).
- Jesus prayed, "[A]lso for those who will believe in Me through their [the disciples'] word, that they may all be one, just as You, Father, are in Me, and I in You. . . . that they may be one as We are one . . . that they may become perfectly one, so that the world may know that You sent Me and loved them even as You loved Me"(John 17:20–23).

It is clear from these and many other passages of the Bible that the almighty God who created the universe and populated it with the first man and woman values highly the concept of oneness between Himself and His creation. The creation of the first human beings was described simply but significantly in these words, that they were created "in the image of God" (Genesis 1:27). We know from our study of Scripture that the oneness between God and His creation at the beginning of time was perfect. God intended man to live at peace with Him and to live forever. There was no sense of separation between God and man until sin entered the world. And with sin came death.

Since then, the oneness that God intended from the dawn of time has been spoiled by mankind's preoccupation with self and things that have no lasting value. While initially man and woman were created to live eternally, the presence of sin and all that accompanies it—selfishness, self-gratification, jealousy toward others, hatred of those we envy or fear, desire to take what belongs to someone else, abuse of the gifts God intended to be for mankind's benefit, rejection of God's desire to bring us back to Himself, and much more—have resulted in continued separation between God and the crown of His creation—man and woman. And the end result of sin is death. *"For the wages of sin is death"* (Romans 6:23a).

Without God's action to restore the unity lost by the fall into sin, this separation between man and God and the death resulting from such separation would last eternally. That action was initiated by God when He sent His Son into the world to accomplish the reunification of God and man. A church marquee I recently saw describes it in these few words: "God so loved the world that He came." The Bible uses these words: "For God so loved the world, that He gave His only Son, that whoever believes in Him should not perish but have eternal life. For God did not send His Son into the world to condemn the world, but in order that the world might be saved through Him" (John 3:16–17).

Jesus lived His life in perfect obedience to God's holy will. His life was spent proclaiming freedom to the captive, hope for the despairing, healing for the sick, forgiveness for the sinner, life for the lifeless. His popularity with the people of the region in which He lived both soared (when He performed any of His many miraculous deeds) and fell (when He spoke of being a king whose kingdom was not of this world). Ultimately, He was accused of being a king in that day's common understanding of that term, arrested, tried, persecuted, beaten, found guilty, and condemned to death on a cross.

It was on that cross that He proclaimed, *"It is finished."* "It" referred to His work of accomplishing for mankind what mankind could never accomplish by itself, namely, a restoration of the unity between God and mankind. That unity is a gift from God Himself, a gift that cannot be earned, a gift that is not dependent upon man's inherent goodness or virtue, a free gift that lasts forever. In addition to what Paul writes about the wages of sin being death, he adds, *"but the free gift of God is eternal life in Christ Jesus our Lord"* (Romans 6: 23b).

Sadly, in the world today and in every generation of the past, not all have heard about or received this gift. The Bible describes the condition of people who have not heard or believed what Jesus has done as "lost." While some might consider "lost" a pejorative term, its intent is to convey concern, care, and eternal love. If someone is lost in our normal understanding of that word, he or she needs to be found, whether he or she realizes it or not. For sooner or later, if not found, the person's lost condition will result in separation from home, deterioration of health, exposure to harmful elements or destructive forces, and, ultimately, death.

The same is true of a person who is lost spiritually. That's exactly why Jesus Himself said, "The Son of Man came to seek and to save the lost" (Luke 19:10). And that brings us to the vision and mission of our church body.

In one way, it's quite simple. My vision for The Lutheran Church—Missouri Synod in this new century is "One Mission, One Message, One People." That vision was officially blessed by the 2004 national convention of our Synod. What does it mean?

First, One Mission. Job number one for our church body always has been, and always must be, seeking to fulfill the Great Commission of our Lord. "Go therefore and make disciples of all nations, baptizing them in the name of the Father and of the Son and of the Holy Spirit, teaching them to observe all that I have commanded you" (Matthew 28:19–20). In that One Mission we are joined as a band of brothers and sisters storming the gates of hell in the name of the ascended Christ.

Second, this mission is based on One Message. "I am the way and the truth and the life," Jesus says. "No one comes to the Father except through Me" (John 14:6). Many people are dying every day and are eternally lost because they have not heard and believed the one saving message.

Third, this message yearns to be lived and shared by One People, demonstrating their God-given unity. "Whatever happens, conduct yourselves in a manner worthy of the gospel of Christ. . . . stand firm in one spirit, contending as one man for the faith of the gospel" (Philippians 1:27 NIV).

So it seems simple enough: "One Mission, One Message, One People." That's not controversial. You might choose some different words or prefer another emphasis, but I believe most of us find "One Mission, One Message, One People" unobjectionable. A vision should be simple but not simplistic. It should be easily remembered but also compelling at the grass roots of congregational life as well as in our Synod's boards, offices, and institutions of higher learning.

Will this vision flourish or fail to be accomplished? Will the giant awaken and arise? Will the giant be able to figure out which roads to take and which roadblocks to avoid in the process of fixing and funding the mission?

The Lutheran Church—Missouri Synod is a church body full of contradictions. In some aspects of our life and work together, it's flourishing, with encouraging evidence of growth. In other places and ministries, revitalization needs desperately to occur.

So the challenge for this vision to flourish comes to this: how to deal with present realities in such a way that the vision is more than a nice set of words but becomes truly compelling for us in every aspect of our life together as The Lutheran Church—Missouri Synod.

That challenge will be met with a continued focus on our historic core values. "Stand at the crossroads and look; ask for the ancient paths, ask where the good way is, and walk in it, and you will find rest for your souls" (Jeremiah 6:16 NIV).

A very important chief core value for us has been and continues to be "Scripture Alone." I believe strongly that we in the LCMS are in agreement on our commitment to Holy Scripture. Beginning with God's creative word in Genesis and ending with a warning not to add or detract from the revelation of Scripture, the Bible from cover to cover attests to the truth and power of God's Word for the life of the world and church. "Sanctify them in the truth; Your word is truth" (John 17:17). "The words that I have spoken to you are spirit and life" (John 6:63).

The Gospel, the revelation of God in the life, death, and resurrection of Jesus Christ, *"is the power of God for salvation to everyone who believes"* (Romans 1:16). So that this power will work among us, we in The Lutheran Church—Missouri Synod have freely and voluntarily bound ourselves by our centuries-old confessional commitment: "We believe, teach, and confess that the prophetic and apostolic writings of the Old and New Testaments are the only rule and norm according to which all doctrines and teachers alike must be appraised and judged" (Formula of Concord, Epitome, Rule and Norm).

Coming closer to our own age in a more contemporary document, the constitution of The Lutheran Church—Missouri Synod states: "The Synod, and every member of the Synod, accepts without reservation: 1. The Scriptures of the Old and the New Testament as the written Word of God and the only rule and norm of faith and of practice; 2. All the Symbolical Books of the Evangelical Lutheran Church as a true and unadulterated statement and exposition of the Word of God" (Article II).

Today, as pastors, teachers, professional church workers, and congregations join our Synod, they subscribe to the cardinal truth of "Scripture Alone" by stating their belief and confession that "the canonical books of the Old and New Testaments [are] the inspired Word of God and the only infallible rule of faith and practice." On this core value—our scriptural and confessional commitment to the efficacious work of God through His Word—we are agreed.

Is this lip service? Not at all. Our history demonstrates this lively commitment. Our investments in maintaining biblical and confessional seminary education, our school system from pre-school through the Concordia University System, and Concordia Publishing House, all go back to the founding of the Synod, in some cases even predating the Synod. When I interact with leaders of other Christian denominations and speak with our people who have ecumenical friendships, I often hear that we are known as a theologically gifted church. It all shows that our lips are in sync with our hearts when we profess "Scripture Alone."

A caution is in order lest we thrive as an earthly institution but find ourselves ashamed before God on the Day of Judgment (1 Corinthians 3:10–15). There will always be a great temptation to substitute human insights for the working of God's Word. Principles drawn from the social sciences are all around us, ready to usurp the role of scriptural and confessional theology as we move forward. I hasten to add, however, and I do so emphatically, that human disciplines do teach many useful things that shed helpful light on how we do our work.

For example, so-called felt needs identified by cultural researchers can indeed guide us to a better understanding of how and where to apply the balm of the Gospel. The temptation, however, is to be more ephemeral than eternal, more empathetic than salvific in speaking about sin and salvation.

Overcoming this temptation requires our pastors and people to join together in personal and corporate study of, and submission to, the authority of Holy Scripture. The role of Holy Scripture in our church means that it's not my vision, or your vision, or even the vision of the "institutional" church that will ultimately prevail. Any vision stated by a churchman and embraced by the church body should be God's vision for the salvation of blood-bought souls. While many people outside the church and, sadly, some within it also, do not accept "Thus says the Lord" as definitive, we must do so. It's our core value, the ancient path in which we have long walked together.

This brings us to the mission of our church body, which has been defined and officially articulated by the 1998 convention of our Synod in these words: "In grateful response to God's grace and empowered by the Holy Spirit through Word and Sacraments, the mission of The Lutheran Church—Missouri Synod is vigorously to make known the love of Christ by word and deed within our churches, communities and the world." To say the obvious, we have our challenges.

Annually, 35 percent of the congregations of our Synod gain not one adult by Baptism or confirmation. Annually, 47 percent of our congregations gain no more than one adult by Baptism or confirmation. Since 1968, the number of annual adult confirmations in our congregations has remained virtually the same, just under 30,000 per year. Statistically, it requires the efforts of 115 members of the LCMS to result in one adult confirmation each year. The national average in Christian churches is 85 adults to add one convert. In all but two of the past 40 years, our congregations together have lost more members than they have gained.

So what's going on here? What's the reason for this 40-year decline? The "Mission 21st Century Task Force" I appointed a few years ago studied the reasons for our decline in baptized membership and offered recommendations to reverse the trend. Here is a brief excerpt from the Task Force's report to the 2004 Synod convention. The summarized report is included as Appendix F in the back of this book:

> The Commission on Theology and Church Relations Statement of 1991 states, "Each of us has received from God's hand grace upon grace, all flowing from the sacrificial service of the One who laid down his life for us on the cross. We cannot, therefore, leave the work of God's mission to 'the church' in general or to 'others' who may appear more gifted for the task or to 'the pastor.' What an honor it is to follow in the footsteps of God's Servant-Son, and to share with others the love He has so freely and fully bestowed on us! Each of us is a personal letter from Christ to the world (2 Cor. 3:2–3), telling all who will listen of His grace, mercy and power." With the CTCR we have affirmed:
>
> - **Mission begins in the heart of God.**
> - **God's mission is necessary because of sin.**
> - **God's mission centers in Jesus Christ.**
> - **God's mission is empowered by the Holy Spirit.**
> - **God's mission is to and for everyone.**
> - **God's mission is our mission.**
> - **God's mission is my mission.**
> - **God's mission is urgent.**
>
> While we as a synod and in many of our congregations have declared our mission to be reaching our communities and the world for Jesus Christ, our history in North America over the past 30 plus years gives a much different message. We continue to decline in membership in the midst of a population that is rapidly growing.
>
> We believe it is time for the LCMS in convention under our theme of One Mission ABLAZE to return to faithfulness as a missional

church in North America. Mission 21st Century is a matter of faithfulness to our Scriptural and Confessional teachings and our commitment to reach each community with the Good News of Jesus Christ.

Acknowledging the realities that led to the appointment of the Task Force and to the conclusions it presented to the 2004 convention, it must also be said with joy that there are ample evidences that the mission of Christ is flourishing among us in many ways. Some intentional and strategic mission endeavors on the national level include:

- **LCMS World Mission, with the approval of our Synod in convention, has undertaken an intensive effort called *Ablaze!*—a movement with a goal to reach 100 million people with the Gospel by 2017, the 500th anniversary of the Reformation.**
- **A corollary capital campaign titled *Fan into Flame* has as its goal to gather $100 million in new gifts and offerings to support the costly aspects of the *Ablaze!* movement.**
- **"Pentecost 2000" was an effort to begin 1,000 new cross-cultural ministries.**
- **"What a Way!" is an initiative to create a new climate of joy and affirmation in the recruitment and retention of professional church workers.**
- **"For the Sake of the Church" is an effort to raise $400 million in endowments to offset the expense of professional church worker preparation and to double the number of students from The Lutheran Church—Missouri Synod in our 10 colleges and universities.**

- **The Next Generation Task Force helped non-synodically trained teachers within our schools receive affordable theological training.**

That, I repeat, is at the national level. There is much more happening at the district and congregation levels that evidences flourishing mission. In all this, the mission of God to save souls must be uppermost, not a mission merely to advance The Lutheran Church—Missouri Synod, which is a human organization.

Thus another caution: The Pharisees were mission-minded. Jesus said to the Pharisees, *"You travel across sea and land to make a single [convert]"* (Matthew 23:15), but then quickly added a word of condemnation: *"and when he becomes a [convert], you make him twice as much a child of hell as yourselves."* The condemnation was prompted by the Pharisees' mission for their self-righteous exaltation, not the Messiah who came to seek and save the lost (Luke 19:10). We dare not assume that our correct doctrinal formulations grant us an exemption from divine censure should we pursue mission for institutional purposes. *"Everything that was written in the past was written to teach us"* (Romans 15:4 NIV). Our mission is a Law and, especially, a Gospel mission through which Jesus seeks and saves the lost of the 21st century.

It is important to note that to be in God's mission we must be one with God's message. The message is simple in its essence: "in Christ God was reconciling the world to Himself, not counting [our] trespasses against [us], and entrusting to us the message of reconciliation" (2 Corinthians 5:19). This message is the power of God to cut through the clutter of the hundreds of messages that bombard Americans every day. Those messages are not only soul-destroying for those who are lost but can be discouraging to us as well.

Yes, we get discouraged:

- **We get discouraged because pluralism suggests that the faith of our Synod is an ethnic inheritance, not relevant for this pluralistic age.**
- **We get discouraged because we no longer live in the "Christian" America of past generations.**
- **We get discouraged because we're told everything is relative. Oprah Winfrey says, "One of the biggest mistakes humans make is to believe that there is only one way. Actually there are many diverse paths leading to what you call God."**
- **We get discouraged because historic values and practices of Judeo-Christian morality have been jettisoned in favor of abortion, euthanasia, living together, homosexual behavior, etc.**

Do these developments in our culture, trends that we all bump up against every day, consign us to founder, or can we hope to flourish? The latter is what I believe. We can confidently promote the Christ-centered message of infallible Scripture because it speaks to basic needs of the human heart through Law and Gospel. The Creator knows His creatures better than the promoters of postmodern thinking. We should be energized, for Lutheran Law-Gospel preaching centered in Jesus Christ can meet "felt needs" in a way no virtual ministry can begin to approach.

Pursuing the vision of this One Message has the most substantial backing known. The Gospel is God's power to convert (Isaiah 55; Hebrews 4:12) and has His promise of progress: "This gospel of the kingdom will be proclaimed throughout the whole world as a testimony to all nations" (Matthew 24:14).

The destructive and discouraging spiritual mush of America at the start of the 21st century will best be met with the wise and winsome confidence that the truth has always enjoined. "Write down the revelation and make it plain on tablets so that a herald may run with it. For the revelation awaits an appointed time; it speaks of the end and will not prove false" (Habakkuk 2:2–3 NIV).

An unknown author wrote something like, "Christianity did not do what it did or get where it got by being a milquetoast faith." Happily, The Lutheran Church—Missouri Synod neither is, nor I pray ever will be, a "milquetoast" church. People know and will always know where we stand on the infallibility of God's Word, on life issues, on marriage and family, on the godly education of our children, on moral absolutes and the reality of sin, and on the fact that faith in Jesus Christ is the only way to salvation and eternal life. While so many are standing at the crossroads and looking for new ways, we will proclaim the ancient paths, where the good way is, where our contemporaries can find rest for their souls.

We look to our pastors and theological faculties to lead us in this engagement. David H. C. Reid, once chaplain at Edinburgh University, described a young pastor who was building the ideal church and manse, or parsonage.

> His church would sit here, and his manse would sit there. He would have his study in the manse and his pulpit in the church connected by a sealed corridor, with his zealous wife guarding the door. There would be no telephone His existence would be hermetically sealed through the week with his clean and chaste theology books. And then on Sundays he would burst from the study door, dash along the corridor and into the pulpit. Nothing would have bothered him, nothing would have upset him. All he would have to do is preach. His gospel would be chaste, pure and

> untrammeled with the world, that is quite true, but how out of touch with things that matter! When asked how he liked his new parson, an old Scot said that he supposed he was all right, in the main, but six days he was invisible and the seventh day he was incomprehensible. It just won't work to shut ourselves off on these tight little islands. (Carlisle Marney, *For All the Saints*, II, 776)

For our vision to become reality, the One Mission and One Message must be shared by One People. The Pharisees knew the Hebrew Scriptures and their traditions but did not hear the revelation of Law and Gospel in the context of their own sinfulness and lost condition. As indicated earlier in this book, in many respects The Lutheran Church—Missouri Synod enjoys great unity in what we believe, teach, and confess. But in other respects we are divided.

In my travels I hear and feel the pain that we are fractured by disagreements, some in doctrine, many others in practice, largely exacerbated by a party spirit and well-organized political groups. In some respects, a lack of harmony, concord, and unity is apparent in our Synod and is demonstrated by specific actions and reactions that cross my desk on a regular basis. The devil is active in those details. Or, is it God in the details?

It is God who wins out in the details when we understand that the Gospel message comes down to this: Jesus died for my sins. Jesus died for your sins. That message of the now-empty cross is the greatest unifying power among us, and it comes to us preeminently through the ministry of Word and Sacraments. There is *"one Lord, one faith, one baptism, one God and Father of all, who is over all and through all and in all"* (Ephesians 4:5–6 NIV). We repentant sinners are united with God through Word and Sacrament, God's gifts to us, through which God makes His fractious people one.

The grace of God to us throughout our history and the desperate need of the 21st century for Jesus Christ, that one "name under heaven given among men by which we must be saved" (Acts 4:12), call us forward to flourishing mission and ministry. I am convinced that we can remain faithful to our doctrine and practice, shining brightly like a city on a hill, as we support one another in love and trust, always seeking to be faithful in mission and ministry.

One Mission, One Message, One People—making known the love of Christ by word and deed, within our church, communities, and the world!

> *Not to us, O LORD, not to us, but to Your name be the glory, because of Your love and faithfulness.* Psalm 115:1 NIV

CHAPTER SEVEN

The Giant Matures and Leads—Leadership, Especially in Difficult Times

One of the most frequently asked questions I hear has to do with leadership. The question often includes an inquiry regarding how I learned to be a leader. The answer is not simple. Much of what I learned about leadership came from my years in the Future Farmers of America and the Corps of Cadets at Texas A&M University. In both cases I learned leadership skills from experienced leaders, skills that were developed and honed in the crucible of life. As a company commander at Texas A&M, I learned to lead by leading. While this may sound strange, the truth is that there is no substitute for experience.

Did you hear the story of the young banker who had just been promoted to bank president? One day he asked for an appointment with the man whose retirement had created the vacancy he was about to fill. When the appointed hour came, the young man asked, "Sir, as I prepare to become president of the bank, I wonder if you would share with me the secret to your success."

The older man replied, "Right decisions."

The young man, expecting greater detail, responded, "Sir, how did you learn to make right decisions?"

The older man said, "Experience."

The young man, hungering for more, asked, "Sir, how did you get experience?"

The older man replied, "Wrong decisions."

In fact, there are many means to help developing leaders learn to make right decisions and gain experience besides living through wrong decisions. In that regard, allow me to share a few thoughts.

Leadership requires a spirit of humility, service, and evangelical persuasion. Richard T. Hinz, former president of the Southeastern District of The Lutheran Church—Missouri Synod, wrote these words about leadership in the Spring 1999 *Issues in Christian Education*:

> The front line of mission and ministry is the local congregation. God gives to the members of the local congregation responsibility for teaching, witness, service, nurture, fellowship, stewardship, worship and administering the sacraments. (The foregoing list of responsibilities is admittedly more illustrative than exhaustive.)
>
> All other levels of church life are to support and enhance, and not hinder, the congregation's pursuit of its fundamental, God-given responsibilities.
>
> The dynamic meaning of "Synod" must allow more than that, encouraging an expression of "partnership" in which congregations necessarily take a front and center role. This "Synod" is the commitment of congregations to support one another in their mission and ministry and to offer that support in as direct a way as possible.
>
> It is interesting to note that this focus on "Synod" seems to have been operative for the first synodical president, Dr. C. F. W. Walther. His first presidential address was titled "How shall we work together when we have no power over each other?"

The question Walther did indeed ask was remarkably perceptive. His answer was no less so. He noted that "Christ not only declares that He alone has the power in His church and exercises it by His Word, but He also expressly denies to all others any other power, any other rule, any other authority to command in His church." He further stated that "We have merely the power to advise one another, that we have only the power of the Word, and of convincing (persuasion)."

If a person observes carefully, Walther was aware that "Synod" could lead to an insatiable interest in defining who has power over whom. How debilitating that pursuit would be for Christ's mission! Walther hoped to replace this human focus with an eagerness to see power used to equip members to serve!

Robert K. Greenleaf, resident management guru with American Telephone and Telegraph, in retirement began writing his reflections on leadership. He was a quiet, but assured, advocate of the concept of "the servant as leader." He provides an answer to the question, "How will you recognize a servant leader?" He writes:

"The best test, and difficult to administer, is:

- **Do those served grow as persons?**
- **Do they, while being served, become healthier, wiser, freer, more autonomous, more likely themselves to become servants?"**

Servant leadership is an often used but frequently misunderstood term. Essentially, servant leadership is embodied in a leader who cares more for others than for himself and is willing to make sacrifices for the good of those he leads.

Louis Pasteur, the pioneer of immunology, lived at a time when thousands of people died each year of rabies. Pasteur had worked for years on a vaccine. Just as he was about to begin experimenting on himself, a 9-year-old, Joseph Meister, was bitten by a rabid dog.

The boy's mother begged Pasteur to experiment on her son. Pasteur injected Joseph for 10 days, and the boy lived. Decades later, of all the things Pasteur could have had etched on his headstone, he asked for just three words: "Joseph Meister Lived."

Leadership is not measured by a wall of credentials or a list of impressive accomplishments. Touching people's lives is what leadership in ministry is all about. What kind of influence will you leave? How many lives will be impacted with the Gospel as a result of decisions you've made and words you've spoken? The human legacy you leave will be reflected in the eternal destiny of those whose lives have been touched by your leadership.

Leadership requires experience, creative ingenuity, and the ability to think on one's feet. Let me demonstrate this truth with a story:

A wealthy old gentleman decides to go on a hunting safari in Africa, taking his faithful, elderly German Shepherd along for the trip. One day the old German Shepherd starts chasing rabbits and, before long, discovers he's lost. Wandering about, he notices a young leopard heading stealthily in his direction with the intention of having lunch.

The old pooch thinks, "Uh, oh! I'm in deep trouble now!" Seeing some bones on the ground close by, he immediately settles down to chew on them, keeping his back to the approaching cat. Just as the leopard is about to pounce, the old German Shepherd exclaims, "Boy, that was one delicious leopard! I wonder if there are any more around here." Hearing this, the young leopard halts his attack in mid-strike, a look of terror comes over him, and he slinks away into the trees. "Whew!" he says, "That was close! That old German Shepherd nearly had me!"

Meanwhile, a monkey who'd been watching the whole scene from a nearby tree figures he can put this knowledge to good use and trade it for protection from the leopard. So off he goes. But the old German Shepherd sees him heading after the leopard and figures something must be up. The monkey soon catches up with the leopard, spills the beans, and strikes a deal for himself with the leopard.

The young leopard is furious at being made a fool of and says, "Here, monkey, hop on my back and see what's going to happen to that conniving canine!"

Now the old German Shepherd sees the leopard coming with the monkey on his back and thinks, "What am I going to do now?" But instead of running, he sits down with his back to his attackers, pretending he hasn't seen them yet. Just when they get close enough to hear, the old German Shepherd says, "Where's that monkey? I sent him off an hour ago to bring me another leopard!"

The moral of this story? Don't mess with old dogs. Age and skill will always overcome youth and treachery! Brilliance only comes with age and experience.

Leadership requires truthfulness. A few years ago Greg Morris of Leadership Dynamics expounded on this characteristic of leaders with these words:

> Early in your leadership journey you must decide the non-negotiables that will both characterize your leadership and also provide the bedrock on which you will build. This will either be a cognizant decision, [to] which you have given thought and consideration or it will be a tacit decision made in the heat of the moment. Either way, you will have made a decision that will impact your leadership and your influence.
>
> One of the foundational bases for leadership must be honesty. Edward R. Murrow observed, "To be persuasive, we must be believable. To be believable, we must be credible. To be credible, we must be truthful." Honesty or truth-telling must be a non-negotiable for your leadership and ministry as it provides the very basis

to lead. Those around you must know that you are trustworthy, and truth-telling communicates trust.

Truth is not decided by a consensus. It is not determined by a popularity contest or public opinion poll. It is not subject to manipulation or personal prerogatives. Honesty is not a majority thing or a 90 percent thing or even a 98 percent thing. Either you are truthful or you're not. There's no middle ground.

And for long-term influence, you must be committed to absolute truth and honesty in all your dealings. Now this is not to be an excuse for verbal cruelty, as truth-telling certainly demands wisdom and discretion. Truth without grace is simply brutality, but truth when accompanied with grace is Christ-like.

There are countless benefits to truthfulness. Here are just a few:

1. Credibility—Truthfulness forms the basis of your credibility, which is foundational for your leadership. You cannot have one without the other.
2. Trust—Truth-telling is the basis for trust. When trust is gone, so is the essence of your leadership.
3. Respect—Others will respect you when they know your words are based not on convenience but on honesty.
4. Example—To get others to be honest, you must first model honesty and truthfulness.
5. Enables others to follow—Only when you demonstrate character will you earn the right to lead.
6. Reference point—In a world of shifting values, truthfulness provides an absolute.
7. Staying Power—Only when your leadership is marked by complete honesty will it have staying power. There's no shortcut or substitute to long-lasting influence and integrity.

Jazz musician Billy Tipton was a gifted pianist and saxophonist, getting his start during the Big Band era of the 1930s. According to *Time* magazine, Billy had a few idiosyncrasies: He refused to give his agent his Social Security number, his three adopted sons could not recall a time when he went swimming with them, and he would never visit a doctor even when suffering serious illness. When Tipton died in 1989 at age 74, his family found out why. The funeral director told one of the adopted sons that Billy Tipton was a woman!

Tipton began living a lie because, during the Big Band era, women were allowed to sing but rarely played in the band. Certainly the prejudice of sexism is sad, but Billy Tipton's story is sad in another way. No matter what a person's motives are for lying, when the truth comes out, confusion, hurt, shame, and heartache are inescapable.

Pontius Pilate posed the cynical question to Jesus: "What is truth?" Christ's words still resonate, "I am the Truth" (John 14:6). As followers of Christ, we must imbue our leadership with truthful communication and behavior. Trust and credibility can be quickly voided by the compromise of partial truthfulness. Truth-telling may not always be convenient, but it is always right.

Leadership requires courage. The great explorer Ferdinand Magellan said: "The sea is dangerous and its storms terrible, but these obstacles have never been sufficient reason to remain ashore. Unlike the mediocre, intrepid spirits seek victory over those things that seem impossible. It is with an iron will that they embark on the most daring of all endeavors . . . to meet the shadowy future without fear and conquer the unknown."

Theodore Roosevelt said: "The credit belongs to those people who are actually in the arena . . . who know the great enthusiasms, the great devotions to a worthy cause; who at best know the triumph of high achievement, and who, at worst, fail while daring greatly . . . so that their place shall never be with those cold and timid souls who know neither victory nor defeat." Throughout history, periods of war and armed conflicts have given opportunity for men to display their courage, their character, and their leadership. Times of crises provide occasion for individuals to display their leadership abilities and talents. One such person who has come to the recent forefront is General Colin Powell. Having served as Chairman of the U.S. Joint Chiefs of Staff (1989–1993), Powell was responsible for Operation Desert Storm, the U.S. military effort against Iraq in 1991.

In an article by Curt Schleier, General Powell shared the following principles gleaned from his own leadership experience:

1. Do your best and work hard—All work is honorable. Always do your best, because someone is watching.
2. Stay focused—Figure out what is crucial then stay focused on that. Never allow side issues, notwithstanding their importance, to knock you off track.
3. Know your strengths and your limitations—A good leader surrounds himself with people who complement his skills. Only an honest and fair assessment of your abilities will allow this to happen.
4. Duty above politics—It is more important to do what is right than to do what is personally beneficial. Whatever the cost, do what is right!
5. Don't be impressed by your own importance—Don't believe your press clippings. To maintain your perspective, work hard on humility.

6. Surround yourself with good people—The best commanders and leaders are backed by the best people. As Admiral Rickover said: "Organizations don't really accomplish anything. Plans don't accomplish anything, either. Theories of management don't much matter. Endeavors succeed or fail because of the people involved. Only by attracting the best possible people will you accomplish great things."
7. Be accessible—This keeps you informed of what's going on as well as allowing others the freedom to express their concerns and complaints.
8. Keep an eye on image—Good relationships with others cannot be underestimated. This is not an empty reputation, but a reflection of your values and commitments.
9. Build bridges, don't burn them—As an outgrowth of the above principle, you cannot afford to alienate others. People are not the means to an end, they are the end.
10. Balance is crucial—Powell never let his career consume or define him, but balanced it with family and outside interests. He operated under the premise, "Never become so consumed by your career that nothing is left that belongs only to you and your family. Don't allow your profession to become the whole of your existence."

Although written for a secular audience, the principles articulated and modeled by Gen. Colin Powell are as significant, valuable, and applicable for ministry as they are for the military. Every congregation, pastor, or leader can either directly apply these principles to its or his own situation or allow these standards to serve as an assessment tool.

Leadership is magnified by learning to trust and to be trusted. When I was a boy of 12, I learned the value of trustworthiness—in a most memorable way. Here's the story.

One Wednesday night during Lent my parents, sisters, and I attended worship and drove home. It was dark, and I was the designated garage-door opener. Mind you, there was no button to push—only a door to lift, manually. Immediately after I had done my duty, the lights of the car illuminated a pair of beady eyes staring at us from the back wall of the garage.

I knew those eyes were attached to the head of an opossum. We lived in the country and were used to seeing these critters, which we simply called "possums." They are not attractive animals, to put it mildly! Their nose, hair, feet, and tail are just plain ugly. Besides that, they can be very mean, especially when backed into a corner by a dog or other adversary. I wanted nothing to do with this creature!

What complicated the scenario was that the possum had chosen to rest for the evening on top of my mother's brand new clothes-washing machine. This was the first such machine my mom had ever owned. She and Dad had saved up a long time to buy it.

The dilemma called for cool heads and clear thinking to persuade the possum to choose a different abode for the night. This was easier said than done, for my mother was visibly upset by this ugly, mean animal roosting on her brand new washing machine. She was not reticent in expressing her desire to my Dad that he do something about the situation—and in short order!

Dad said, "Jerry, go upstairs and get your .22 rifle and bring it back down here." Now when my dad spoke, I listened and did what he told me to do. In order to keep from disturbing or angering the possum, I entered the house through the front door, went upstairs, got my .22 rifle (which had been a Christmas gift the year before) along with several shells, went back downstairs, out the front door, and over to the garage. Mom and my three sisters were still in the car; Dad was standing beside it awaiting my return with the weapon of choice.

When I got there, I handed the rifle and shells to him and said something like, "OK, Dad. Here you go." My natural thought was that he was going to fire a shot into the ground outside the garage, hoping the noise would startle the intruder into moving to a different resting place. Imagine my surprise at what actually happened.

"Jerry," Dad said, "shoot the possum."

My response was something profound like, "Say what?"

"Shoot the possum!"

"But the possum is on top of Mother's brand new washing machine! What if I miss the possum and hit the machine instead?"

He said, "You earned a Boy Scout merit badge in marksmanship with a .22. I know you can hit the possum and not Mother's washing machine. I trust you to do so. Go ahead and shoot the possum."

With those words, I somehow mustered the courage to load three shells in the chamber of my bolt-action Remington single-shot .22 rifle. I looked around for something to help steady my aim, but there was nothing in the driveway to lean against and no convenient way to support the rifle on the roof or hood of the car. I was on my own, aiming the rifle at those beady eyes, praying for mercy in case I missed. I had never heard the sound of a .22 shell hitting the metal chassis of a clothes-washing machine and wasn't looking forward to hearing it now.

I held my breath and squeezed the trigger. The sound I heard after the gunshot sound was not lead hitting steel. Instead, I refocused my eyes and saw that the bullet had found its intended target—right between the eyes of the possum. And because the animal was on top of the instrument panel of the machine, the bullet's penetration did not affect the machine in any way. Although I'm considered a fairly accurate marksman, after all these years, there's still a part of me that believes my possum shot was nothing short of a miracle!

The real lesson I want to convey here is that of trustworthiness. Fathers, trust your children and let them know of your trust. Doing so may very well require taking a risk. The risks we take in placing trust in our children or others may include varying degrees of consequence if the risk turns out to be greater than the reward. Some such risks involve matters of life and death. The risk my father took involved only the life of a possum, but it also involved the well being of a precious piece of equipment and, more importantly, his relationship with my dear mother, who also just happened to be his dear wife.

My father could easily have communicated to me at that formative moment in my life that he didn't trust me to make that difficult and dangerous shot. And though I never confirmed this with him before he went to heaven on New Year's Day 1983, I have pretty good reason to believe that his dear wife, my dear mother mentioned above, may not have been at all pleased with his decision to put the safekeeping of her washing machine in the hands and rifle aim of her 12-year-old son. I suspect he had some "tall talking" to do to convince her of the wisdom of that decision.

Leadership requires compassion. Sometime ago I received an e-mail with a story titled, "Learning Disabled Shay's First Baseball Game."

At a fund-raising dinner for a school that serves learning-disabled children, the father of one of the students delivered a speech that would never be forgotten by all who attended. After extolling the school and its dedicated staff, he offered a question.

"When not interfered with by outside influences, everything nature does is done with perfection. Yet my son, Shay, cannot learn things as other children do. He cannot understand things as other children do. Where is the natural order of things in my son?" The audience was stilled by the query.

The father continued. "I believe that when a child like Shay comes into the world, an opportunity to realize true human nature presents itself, and it comes in the way other people treat that child."

Then he told the following story: Shay and his father had walked past a park where some boys Shay knew were playing baseball. Shay asked, "Do you think they'll let me play?"

Shay's father knew that most of the boys would not want someone like Shay on their team, but he also understood that if his son were allowed to play, it would give him a much-needed sense of belonging. Shay's father approached one of the boys on the field and asked if Shay could play.

The boy looked around for guidance and, getting none, took matters into his own hands and said, "We're losing by six runs and the game is in the eighth inning. I guess he can be on our team and we'll try to put him in to bat in the ninth inning."

In the bottom of the eighth inning, Shay's team scored a few runs but was still behind by three. In the top of the ninth inning, Shay put on a glove and played in the outfield. Even though no hits came his way, he was obviously ecstatic just to be in the game and on the field, grinning from ear to ear as his father waved to him from the stands.

In the bottom of the ninth inning, Shay's team scored again. Now, with two outs and the bases loaded, the potential winning run was on base and Shay was scheduled to be next at bat. At this juncture, would the team let Shay bat and give away their chance to win the game?

Surprisingly, Shay was given the bat. Everyone knew that a hit was all but impossible because Shay didn't even know how to hold the bat properly, much less connect with the ball. However, as Shay stepped up to the plate, the pitcher moved in a few steps to lob the ball in softly so Shay could at least be able to make contact.

The first pitch came and Shay swung clumsily and missed. The pitcher again took a few steps forward to toss the ball softly towards Shay. As the pitch came in, Shay swung at the ball and hit a slow ground ball right back to the pitcher. The pitcher picked up the soft grounder and could have easily thrown the ball to the first baseman. Shay would have been out and that would have been the end of the game.

Instead, the pitcher took the ball and turned and threw it on a high arc to right field, far beyond the reach of the first baseman. Everyone started yelling, "Shay, run to first! Run to first!" Never in his life had Shay ever made it to first base. He scampered down the baseline, wide-eyed and startled.

Everyone yelled, "Run to second, run to second!" By the time Shay rounded first base, the right fielder had the ball. He could have thrown the ball to the second-baseman for the tag, but he understood the pitcher's intentions and intentionally threw the ball high and far over the third-baseman's head.

Shay ran toward second base as the runners ahead of him deliriously circled the bases toward home. Shay reached second base, the opposing shortstop ran to him, turned him in the direction of third base, and shouted, "Run to third!" As Shay rounded third, the boys from both teams were screaming, "Shay, run home!"

Shay ran to home, stepped on the plate, and was cheered as the hero who hit the "grand slam" and won the game for his team.

"That day," said the father softly with tears now rolling down his face, "the boys from both teams helped bring a piece of true love and humanity into this world."

Shay's father was a man of compassion who cared enough about his son to take the risk of asking a baseball team if they would allow Shay to play. And when the opposing team saw Shay, they had compassion on him in a remarkable, selfless way.

Christ was moved with compassion when He saw the crowds harassed and helpless like sheep without a shepherd (Mark 6:34). God has established leadership and leaders to enable, to direct, to equip and to care for His people. Leadership, then, is not a matter of status, rank, or position but a privileged responsibility ordained by God. And only when viewed in light of eternity will our leadership begin to take on those characteristics that God has in mind for our influence and effectiveness!

Having shared these observations, experiences, and principles of leadership, I am mindful of one probing question: How do leaders lead in uncertain and difficult times such as those we are experiencing now? Let's explore this topic.

Perhaps by the time this book is published, the American economy will have righted itself to some degree. But as I write this today, many people are still in dire and depressing circumstances. Today the fear of being hit by the financial crisis is still very real. And the economy is but one example of many issues that overwhelm people and grip them with fear. With every natural disaster that strikes—hurricanes, tornadoes, floods, wildfires, and others—the lives of people are thrown into turmoil with the loss of possessions and, in some cases, the loss of loved ones. Fear of terrorism preys on the minds of people and brings its own brand of panic and dread. For some, life becomes so filled with despair that they choose to end their own lives, leaving those who remain overwhelmed with grief and sadness.

One of the things that struck me during the 2008 presidential campaign was how the candidates and their respective political parties chose to exploit people's fears. Meanwhile, the same candidates worked to convince the public that they would be the best leader for such turbulent times. I am not certain that one who chooses to capitalize on another's fears is one who should be trusted with the helm of leadership. Surely there is a better way.

That being said, reflecting on these turbulent times leads me to ask, "How should one lead in overwhelming times?" This question is apropos not only of leadership in our country but also and particularly in the context of leadership in the church.

The answer to this question begins where I believe we should begin every undertaking in life—with Jesus. The typical response many may have is to ask, "What Would Jesus Do?" But I don't think that is the proper question for this scenario. Rather, the proper question is, "What DID Jesus Do?"

Jesus dealt with people in tumultuous moments and overwhelming times. A familiar example of the former occurred as He slept in a boat while His disciples struggled to cope with a sudden storm. This is the account of that setting from the Gospel of Mark, the fourth chapter:

> That day when evening came, [Jesus] said to His disciples, "Let us go over to the other side." Leaving the crowd behind, they took Him along, just as He was, in the boat. There were also other boats with Him.
>
> A furious squall came up, and the waves broke over the boat, so that it was nearly swamped. Jesus was in the stern, sleeping on a cushion. The disciples woke Him and said to Him, "Teacher, don't you care if we drown?"
>
> He got up, rebuked the wind and said to the waves, "Quiet! Be still!" Then the wind died down and it was completely calm. He

> said to His disciples, "Why are you so afraid? Do you still have no faith?"
>
> They were terrified and asked each other, "Who is this? Even the wind and the waves obey Him!" (Mark 4:35–41 NIV)

I find this to be a very compelling account of calm leadership in the midst of a storm, and I believe there are a couple of key leadership points that can be drawn from it. One focuses on the power of Jesus. The other focuses on the matter of faith. I highlight these two aspects because I believe they are the main points Jesus was teaching His future church leaders that day on the Sea of Galilee.

In like manner, we need to remember in our present time that no matter what overwhelming issues may be challenging us or the people we are called to lead, we are in the same boat with a man named Jesus. No matter the situation, we are not facing it by ourselves. We are not alone. The Lord is by our side, even if it seems in our minds that He may be sleeping.

This means that the Lord of the universe, the One who with a word can calm the angry seas, the One who has been given all authority in heaven and on earth, has all power at His disposal to resolve any crisis we may face in this world. We do not need to be concerned about whether there is a solution in a crisis. We know that in Jesus, there is a solution.

So, how does this truth and knowledge of our almighty and all-powerful God affect our leadership? This question directs us to the matter of faith.

Faith, as we know from the Bible, is *"being sure of what we hope for and certain of what we do not see"* (Hebrews 11:1 NIV). Faith in Almighty God and the Lord Jesus Christ means that we have hope in every circumstance, even when we do not know how the future will unfold. This is the kind of faith that we, as leaders, need to exhibit in our lives. This is the kind of faith by which leaders, with the help of the Holy Spirit, can inspire others to overcome their fears.

Consider the questions Jesus posed to His disciples: *"Why are you so afraid? Do you still have no faith?"* Clearly the disciples, in their storm-driven terror, lacked sufficient faith in Jesus. They failed to see that the Lord of wind and wave had the power and authority to deal with any life circumstance.

A key to being an effective Christian leader in overwhelming times is having an overwhelming faith in Jesus. Know and believe without a doubt that Jesus can handle anything and everything life throws at you. He spent considerable time teaching that lesson by saying things like:

> "Therefore I tell you, do not worry about your life, what you will eat or drink; or about your body, what you will wear. Is not life more important than food, and the body more important than clothes? Look at the birds of the air; they do not sow or reap or store away in barns, and yet your heavenly Father feeds them. Are you not much more valuable than they? Who of you by worrying can add a single hour to his life?
>
> "And why do you worry about clothes? See how the lilies of the field grow. They do not labor or spin. Yet I tell you that not even Solomon in all his splendor was dressed like one of these. If that is how God clothes the grass of the field, which is here today and tomorrow is thrown into the fire, will He not much more clothe you, O you of little faith? So do not worry, saying, 'What shall we eat?' or 'What shall we drink?' or 'What shall we wear?' For the pagans run after all these things, and your heavenly Father knows that you need them. But seek first His kingdom and His righteousness, and all these things will be given to you as well. Therefore do

> not worry about tomorrow, for tomorrow will worry about itself. Each day has enough trouble of its own." (Matthew 6:25–34 NIV)

When we as leaders live with this kind of faith and confidence in our own lives, the people we lead will observe it and learn from our example that there is nothing to fear when one is in the boat with Jesus. Such faith and confidence enable us to lead with assurance and, in similar accord, set a godly course for the church in the midst of overwhelming times.

I am sure there were many Christians who modeled such leadership during the time of the Great Depression, the worst economic period ever to besiege our country, far worse than anything we have yet to experience today. One shining exemplar of leadership during that time was the president of what was then called the Evangelical Lutheran Synod of Missouri, Ohio, and Other States, Dr. Friedrich Pfotenhauer, who served as Synod president for 24 years, from 1911–1935, retiring at the tender age of 76.

At the 35th Regular Convention of the Synod in 1932, Dr. Pfotenhauer exhibited confident and unwavering leadership in his report to that convention. Through his faith in the Lord, he set a direction for the church in the midst of troubled times. He said:

> Some attention must also be given to the problem of finances. Now all this business stands in direct relation to our great Christian desire to bring Christ's rest to a sin-weary world. It is true that the present economic conditions throughout the world induce us, if we do not keep our vision clear, to curtail our church activities. No doubt money is more scarce than in previous years. All the more must we keep before us the lesson of history: first, that, the more evil the days, the greater our prospect of success in our Christian work; and secondly, that, when children of God are eager to pro-

> mote their Savior's glory, the Lord supplies the necessary means and blesses them.
>
> We pray that in these days of our convention the Holy Spirit may above all let us taste and experience the sublime rest of Christ, and may He in this experience keep us safe from follies and enkindle in us that blessed restlessness of spirit which impels us to apply every ounce of consecrated energy to the task of bringing to our fellow-men that great blessing of God, Christ's gift of rest for weary souls. (Presidential Address, Proceedings of the Thirty-Fifth Regular Convention, 1932, p. 8)

Dr. Pfotenhauer provided great leadership for the church during an overwhelming time, and his words of wisdom still serve us well in our own difficult time. I am especially appreciative of these words: "the present economic conditions throughout the world induce us, if we do not keep our vision clear, to curtail our church activities . . . [and] when children of God are eager to promote their Savior's glory, the Lord supplies the necessary means and blesses them."

"Keep our vision clear." Leadership in overwhelming times calls for clear vision. When we keep our eye on the goal and our people focused on that goal, trusting that the Lord will provide, we will not be swayed from that which the Lord would have us do. As we "keep the vision clear," we will not be afraid of what we cannot do. Rather, we will look forward with expectation to what God will do. The Scriptures teach us: "Trust in the LORD with all your heart and lean not on your own understanding; in all your ways acknowledge Him, and He will make your paths straight" (Proverbs 3:5–6 NIV).

In times such as these, it is essential to foster an environment of "trust in the Lord" whereby "the children of God *are eager* to promote their Savior's glory." I recently read a quote, author unknown, which said: "Setting an exciting goal is like setting a needle in your compass. From then on, the compass knows only one point, its ideal. And it will faithfully guide you there through the darkest nights and the fiercest storms."

Placing that quote in the context of Christian leadership, it teaches us to point the needle toward the mission of our Lord Jesus Christ. Then, whether we are in the darkest of times or the fiercest of storms, we will know the direction we need to lead, being certain that "the Lord will provide."

The mission statement of The Lutheran Church—Missouri Synod is:

> *In grateful response to God's grace and empowered by the Holy Spirit through Word and Sacraments, the mission of the LCMS is vigorously to make known the love of Christ by word and deed within our churches, communities and the world.*

We have set our compass. Its direction is "vigorously to make known the love of Christ." As leaders in overwhelming times, we keep moving in that direction. Our vision is clear and distinctive: One Mission: reaching people for Christ—One Message: Christ alone is Savior of the world—One People: forgiven and united by God's love in Christ.

We need not be afraid. We are focused on the work our Lord has given us to do. We need not fear. We have faith in the Lord who rules over every wind and wave that comes our way. This is the confidence we have in overwhelming times—that *"He who began a good work in [us] will bring it to completion at the day of Jesus Christ"* (Philippians 1:6).

In the month of April in the year of our Lord 2001, I was in my fourth three-year term as President of the Texas District of The Lutheran Church—Missouri Synod, about to complete my 10th year of service. About a month earlier I had received word that I was one of the nominees for the Office of the President of The Lutheran Church—Missouri Synod, the election for which would occur at the Synod's national convention in July in St. Louis.

That morning I had spent some time in my office at home preparing an article for the Texas District edition of *The Lutheran Witness*, our church body's national monthly magazine. I had also perused the mail from the previous week. In the days since learning of my nomination and even quite some time prior to that, I had been the target of some communications that, to put it gently, were not supportive of my election.

Reading this material left me deeply saddened and frustrated. My integrity and beliefs had been called into question. But then I thought about the fact that, just three months hence, I would be involved in an election to a national office that might change my life. Were I to be elected, my wife, Terry, and I would need to move to St. Louis, the location of the International Center of The Lutheran Church—Missouri Synod, leaving behind in Texas our children and grandchildren, parents and siblings. And I knew that the allegations and accusations would not cease but might well increase, and exponentially at that.

After a few moments of reflection and silent prayer, I turned off my computer, packed my briefcase, and walked down the hall from my office to the garage. After putting my briefcase and coat in the back seat, I opened the front door, sat in the driver's seat, put the key in the ignition, and started the car. I had forgotten that when I had driven home from the office the night before, I had been listening to a CD by a Christian artist. As soon as the car started, so did the CD. Here are the words of the song I heard: "He who began a good work in you will be faithful to complete it. He who started the work will be faithful to complete it in you!"

Immediately I recognized these words from the apostle Paul to the Christians in Philippi: "I am sure of this, that He who began a good work in you will bring it to completion at the day of Jesus Christ" (Philippians 1:6).

Before backing my car out of the garage, I listened to the rest of the song, eyes closed, with a sense of peace enveloping my being. I remembered the words I'd heard so often from my childhood pastor at the conclusion of each of his sermons: "May the peace of God that passes all understanding keep your hearts and minds through faith in Christ Jesus our Lord!" With that reminder of God's promise and the presence of His peace, I drove to the office, the feelings of sadness and frustration replaced by quiet assurance and confident hope in God's grace, mercy, and peace.

From that day until the election occurred on July 12, 2001, and since that time, I have often remembered that day in April 2001. There have been many other days of sadness and frustration. I've come to know and at least partially accept the fact that leaders always disappoint someone. But the promise of God has been constant and sure, providing a quiet sense of peace, even in the midst of the trouble and turmoil associated with life in the church militant.

Leadership in overwhelming times is grounded in the principles of trust in the Almighty God, the Lord of heaven and earth, of faith that does not waver though the earth give way, and of clear vision for the work of His mission, promoting our Savior's glory.

Therefore, I appeal to those who read these words, leaders of The Lutheran Church—Missouri Synod and other Christian church bodies, ambassadors of the Almighty God. Lead with faith and trust in your hearts and with boldness and confidence on your lips. Constantly and unwaveringly point those whom you lead to the greater purpose of our Lord Jesus Christ. In times of economic uncertainty, in the face of natural disasters, or in the turmoil of any of life's circumstances, point the people to Jesus. He will calm their fears. He will assure them that He "will not leave them nor forsake them." Work through them to promote the Savior's glory. That is leadership in overwhelming times.

In conclusion of this chapter and nearing the end of this book, I share with you two hymn verses that Dr. Pfotenhauer used when he concluded his report to the Synod convention in 1932. These verses are from the hymn, "To God the Holy Spirit Let Us Pray."

Shine in our hearts, O most precious Light,
That we Jesus Christ may know aright,
Clinging to our Savior, whose blood has bought us,
Who again to our true home has brought us.
Lord, have mercy!
Thou sweetest Love, grace on us bestow,
Set our hearts with heavenly fire aglow
That with hearts united we love each other,
Of one mind, in peace with every brother.
Lord have mercy! Amen.

CONCLUSION

The Future of the LCMS—Tying It All Together

As stated at the outset of this book, over the years, a number of Missouri Synod speakers have been fond of quoting a statement attributed to Billy Graham, who reportedly referred to The Lutheran Church—Missouri Synod as "a sleeping giant." In many respects—again, as I said in the Introduction—we are, relatively speaking, "large, strong, and laden with talent and purpose, and yet we don't seem to accomplish as much as we might." Why is that? In my opinion, a chief reason is because we spend too much time in introspection and internal housekeeping.

Let's leave the "giant" for a moment and try a different metaphor. It comes from a favorite poem of mine by Robert Frost.

In the poem, called "The Woodpile," Mr. Frost is walking through a snowy marsh somewhere in New England. Suddenly he happens upon a stack of firewood, a cord of maple, cut, split, and neatly piled. It's sitting all by itself in the lonely swamp, with no tracks or footprints or any other sign that it's being used.

Upon closer inspection, Frost notices that the wood is old. It's not this year's cutting, or last year's cutting, or even the cutting from the year before. The wood has turned gray, its bark is warping off, and creeping, climbing vines have intertwined themselves between and among the logs.

Who would spend the labor of his ax, Frost wonders, only to leave his work so far from a useful fireplace?

This woodpile, one might say, is The Lutheran Church—Missouri Synod. Compared with many church bodies, it is big and impressive. It is more than 160 years old—seasoned and ready. It is full of potential to bring the light and warmth of Jesus Christ to a cold, gloomy, sin-filled world. And yet, too often, ignition that could lead to a roaring blaze is doused by our own hand. We pour water on our own wood. We pour water on one another's fires because we don't like the way our brother is going about building and burning his. It's not exactly how *we* would do it, and so for some reason it isn't right. We meddle in so many other fires that we fail to tend to our own.

And so our woodpile sits, in Frost's words,

To warm the frozen swamp as best it could
With the slow, smokeless burning of decay.

The Lutheran Church—Missouri Synod is not about "the slow, smokeless burning of decay." Our history, our present, and our future are too vital and too promising for that. I am convinced, brothers and sisters in Christ, that we can keep our cord of wood—namely, our doctrine and practice—neatly stacked, perfectly tidy, carefully arranged, and ready to be used for the purpose for which a stack of wood is intended—not "to warm the frozen swamp . . . with the slow, smokeless burning of decay," but with the light and warmth and energy produced by a roaring fire. I firmly believe we can do all that and yet be supportive of one another in the various and creative ways we seek, and sometimes need, to use our stack of wood to warm and light a cold, dark world. And when honest disagreements arise, whether over doctrine or practice or style or methods, I am convinced that we can learn to deal with those disagreements in love and trust, rather than letting them fester into major squabbles that embarrass the church and stymie our proclamation of the Gospel.

When the day comes that we are able to do that, and I believe it is not only coming but has already begun, the sleeping giant will rise. He will gather up logs in his powerful arms and feed them into many fires. And we, the children of the Light, the people of the church who collectively are that giant, will carry our torches like lamps throughout the world. For that is what the God of the universe has called us to be. And that is what He has called us to do, by the power of His grace, in His most holy name.

In closing, I share with you the words of St. Paul that appear in a number of places in this book, but which cannot be overemphasized in our midst:

> For this reason I bow my knees before the Father, from whom every family in heaven and on earth is named, that according to the riches of His glory He may grant you to be strengthened with power through His Spirit in your inner being, so that Christ may dwell in your hearts through faith—that you, being rooted and grounded in love, may have strength to comprehend with all the saints what is the breadth and length and height and depth, and to know the love of Christ that surpasses knowledge, that you may be filled with all the fullness of God. . . .
>
> I therefore, a prisoner in the Lord, beg you to lead a life worthy of the calling to which you have been called, with all humility and gentleness, with patience, bearing with one another in love, making every effort to maintain the unity of the Spirit in the bond of peace. There is one body and one Spirit, just as you were called to the one hope of your calling, one Lord, one faith, one baptism, one God and Father of all, who is above all and through all and in all. (Ephesians 3:14–19; 4:1–6)

To this God alone be the glory, through Jesus Christ our Lord!

APPENDIX A

An Introduction to The Lutheran Church—Missouri Synod

Rev. Dr. Samuel H. Nafzger

Preface

Nearly two thousand years after the birth of Christ, His life and teachings continue to form the foundation for the religious identity of millions, even billions, of people from every corner of planet earth. According to the best statistics available, about one-third (2.1 billion) of the world's 6.6 billion people are identified as in some sense Christian. Islam has 1.5 billion followers. The third largest grouping of people by religious identity may be referred to as those who claim no religion (atheist, agnostic, secular humanist, etc.), numbering just over one billion. Hinduism embraces slightly under one billion adherents. Judaism is the twelfth largest world religion with 14 million followers and there are approximately 400,000,000 Buddhists in the world today.

More than half of the world's Christians (just over one billion) are Roman Catholic. About eleven percent claim adherence to the Orthodox faith. Anglicans with approximately 80 million members and Lutherans with slightly over 70 million each, represent about three percent of the Christian population of the world.

The world's 70 million Lutherans belong to some 250 different Lutheran denominations around the world. Not surprisingly, about half of all Lutherans find their home in northern Europe, where the Lutheran tradition has its 16th century roots. There are 12.7 million Lutherans in Germany (where Lutheranism began), 6.9 in Sweden, 4.6 in Finland, 4.5 in Denmark, and 3.9 in Norway.

Today the Lutheran church is growing most rapidly in Africa and Asia with the result that there are now more Lutherans in Africa—over 15 million—than there are in either Germany or North America. Asia has more than 8 million Lutherans, and that number is also increasing at a rapid pace.

In North America 8 million Lutherans belonging to 12 different Lutheran church bodies (not counting a number of other very small, locally organized bodies). The largest is the Evangelical Lutheran Church in America (ELCA), with 4.8 million members. This church body came into being in 1988 as the result of a merger of the Lutheran Church in America, the American Lutheran Church, and the Association of Evangelical Lutheran Churches. The Lutheran Church—Missouri Synod, with 2.4 million baptized members, ranks as the second largest Lutheran church body in North America and the 13th largest Christian denomination in the USA. The Wisconsin Evangelical Lutheran Synod (WELS) has 400,000 members and is the third largest Lutheran Church in the USA.

The purpose of this introduction is to present: 1) a brief overview of the history, mission, and ministry of The Lutheran Church—Missouri Synod (LCMS); 2) a discussion of the foundational Lutheran beliefs as held and taught by the Missouri Synod; and 3) the LCMS' understanding of the nature and mission of the church and its relationship with other Christian denominations.

The History, Mission, and Ministry of the LCMS

The Lutheran Church—Missouri Synod traces its origin to 750 German immigrants who came to Missouri in 1839 seeking freedom from the religious and political pressures and constraints of 19th century Germany. Under the leadership of a young pastor named C. F. W. Walther, these Saxon immigrants joined together with a number of other German pastors sent to America by Wilhelm Loehe from Bavaria to form "The German Evangelical Lutheran Synod of Missouri, Ohio, and Other States."

The constitutional convention of the new synod was held in Chicago on April 25–May 6, 1847. Twelve pastors, with their congregations, adopted a constitution. Ten other pastors added their signatures as advisory members, since their congregations had not yet voted to join. Of these 22 pastors, 4 served congregations in Missouri, 6 in Ohio, 5 in Indiana, 3 in Illinois, 2 in Michigan, and 2 in New York. The twelve original congregations which formed the Missouri Synod comprised a total membership of about 3,000 persons. Dr. Walther was elected to serve as the first president of the new Synod. One hundred years later in 1947 the Synod officially changed its name to The Lutheran Church—Missouri Synod.

The Lutheran Church—Missouri Synod remained largely German in its make-up and even in language until the end of the First World War. It grew dramatically during the late 19th and early 20th centuries. In 1897, 50 years after its founding, the Synod reported a membership of 685,000. During the next 50 years, it more than doubled in size. The LCMS currently has a membership of 2.4 million members belonging to 6,150 congregations throughout the USA. The LCMS International Center is located in the St. Louis suburb of Kirkwood, Missouri. Dr. Gerald Kieschnick, the 12th president of the

Synod during its 160 years of existence, has served in this position since 2001.

The Synod owns and operates 10 colleges and universities as part of its Concordia University System (CUS), together with two seminaries. It also has more than 100 high schools and the nation's largest Protestant elementary school system with over 1,000 elementary schools and 1,300 preschools. The Synod's congregations and schools are served by 9,000 pastors and almost 30,000 educators and other full-time workers, such as deaconesses and directors of Christian education. While the Synod holds that, according to the Bible, women are not to serve as pastors, nearly half of its full-time professional church workers are women.

The LCMS is well known for its emphasis on Biblical doctrine and faithfulness to the historic Lutheran Confessions. At the same time, it has sought to make use of new ways to share the love of Christ in an ever-changing world. The reason for the Synod's existence is summarized in its mission statement as follows: "*In grateful response to God's grace and empowered by the Holy Spirit through Word and Sacraments, the mission of The Lutheran Church—Missouri Synod is vigorously to make known the love of Christ by word and deed within our churches, communities, and the world.*"

The LCMS has more than 110 years of experience of proclaiming the Gospel in foreign mission fields. It commissioned its first overseas missionary to India in the 1890s. Today, LCMS World Mission works with partner church bodies and emerging church bodies worldwide. It has active work or mission relationships in approximately 85 countries in Africa, Asia, Eurasia, and Latin America. The LCMS is strongly committed to a global Lutheran mission movement called *Ablaze!* which has as its goal the sharing of the Gospel with

100 million unreached or uncommitted people by the year 2017 (the 500th anniversary of the Lutheran Reformation).

In the early 1990s the LCMS declared the United States itself to be a "world mission field." Through its National Mission Affiliates, the Synod conducts national mission work in many specialized ethnic and cultural contexts: e.g., among Hispanics (Latinos), African immigrants, Arabic speaking groups, Native Americans, Asians, and those of Jewish heritage and background. It also maintains its long-standing work in black ministry (over 100 years), ministry to the deaf (also over 100 years) and ministry to the blind (over 60 years). Each month, for example, 800 volunteers in 60 work centers distribute 2,000 Braille magazines, 6,500 large print publications and 1,200 cassettes containing educational and devotional material for the sight-impaired. The Synod's first military chaplain served in the American Civil War in the year 1862. Through its Ministry to the Armed Forces the LCMS continues to provide military chaplains to serve on the field and in veteran's hospitals, and it works with pastors and congregations to meet the spiritual, emotional and physical needs of their members in uniform.

Since the early 1900s, LCMS World Relief and Human Care has sought to "make a world of difference" in the lives of people who have been touched by need, whether because of war or natural disaster or because of oppressive poverty. In its human care efforts the LCMS acts in partnership with a number of other assistance organizations, such as Lutheran World Relief (LWR), Lutheran Immigration and Refugee Services (LIRS), Lutheran Services in America (LSA), and Lutheran Disaster Response (LDR). The Synod also works closely with over 60 Recognized Service Organizations (RSOs) which provide specialized mission and ministry for a wide range of needs (e.g., Bethesda Lutheran Homes and Services, Lutherans for Life, Wheat

Ridge Ministries, Lutheran Child and Family Services, Lutheran camps and retreat centers, etc.).

The LCMS was the first denomination in the United States to urge its members (in 1981) to donate body organs at death for transplant. The Synod holds a strong pro-life position and supports efforts calling for constitutional protection of all human life, including the unborn. For this reason it also opposes embryonic stem cell research, even while encouraging other forms of stem cell research (e.g., the use of adult stem cells) that do not involve the creation and destruction of human life. With regard to the end of life, the Synod believes that the Scriptures teach that Christians are always to care for the dying, but never to aim to kill them. Therefore the LCMS strongly opposes euthanasia and assisted suicide, but also believes that when the body's ability to sustain itself is no longer possible, and when doctors conclude that there is no hope for recovery, Christians may in good conscience forego the use of life support systems. While rejecting homosexual behavior as contrary to God's will, the Synod has also prepared resources encouraging and equipping its church workers and members to minister to homosexuals and their families. The Synod holds that marriage, as instituted by God, is to be understood and upheld as a lifelong union between a man and a woman.

The Synod's publishing arm, Concordia Publishing House (CPH), is one of the nation's largest Christian publishers. More than 300,000 adults have spent an estimated 20 million hours in Bible study using its *LifeLight* materials as a means to a deeper understanding of the Scriptures. In order to meet the changing needs of God's people, CPH also develops materials in Spanish, Laotian, Russian, Vietnamese and other languages.

A pioneer in radio and television work, the Synod operates the world's oldest religious radio station, KFUO, headquartered in

St. Louis, Missouri. Its program, "The Lutheran Hour," produced by the Synod's International Lutheran Layman's League, has been aired in North America since 1930 and is broadcast each week in more than 40 languages in 40 different countries. The Lutheran Women's Missionary League (LWML) serves as the Synod's auxiliary for women and has been a leader in supporting missionary outreach for over 65 years. Throughout its history, the Synod has been strongly committed to nurturing and encouraging young people in their faith. In 2007 the LCMS celebrated 30 years of triennial national youth gatherings which in recent years have been attended by as many as 35,000 youth and adults.

Unlike many other churches, the LCMS has never been involved in a major merger. It was, however, a member of the Lutheran Council in the U.S.A. (LCUSA) until the Council went out of existence in 1988 with the formation of the Evangelical Lutheran Church in America. The Synod is a member of the International Lutheran Council, a worldwide association of 34 established Lutheran church bodies which support one another in proclaiming the Gospel on the basis of God's Word and the Lutheran Confessions. The LCMS does not belong to the Lutheran World Federation, the National Council of Churches or the World Council of Churches, but regularly sends representatives to attend meetings of these organizations as non-member participants.

WHAT DO LUTHERANS BELIEVE?

Lutheran churches, including the LCMS, are creedal or "confessional" churches. Lutherans do not define themselves by organizational structure. Many Lutheran churches, such as the LCMS, are basically congregational in polity, but some have a more hierarchical form. Styles of worship vary from strongly liturgical to contemporary, or may be a "blended" mix between the two. But all Lutherans subscribe to creeds or confessions that state what they understand the Bible to teach.

The Lutheran church derives its name from Martin Luther (1483–1546), a German monk (of the Augustinian order) whose posting of the 95 Theses on October 31, 1517, sparked the Reformation. The documents that set forth what Lutherans believe, teach and confess were assembled and published in 1580 in what is called The Book of Concord. For more than 425 years, these documents have served as a normative statement of the Christian faith as Lutherans confess it. The foundational article of the constitution of The Lutheran Church—Missouri Synod states that "the Synod and every member of the Synod, accepts without reservation the Scriptures of the Old and New Testament as the written Word of God and the only rule and norm of faith and of practice" and all the writings in the Book of Concord as "a true and unadulterated statement and exposition of the Word of God" (Article II, Confession).

Significantly, the very first documents included in *The Book of Concord* are the three ancient creeds compiled during the early, formative years of the Christian era. The Apostles' Creed (ca. third century A.D.), the Nicene Creed (fourth century), and the Athanasian Creed (fifth and sixth centuries) are called the "ecumenical" (i.e., "church-wide") creeds because they set forth what Christians everywhere have believed, taught, and confessed since the earliest days of the Christian church. In addition, *The Book of Concord* includes Luther's Small Catechism (1529), the Augsburg Confession (1530), and five other 16th century statements, including Luther's Large Catechism and the Formula of Concord.

Luther and the other writers of these confessions did not want to be doctrinal innovators. They, together with their contemporary descendants, have maintained that Lutherans believe and teach nothing more and nothing less than what the Scriptures themselves teach and what Christians through the ages have always believed. We Lutherans therefore consider ourselves to be catholic (small "c"), which means "universal." At the same time, we have always thought of ourselves as "evangelical" Christians. In some countries, in fact, the Lutheran Church is still referred to as simply the Evangelical Church. We consider ourselves "evangelical" because it is the *evangel*—the Gospel, the good news of the death and resurrection of Jesus Christ for the sins of the world—that lies at the heart and core of everything we believe, teach and confess. In this sense, therefore, Lutherans can rightly be regarded as evangelical catholics. Standing firmly in the tradition of the trinitarian and christological confessions of the 4th and 5th centuries, we believe that sinners are justified (declared right) with the Creator God by grace alone (*sola gratia*), through faith alone (*sola fide*), on the basis of Scripture alone (*sola scriptura*). These three great "Reformation *solas*" form a concise and useful outline of what Missouri Synod Lutherans believe, teach, and confess.

GRACE ALONE

At the heart of what Lutherans believe is the conviction that salvation is the free gift of God's grace (undeserved love and mercy) alone for the sake of Christ alone. "Since the fall of Adam," says the Augsburg Confession, "all human beings who are born in the natural way are conceived and born in sin" (AC II, 1). This "innate disease and original sin" makes it completely impossible for anyone to *earn* God's love and forgiveness. If salvation were dependent on human initiative and effort, there would be no hope for anyone. But God forgives our sins, says Luther in his Large Catechism, "altogether freely, out of pure grace" (LC III, 96).

God's grace *alone* gives hope to sinful human beings. And the sole basis for God's grace is the life, death and resurrection of His

Son, Jesus Christ. We believe, as Luther says in his explanation of the Apostles' Creed, "that Jesus Christ, true God, begotten of the Father from eternity, and also true man, born of the Virgin Mary, is my Lord, who has redeemed me, a lost and condemned person ... not with gold or silver but with His holy, precious blood and with His innocent suffering and death" (*Luther's Small Catechism with Explanation,* 14).

We Lutherans believe the Bible's teaching that God's grace in Christ Jesus embraces all people of all times, ages, races, and places. There is no sin for which Christ has not died. The Formula of Concord says: "We must always firmly and rigidly insist that, like the proclamation of repentance, so the promise of the Gospel is *universalis,* that is, it pertains to all people (Luke 24:47). . . . Christ has taken away the sin of the world (John 1:29)" (FC SD XI, 28). There need be no question, therefore, in any sinner's mind whether Christ has died for each and every one of his or her personal sins.

Faith Alone

While God's grace is universal and embraces all people, this great gift (says the Bible) can be received by sinful human beings only through faith. This is where Luther, through his study of Scripture, broke decisively with the teaching about salvation that had generally prevailed in the Roman Catholic Church during the Middle Ages.

A thousand years before the Reformation, St. Augustine (A.D. 354–430) had fought strongly against the errors of a monk named Pelagius. Pelagius taught that sinners could contribute to their salvation by their own efforts, apart from God's grace in Christ. Relying on St. Paul's letter to the Romans, Augustine held that Adam's fall into sin had so corrupted human nature that the human will was completely depraved and enslaved to sin and to the devil. But Augustine believed that sinners, following their conversion and infused with renewing grace by means of baptism, begin to be healed. They are then empowered by God's grace to do what is truly good and pleasing to God. Christians, according to Augustine, continue to commit some sins, but they are gradually justified by God as the Holy Spirit enables them to do more good things and fewer bad things.

Augustine's understanding of justification as a gradual process of being "infused" with God's grace was ultimately rejected by Luther. But it was of great help to him at the beginning of his search for the truth of the Gospel, as he fought against crass forms of work-righteousness (such as buying indulgences to secure God's favor). Try as he might, however, Luther's troubled heart would give him no rest. Despite his best efforts, he could not find in himself that pure love that Augustine said Christians were capable of manifesting following conversion. After years of struggle over this question, Luther finally discovered Scripture's teaching that sinners are saved "through faith *alone*." God's grace is the sole basis of salvation for the sinner only when it is appropriated solely through faith.

Luther had learned from Augustine that only the grace of God could save him. But Luther's rediscovery of the Gospel in all its clarity took place when he came to understand that he did not first have to *do* something to merit God's saving grace. Philip Melanchthon, Luther's colleague at the University of Wittenberg, writes in the Augsburg Confession: "It is taught among us that we cannot obtain forgiveness of sin and righteousness before God through our merit, work, or satisfactions, but that we receive forgiveness of sin and become righteous before God out of grace for Christ's sake through faith when we believe that Christ has suffered for us and that for his sake our sin is forgiven and righteousness and eternal life are given to us. For God will regard and reckon this faith as righteousness in his sight, as Paul says in Romans 3 and 4" (AC IV, 1–3).

The implications of salvation "through faith alone" permeate everything we Lutherans believe and teach. We believe, for example, that the conversion of sinners is a gift of God and not the result of any human effort or decision. Lutherans therefore confess in the words of Luther's explanation to the third article of the Apostle's Creed: "I believe that I cannot by my own reason or strength believe in Jesus Christ, my Lord, or come to Him; but the Holy Spirit has called me by the Gospel" (*Luther's Small Catechism with Explanation,* p. 15).

We Lutherans are by no means anti-intellectual. We thank God for the gift of human reason. We use it to seek to understand the wonders of God's creation and to present and defend what we believe the Bible teaches. We do reject, however, all suggestions that scientific evidence or rational arguments can prove Christian truth claims. Similarly, we uphold the importance of emotion and feeling in the life of the Christian, but we steadfastly repudiate any reliance on conversion experiences or "charismatic gifts" for the certainty of salvation. We believe that, according to Scripture, the sole object of saving faith is Jesus Christ and His resurrection. We believe that a true Christian can say, "I believe" only by the miraculous power of God the Holy Spirit. Faith is not a human work but a gift from God.

"Through faith alone" also implies that it is only through the proclamation of the Gospel—in Word and Sacrament—that the Holy Spirit gives the gift of faith. The proclamation of the Gospel Word in public preaching therefore occupies a central place in Lutheran theology. Missouri Synod Lutheran churches are preaching churches. But they are also sacramental churches, for the sacraments—Baptism and the Lord's Supper—are the Gospel made visible.

Lutherans believe that Baptism has God's command and promise. Baptism is "God's Word in the water," Luther taught (Smalcald Articles, Part III, V, 1). We believe that it is precisely in the Baptism of infants, who are included in Christ's Great Commission (Matt. 28:19–20), that we can see the full meaning of "through faith alone." We believe that those who deny that God gives faith to infants through Baptism also deny (perhaps without intending to do so) salvation by grace *alone*. God's action in Baptism, apart from any human initiative, creates and bestows the gift of faith through which the Christian is "born again" and receives the gift of God's grace. We also believe that the Scriptures teach that the bread and the wine in the Lord's Supper are the true body and blood of Christ. Although we do not presume to understand how this takes place, we confess that in, with, and under the earthly elements God gives the true body and blood of Christ for the forgiveness of sins. In public worship, therefore, Missouri Synod Lutherans emphasize both the verbal proclamation of the Gospel and God's grace made "visible" in the sacraments. It is only through these "means of grace" that sinners are brought to faith in Jesus Christ and preserved in it.

Finally, to say "through faith alone" means, to use a phrase Luther made famous, that Christians are both sinners and saints at the same time (*simul justus et peccator*). Justification is a gracious act of God, a divine declaration. It is not a process. Through faith in Christ, and only through faith, sinners are declared to be forgiven and to be perfectly right with God. This declaration is whole and complete, totally independent of any inherent goodness in us sinners. In short, because of God's act on the cross received through faith, we sinners are declared to be perfect saints in God's sight. This does not mean, however, that forgiven sinners do not continue to be sinners when viewed and judged in the light of God's holy Law. Lutherans are not "perfectionists." We do not teach that Christians, following their conversion, reach a point where they stop sinning. "Forgiveness is constantly needed," says Luther. "We are never without sin because we carry our flesh around our neck" (Large Catechism II, 54).

Because of our emphasis on justification through faith alone, we Lutherans have sometimes been understood to advocate, or at least to condone, what the German Lutheran theologian Dietrich Bonhoeffer condemned as "cheap grace." Lutherans, some might say, simply take sin for granted and are not concerned with striving to live a holy life. But such notions are a serious distortion of what we believe. "Love and good works ought to follow faith," writes Melanchthon, because "God requires them" and "faith is exercised in them." Through love and good works our faith "is shown to others, in order that others may be invited to godliness by our confession" (Apology of the Augsburg Confession IV, 74 and 189). In other words, Lutherans believe that good works are necessary—but they are not necessary for salvation.

Because we believe that salvation is both "by grace alone" and "through faith alone," we Lutherans refuse to give a logically satisfying answer to the age-old question of why some people are saved and others are not. We disagree with those who (like the reformer John Calvin) teach that since salvation is God's free gift, the damnation of those who do not believe must be proof that God does not want everyone to be saved. In opposition to this view, we maintain that the Scriptures clearly teach that God desires "all people to be saved and to come to the knowledge of the truth" (1 Tim. 2:4). Yet we also disagree with those who answer the question "why some and not others" on the basis of something that human beings do or possess, as if the ultimate cause of a person's salvation is striving or cooperating or "deciding" for Christ. The Scriptures teach that all people by nature are "dead in . . . trespasses and sins" (Eph. 2:1), utterly incapable of contributing anything to their conversion or salvation. If sinners, therefore, come to believe in Christ, this is the result of God's power at work in them through the means of grace (Word and sacrament). If they continue to reject the Gospel, this is their own fault. We do not regard this response as a "cop-out" but simply as faithfulness to what the Scriptures themselves teach about the doctrine of election. This brings us to the final *sola*, "Scripture alone."

Scripture Alone

Luther's insight that salvation comes by *grace alone* through *faith alone* cannot be divorced from "on the basis of *Scripture alone*." His rediscovery of justification by grace alone through faith alone came as a direct result of his commitment to Scripture alone. Together with his contemporaries, Luther held that the Bible is the Word of God and that it does not mislead or deceive us. But unlike his opponents in the Roman Catholic Church, Luther rejected the notion that an infallible magisterium of the church is necessary for the right interpretation of the Bible. Scripture alone, said Luther, is infallible. The institutional church and its councils, as well as its bishops and teachers (including the office of the papacy) can and do err. But Scripture, says Luther, "will not lie to you" (Large Catechism V, 76).

Missouri Synod Lutherans maintain a deep appreciation for the catholic or "universal" church. But they believe that Scripture alone—not Scripture *and* tradition, Scripture *and* the church, Scripture *and* human reason, or Scripture *and* experience—stands as the final standard for what the Gospel is. At the same time, we believe that confidence in the reliability of the Bible is not possible apart from faith in Jesus Christ. Christians believe what the Scriptures teach because they first believe in Jesus Christ. Christ is the object of saving faith, not the Bible. Inverting this order, we believe, undermines the principle of "Scripture alone" and ultimately results in futile attempts to "prove" that the Bible is true. Lutherans do not believe that human efforts to verify or demonstrate the Bible's truthfulness and reliability—by discovering, for example, a piece of Noah's ark—can provide a foundation for faith in the Gospel. The Bible remains a dark book apart from faith in Christ, for He is its true content. But when sinners are brought to faith in Him, Christ points them back to the writings of the prophets and apostles as the sole authoritative source for all that the church believes, teaches, and confesses.

The key to understanding Scripture properly, we believe, is the careful distinction between the Law and the Gospel. Walther, the first president of the LCMS, wrote a classic book on this critical issue called *The Proper Distinction Between Law and Gospel.* The Law tells what God demands of sinners if they are to be saved. The Gospel reveals what God has already done for our salvation. The chief purpose of the Law is to show us our sin and our need for a Savior. The Gospel offers the free gift of God's salvation in Christ. The whole Bible can be divided into these two chief teachings. When Law and Gospel are properly distinguished the purity of the Gospel is preserved and the three *solas* of "grace alone," "faith alone," and "Scripture alone" are united.

Doctrinal differences among contemporary Lutherans are rooted primarily in disagreements about the meaning and implications of this third *sola.* While all Lutheran churches profess allegiance to "Scripture alone," they do not all agree on what this means in practice. The Lutheran Church—Missouri Synod believes that "Scripture alone" is compromised when the inerrancy of the Bible is denied, and this in turn endangers both "by grace alone" and "through faith alone." In discussions with the ELCA and its predecessor bodies, the LCMS has expressed serious disagreement with methods of interpretation (called "historical criticism") that presuppose that the Bible is not necessarily without error in matters of history and science. This view of the Bible has direct implications for other points of difference between the LCMS and the ELCA, such as the ordination of women to the pastoral office, official positions on moral issues like abortion and homosexual behavior, and the understanding of the basis of church fellowship.

The LCMS Understanding of the Church

The Nature and Mission of the Church

In addition to the three "*solas*," we Lutherans believe that there is "one holy, Christian church" on earth (Augsburg Confession VII, 1), which is made up of all believers in Jesus Christ wherever they may be found. This one church, which is not to be identified with any institution or denomination, is present wherever the Gospel is preached and the sacraments administered. All Christians are members of this one church, and they are all members of the "royal priesthood" of all believers (1 Peter 2:9–10). At the same time, Lutherans believe that God has instituted the office of the public ministry (the pastoral office) for the preaching of the Gospel and the administration of the sacraments on behalf of and with accountability to the church. Rankings and distinctions among those holding this office (between pastors and bishops, for example) are of human, not divine, origin.

The primary mission of the church, Lutherans believe, is the preaching of the Gospel and the administration of the sacraments. The government, on the other hand, has the divinely given mandate to provide for the temporal peace and tranquility of its citizens. So we Lutherans advocate a certain institutional separation but functional interaction between church and state as two distinct "realms" through which God works to provide for people's spiritual and temporal needs.

Congregations, pastors, teachers, and other professional church workers who have signed the constitution of the Synod make up the official membership of the LCMS. The polity of the LCMS might best be described as a modified congregational structure. We speak of congregational autonomy. Congregations call their pastors, but as members of the Synod they agree to call only pastors certified for ministry on the pastoral roster of the Synod and to honor and uphold the doctrinal position of the Synod.

In order to carry out the mission of the church, the Synod has divided itself into 35 districts, all but two of which are geographical. The two non-geographical districts are the English District, which takes its name from the late 19th century beginning of a transition from the German language to English, and the Slovak Evangelical Lutheran Church, which joined the LCMS as a district in 1971. District congregations are in turn organized into some 600 circuits throughout the Synod, with each circuit including 7–20 congregations.

Meetings of the members of the Synod take place in a three-year cycle. During the first year, convocations of circuit congregations are held. These meetings are largely inspirational and informative. Conventions of districts, to which each congregation sends one voting lay and one voting pastoral delegate, are held in the second year of the cycle. Each district elects its own officers including a district president, vice presidents, and a board of directors. National assemblies, called synodical conventions, take place every third year. Each electoral circuit selects one lay person and one pastor to serve as voting representatives to these national assemblies. The synodical convention is the highest governing body in the Synod. It elects the synodical President to renewable 3 year terms, 5 vice presidents, the members of the Board of Directors and the members of various boards and commissions.

Relationships with Other Christian Churches

Despite all of the external divisions in contemporary Christendom, we Lutherans believe that there is, properly speaking, only one church in heaven and on earth. St. Paul describes this unity of the church most beautifully in his letter to the Ephesians: "There is one body and one Spirit—just as you were called to the one hope that belongs to your call—one Lord, one faith, one baptism, one God and Father of all, who is over all and through all and in all" (Eph. 4:4–6). We join Christians of all ages, therefore, in confessing in the words of the Nicene Creed (381 A.D.) that we "believe in one, holy, Christian, and apostolic church." This one church is, as the Augsburg Confession puts it, "the assembly of all believers among whom the gospel is purely preached and the holy sacraments are administered according to the gospel" (VII, 1). This true spiritual unity of the church transcends space and time. It binds together all believers in Christ, wherever they may be, in a relationship that "will remain forever" (Augsburg Confession VIII, 1).

Although this spiritual unity (the unity *of* the church) is a present reality, external unity (unity *in* the church) most certainly is not. Already in the New Testament, Jesus warned His disciples about those who would "lead many astray" with their false teachings (Matt. 24:5). St. Paul in his letters warns his readers to be on guard against "false apostles, deceitful workmen, disguising themselves as apostles of Christ" (2 Cor. 11:13). He also warned against sinful divisions (1 Cor. 1:11–12), admonishing the Corinthians "that all of you agree and that there be no divisions among you, but that you be united in the same mind and the same judgment" (1 Cor. 1:10). Seeking to be faithful to what the Scriptures teach about both the unity *of* the church and unity *in* the church, the Lutheran Confessions hold that the way to achieve external unity in the church is to confess the truth and to expose error. The authors of the Formula of Concord write: "Fundamental, enduring unity in the church requires above all else a clear and binding summary and form in which a general summary of teaching is drawn together from God's Word" (FC SD Rule and Norm, 1).

The LCMS seeks to be faithful to what the Bible says about the spiritual unity *of* the church and external unity *in* the church as it relates to other Lutherans and to other Christian churches. On the one hand, we believe that divisions in Christendom ultimately stem from sin and are contrary to God's will. The first objective of the Synod therefore sets forth the goal of working "through its official structure toward fellowship with other Christian church bodies" and of providing a united defense against schism and sectarianism (LCMS Constitution, Article III, 1). As one way of striving toward this objective, the Missouri Synod has taken part in all of the Lutheran bilateral dialogues held in the United States to this date, beginning with the Lutheran/Roman Catholic Dialogue in 1965, and including official discussions with the Orthodox, with Reformed Churches, the Anglicans, Methodists, Baptists, and conservative Evangelicals.

At the same time, LCMS Lutherans believe that the way to external unity in the church is by confronting differences in doctrine and resolving these differences, not by ignoring them or by agreeing to disagree. We believe that, according to Scripture, external unity in the church is a matter of right confession of the Gospel of Jesus Christ. We therefore hold that church fellowship or merger between church bodies in doctrinal disagreement with each other is not in keeping with what the Bible teaches about church fellowship. For this reason, the LCMS representatives to the third round of discussions between Lutherans and Episcopalians in the USA, as well as to the discussions between Lutherans and Reformed church bodies, did not join in with ELCA representatives in recommending full altar and pulpit fellowship with these churches. We believe that genuine unity in the confession of the Christian faith exists only where there is agreement in the confession of the Gospel of Jesus Christ in all its articles.

Conclusion

At its 2004 convention, the Synod heartily endorsed the theme of "One Mission—One Message—One People" as set forth by its current president, Gerald Kieschnick, as a way of summarizing the Synod's reason for existence. In the words of President Kieschnick:

> We are called to be a Synod with One Mission . . . The Great Commission. Jesus said, "Go and make disciples of all nations, baptizing them in the name of the Father and of the Son and of the Holy Spirit, teaching them to obey everything I have commanded you" (Matthew 28:19–20). Accomplishing the mission of the church to disciple, baptize and teach the nations of the world is and must continue to be Job One among us!
>
> We are called to be a Synod proclaiming One Message . . . the message of Jesus Christ and Him crucified . . . the message of sins forgiven . . . the message of the free gift of eternal life. For "God was in Christ, reconciling the world to himself, not counting mankind's sins against them" (2 Corinthians 5:19). We have the greatest message in the world!
>
> We are called to live and act as One People. St. Paul, through the Holy Spirit, acknowledges "One Lord, one faith, one baptism, one God and Father of all, who is over all and through all and in all" (Ephesians 4:5–6). We have a long way to go in this regard, yet I

> implore you, in the words of St. Paul to the Philippians, "Whatever happens, conduct yourselves in a manner worthy of the gospel of Christ . . . stand firm in one spirit, contending as one man for the faith of the gospel" (Phil. 1:27). We need to work together—as one—to meet the challenges before us!

Simply stated, The Lutheran Church—Missouri Synod believes, teaches, and confesses that in Christ alone is there salvation: by grace alone, through faith alone, on the basis of Scripture alone. To share this message with the world is the mission of the church and the reason for its existence.

Dr. Samuel Nafzger is the former Executive Director of the Commission on Theology and Church Relations and currently serves as Director of Church Relations—Assistant to the President of The Lutheran Church—Missouri Synod.

APPENDIX B

A Brief Summary of the Crisis for the Synodical Higher Education System from Within: the Seminary-Synodical Conflict

From *Heritage in Motion: Readings in the History of The Lutheran Church—Missouri Synod, 1962–1995* (CPH 1998), edited by August R. Suelflow, former director of the Concordia Historical Institute.

In the late 1960s there was a movement in the Missouri Synod to resist what some saw as liberalizing tendencies. The response of the conservatives was to rally behind the support of Dr. J. A. O. Preus II for President of Synod in 1969. This set the stage for the crisis that prevailed during much of the 1970s as Synod sought to reaffirm its belief in the verbal inspiration and inerrancy of Scripture and to condemn the aberrant use of higher criticism in the interpretation of Scripture. While the theological issues were an issue at other schools, such as the colleges at River Forest and Seward and the seminary at Springfield, Concordia Seminary under Dr. John H. Tietjen became the focal point of the controversy. By the time the dust settled in 1979, Synod had lost three percent of its congregations, and several District and college presidents had resigned. The seminary, which had been nearly decimated, had rebounded beyond many people's expectations. In fact, one national news organization claimed that this was the first time a major American denomination had successfully reversed its liberalizing drift and returned to its traditional, conservative position.

The crisis had its roots already in the early 1950s when a memorial was submitted to Synod requesting an investigation of the seminary faculty in St. Louis. Similar requests were sent to subsequent conventions and with increasing frequency. The presidencies of Drs. John W. Behnken and Oliver Harms were troubled by the theological problems that were developing within Synod, but primarily at Concordia Seminary. During the 1960s the Board of Control of Concordia Seminary in St. Louis spent considerable time discussing problems of Biblical interpretation, such as the Genesis accounts of creation and the Fall, the nature of Old Testament prophecies, the proper understanding of the book of Jonah, and principles of hermeneutics and exegesis.

The situation became more serious in late 1969 when it became apparent in a meeting of the Council of Presidents and the faculties of both seminaries that there was considerable disagreement in the proper understanding of the authority and interpretation of Scripture. A few months later, in early 1970, three members of the St. Louis faculty formed a Committee for Openness and Trust which issued the document "Call to Openness and Trust." This document advocated open Communion on the basis of a new understanding of the Lord's Supper and attacked Synod's position on the inerrancy of Scripture. It was repudiated at the 1971 Milwaukee convention. These and similar events motivated the synodical President to appoint a Fact-Finding Committee.

The Fact-Finding Committee submitted its report to the synodical President on June 15, 1971. After interviewing 45 men, studying their writings and course syllabi, and visiting classes and chapel, members of the committee concluded that there was considerable diversity in theological positions within the faculty and that there clearly was divergence from the established doctrinal position of Synod. As a result of these findings, President Preus asked the Board of Control to direct the faculty during the 1972–73 school year to refrain from using any avenue, such as class lectures, student consultations, and pastoral conferences, to cast doubt on the divine authority of Scripture, the historicity and factuality of biblical events, the reality of Jesus' miracles, and the Gospel message.

In March of 1972, Dr. Preus, in consultation with the Vice-Presidents, issued *A Statement of Scriptural and Confessional Principles* as a guideline for the Board of Control to use in fulfilling its responsibilities. On September 1, 1972, Preus issued his "Report of the Synodical President" to inform the church of the results of the Fact-Finding Committee's work. One week later the seminary's president, Dr. John H. Tietjen, responded with his *Fact Finding or Fault Finding?* in which he rejected the validity of Preus' report. Late in 1972 the faculty majority responded to the Council of Presidents' recommendation that "each of the professors of Concordia Seminary, St. Louis, . . . assure the Church of his Biblical and confessional stance" with *Faithful to Our Calling, Faithful to Our Lord.* Each faculty member also prepared a statement of faith.

At the 1973 convention, Synod passed Resolution 3-09, which declared that the majority of the faculty at the St. Louis seminary was in violation of Article II of the synodical Constitution, which requires unequivocal acceptance of the Old and New Testaments and all the symbolical books of the Evangelical Lutheran Church. The Preamble restates the three primary errors of the faculty majority, namely, rejection of the *sola Scriptura* principle, Gospel reductionism, and setting aside of the third use of the Law in the manner of neo-Lutheranism.

On July 24, 1973, the faculty majority protested Resolution 3-09 of the 1973 synodical convention which condemned several positions of the faculty as false doctrine and directed that these matters be turned over to the seminary's Board of Control. This protest electrified the seminary community during the 1973–74 school year. The seminary community was encouraged to take a "strong and concerted action" by way of posters, campus newspapers, and the activities of special committees. The situation became more tense after the board in its November 19, 1973, meeting refused to renew the contract of one professor, resolved to implement Synod's retirement policy for faculty members 65 years of age, and resolved to review the doctrinal content of course syllabi. On December 13 over 400 students protested the board's action and hinted that they might leave the seminary.

When the Board of Control suspended President Tietjen on January 20, 1974, the students declared a moratorium on all classes until the board would identify which faculty members it considered false teachers. Later that same day the faculty went on strike. In a letter of January 22 to President Preus, the faculty blamed the Board of Control for bringing the seminary to a standstill. The faculty understood Dr. Tietjen's suspension as condemnation. On January 28 Dr. Preus urged the faculty to return to class and adjudicate the differences through channels provided by Synod. On February 12 the faculty gave the board an ultimatum: for classes to resume on February 19, the board would have to reverse the suspension of Dr. Tietjen and the department heads, renew the contract of one professor, reverse implementation of the retirement policy, and acknowledge the faculty's teaching as being in harmony with Synod's position. The board did not yield and on February 17 asked the faculty to indicate by noon on February 18 whether or not they would resume teaching on the 19th. If they should refuse to return to the classroom, they would be held in breach of contract.

On February 18, 1974, the majority of the faculty and students exited the campus and on February 19, as promised, founded Concordia Seminary in Exile (Seminex) with over 400 students and all but five members of the faculty. On October 12, 1974, the Board of Control officially removed Dr. Tietjen from office.

Concordia Seminary continued to function with 100 students and five professors. Rebuilding the seminary was an intense and demanding process, but it succeeded beyond many people's expectations. The 1974–75 school year began with nearly 200 students and a faculty and executive staff of almost 25. Within a few years the seminary had fully recovered, and its reputation as a solidly conservative Lutheran seminary faithful to Scripture and the Confessions was restored.

The history of the seminary crisis of 1974, which deserves a book in itself, may be summarized by the Majority Report and the Minority Report of the Board of Control of Concordia Seminary, St. Louis. Four members of the seminary's Board of Control issued a minority report over which they had agonized because of the negative connotations often associated with such reports. The minority report charged the board majority with not acting in a loving, brotherly, and evangelical manner and with the best interests of the Synod in mind. The report claims that the board had been "out of control" since the New Orleans convention and that some of the most crucial decisions had been approved by a very narrow majority, as little as one vote. It should be noted that while the board minority did not condone the position of the faculty majority or the student walkout, it faulted the board for the manner in which the board majority handled the conflict.

APPENDIX C

The Lutheran Confessions on the Sacrament of Holy Communion[1]

The Augsburg Confession

V. [The Office of the Ministry]

1 To obtain such faith God instituted the office of the ministry, that is, provided the Gospel and the sacraments. 2 Through these, as through means, he gives the Holy Spirit, who works faith, when and where he pleases, in those who hear the Gospel. 3 And the Gospel teaches that we have a gracious God, not by our own merits but by the merit of Christ, when we believe this.

4 Condemned are the Anabaptists and others who teach that the Holy Spirit comes to us through our own preparations, thoughts, and works without the external word of the Gospel.

VII. [The Church]

1 It is also taught among us that one holy Christian church will be and remain forever. This is the assembly of all believers among whom the Gospel is preached in its purity and the holy sacraments are administered according to the Gospel. 2 For it is sufficient for the true unity of the Christian church that the Gospel be preached

---

1 Theodore G. Tappert, *The Book of Concord* (Philadelphia: Fortress Press, 1959).

in conformity with a pure understanding of it and that the sacraments be administered in accordance with the divine Word. [3] It is not necessary for the true unity of the Christian church that ceremonies, instituted by men, should be observed uniformly in all places. [4] It is as Paul says in Eph. 4:4, 5, "There is one body and one Spirit, just as you were called to the one hope that belongs to your call, one Lord, one faith, one baptism."

X. The Holy Supper of Our Lord

[1] It is taught among us that the true body and blood of Christ are really present in the Supper of our Lord under the form of bread and wine and are there distributed and received. [2] The contrary doctrine is therefore rejected.

XIII. The Use of the Sacraments

[1] It is taught among us that the sacraments were instituted not only to be signs by which people might be identified outwardly as Christians, but that they are signs and testimonies of God's will toward us for the purpose of awakening and strengthening our faith. [2] For this reason they require faith, and they are rightly used when they are received in faith and for the purpose of strengthening faith.

XIV. Order in the Church

It is taught among us that nobody should publicly teach or preach or administer the sacraments in the church without a regular call.

XXII. Both Kinds in the Sacrament

[1] Among us both kinds are given to laymen in the sacrament. The reason is that there is a clear command and order of Christ, "Drink of it, all of you" (Matt. 26:27). [2] Concerning the chalice Christ here commands with clear words that all should drink of it.

[3] In order that no one might question these words and interpret them as if they apply only to priests, Paul shows in 1 Cor. 11:20ff. that the whole assembly of the congregation in Corinth received both kinds. [4] This usage continued in the church for a long time, as can be demonstrated from history and from writings of the Fathers.[5] In several places Cyprian mentions that the cup was given to laymen in his time. [6] St. Jerome also states that the priests who administered the sacrament distributed the blood of Christ to the people. [7] Pope Gelasius himself ordered that the sacrament was not to be divided. [8] Not a single canon can be found which requires the reception of only one kind. Nobody knows when or through whom this custom of receiving only one kind was introduced, although Cardinal Cusanus mentions when the use was approved. [10] It is evident that such a custom, introduced contrary to God's command and also contrary to the ancient canons, is unjust. [11] Accordingly it is not proper to burden the consciences of those who desire to observe the sacrament according to Christ's institution or to compel them to act contrary to the arrangement of our Lord Christ. [12] Because the division of the sacrament is contrary to the institution of Christ, the customary carrying about of the sacrament in processions is also omitted by us.

XXIV. The Mass

[9] We are unjustly accused of having abolished the Mass. Without boasting, it is manifest that the Mass is observed among us with greater devotion and more earnestness than among our opponents. [7] Moreover, the people are instructed often and with great diligence concerning the holy sacrament, why it was instituted, and how it is to be used (namely, as a comfort for terrified consciences) in order that the people may be drawn to the Communion and Mass. The people are also given instruction about other false teachings concerning the sacrament. [2] Meanwhile no conspicuous changes have been

made in the public ceremonies of the Mass, except that in certain places German hymns are sung in addition to the Latin responses for the instruction and exercise of the people. [3] After all, the chief purpose of all ceremonies is to teach the people what they need to know about Christ.

[10] Before our time, however, the Mass came to be misused in many ways, as is well known, by turning it into a sort of fair, by buying and selling it, and by observing it in almost all churches for a monetary consideration. Such abuses were often condemned by learned and devout men even before our time. [12] Then when our preachers preached about these things and the priests were reminded of the terrible responsibility which should properly concern every Christian (namely, that whoever uses the sacrament unworthily is guilty of the body and blood of Christ), [13] such mercenary Masses and private Masses, which had hitherto been held under compulsion for the sake of revenues and stipends, were discontinued in our churches.

[21] At the same time the abominable error was condemned according to which it was taught that our Lord Christ has by his death made satisfaction only for original sin, and had instituted the Mass as a sacrifice for other sins. [22] This transformed the Mass into a sacrifice for the living and the dead, a sacrifice by means of which sin was taken away and God was reconciled. [23] Thereupon followed a debate as to whether one Mass held for many people merited as much as a special Mass held for an individual. Out of this grew countless multiplication of Masses, by the performance of which men expected to get everything they needed from God. Meanwhile faith in Christ and true service of God were forgotten.

[24] Demanded without doubt by the necessity of such circumstances, instruction was given so that our people might know how

the sacrament is to be used rightly. [26] They were taught, first of all, that the Scriptures show in many places that there is no sacrifice for original sin, or for any other sin, except the one death of Christ. [27] For it is written in the Epistle to the Hebrews that Christ offered himself once and by this offering made satisfaction for all sin. [25] It is an unprecedented novelty in church doctrine that Christ's death should have made satisfaction only for original sin and not for other sins as well. Accordingly it is to be hoped that everyone will understand that this error is not unjustly condemned.

[28] In the second place, St. Paul taught that we obtain grace before God through faith and not through works. [29] Manifestly contrary to this teaching is the misuse of the Mass by those who think that grace is obtained through the performance of this work, for it is well known that the Mass is used to remove sin and obtain grace and all sorts of benefits from God, not only for the priest himself but also for the whole world and for others, both living and dead.

[30] In the third place, the holy sacrament was not instituted to make provision for a sacrifice for sin—for the sacrifice has already taken place—but to awaken our faith and comfort our consciences when we perceive that through the sacrament grace and forgiveness of sin are promised us by Christ. Accordingly the sacrament requires faith, and without faith it is used in vain.

[34] Inasmuch, then, as the Mass is not a sacrifice to remove the sins of others, whether living or dead, but should be a Communion in which the priest and others receive the sacrament for themselves, it is observed among us in the following manner: On holy days, and at other times when communicants are present, Mass is held and those who desire it are communicated. [35] Thus the Mass is preserved among us in its proper use, the use which was formerly observed in the church and which can be proved by St. Paul's statement in

1 Cor. 11:20ff. and by many statements of the Fathers. [36] For Chrysostom reports how the priest stood every day, inviting some to Communion and forbidding others to approach. [37] The ancient canons also indicate that one man officiated and communicated the other priests and deacons, [38] for the words of the Nicene canon read, "After the priests the deacons shall receive the sacrament in order from the bishop or priest."

[40] Since, therefore, no novelty has been introduced which did not exist in the church from ancient times, and since no conspicuous change has been made in the public ceremonies of the Mass except that other unnecessary Masses which were held in addition to the parochial Mass, probably through abuse, have been discontinued, this manner of holding Mass ought not in fairness be condemned as heretical or unchristian. [41] In times past, even in large churches where there were many people, Mass was not held on every day that the people assembled, for according to the Tripartite History, Book 9, on Wednesday and Friday the Scriptures were read and expounded in Alexandria, and all these services were held without Mass.

XXV. Confession

[1] Confession has not been abolished by the preachers on our side. The custom has been retained among us of not administering the sacrament to those who have not previously been examined and absolved. [2] At the same time the people are carefully instructed concerning the consolation of the Word of absolution so that they may esteem absolution as a great and precious thing. [3] It is not the voice or word of the man who speaks it, but it is the Word of God, who forgives sin, for it is spoken in God's stead and by God's command. [4] We teach with great diligence about this command and power of keys and how comforting and necessary it is for terrified consciences. We also teach that God requires us to believe this absolution as much

as if we heard God's voice from heaven, that we should joyfully comfort ourselves with absolution, and that we should know that through such faith we obtain forgiveness of sins. [5] In former times the preachers who taught much about confession never mentioned a word concerning these necessary matters but only tormented consciences without long enumerations of sins, with satisfactions, with indulgences, with pilgrimages and the like. [6] Many of our opponents themselves acknowledge that we have written about and treated of true Christian repentance in a more fitting fashion than had been done for a long time.

[7] Concerning confession we teach that no one should be compelled to recount sins in detail, for this is impossible. [8] As the psalmist says, "Who can discern his errors?" Jeremiah also says, "The heart is desperately corrupt; who can understand it?" Our wretched human nature is so deeply submerged in sins that it is unable to perceive or know them all, [9] and if we were to be absolved only from those which we can enumerate we would be helped but little. On this account there is no need to compel people to give a detailed account of their sins. [10] That this was also the view of the Fathers can be seen in Dist. I, *De poenitentia*, [11] where these words of Chrysostom are quoted: "I do not say that you should expose yourself in public or should accuse yourself before others, but obey the prophet who says, 'Show your way to the Lord.' Therefore confess to the Lord God, the true judge, in your prayer, telling him of your sins not with your tongue but in your conscience." Here it can be clearly seen that Chrysostom does not require a detailed enumeration of sins. [12] The marginal note in *De poenitentia*, Dist. 5, also teaches that such confession is not commanded by the Scriptures, but was instituted by the church. [13] Yet the preachers on our side diligently teach that confession is to be retained for the sake of absolution (which is its chief and most

important part), for the consolation of terrified consciences, and also for other reasons.

THE APOLOGY OF THE AUGSBURG CONFESSION

[ARTICLES VII AND VIII.] THE CHURCH

[1] The authors of the Confutation have condemned the seventh article of our Confession in which we said the church is the assembly of saints. And they have added a lengthy dissertation, that the wicked are not to be separated from the church since John compared the church to a threshing floor on which chaff and wheat are heaped together (Matt. 3:12) and Christ compared it to a net in which there are both good and bad fish (Matt. 13:47).

[2] The saying is certainly true that there is no defense against the attacks of slanderers. Nothing can be said so carefully that it can avoid misrepresentation. [3] That is why we added the eighth article, to avoid the impression that we separate evil men and hypocrites from the outward fellowship of the church or deny efficacy to the sacraments which evil men or hypocrites administer. Thus we do not need to defend ourselves at any length against this slander. The eighth article exonerates us enough. We concede that in this life the hypocrites and evil men are mingled with the church and are members of the church according to the outward associations of the church's marks—that is, Word, confession, and sacraments—especially if they have not been excommunicated. The sacraments do not lose their efficacy when they are administered by evil men; indeed, we may legitimately use sacraments that are administered by evil men. [4] Paul also predicts that Antichrist will "take his seat in the temple of God" (2 Thess. 2:4), that is, that he will rule and hold office in the church.

[5] The church is not merely an association of outward ties and rites like other civic governments, however, but it is mainly an

association of faith and of the Holy Spirit in men's hearts. To make it recognizable, this association has outward marks, the pure teaching of the Gospel and the administration of the sacraments in harmony with the Gospel of Christ. This church alone is called the body of Christ, which Christ renews, consecrates, and governs by his Spirit, as Paul testifies when he says (Eph. 1:22, 23), "And he has made him the head over all things for the church, which is his body, the fullness," that is, the whole congregation "of him who fills all in all." Thus those in whom Christ is not active are not members of Christ. This much our opponents also admit, that the wicked are dead members of the church. [6] We wonder why they criticize our description, which speaks of living members.

[7] We have not said anything new. Paul defined the church in the same way in Eph. 5:25–27, saying that it should be purified in order to be holy. He also added the outward marks, the Word and the sacraments. He says, "Christ loved the church and gave himself up for it, that he might sanctify it, having cleansed it by the washing of water with the word, that the church might be presented before him in splendor, without spot or wrinkle or any such thing, that it might be holy and without blemish." We have repeated this statement almost verbatim in our Confession. The Creed also defines the church this way, teaching us to believe that there is a holy, catholic church. Certainly the wicked are not a holy church! [8] The following phrase, "the communion of saints," seems to have been added to explain what "church" means, namely, the assembly of saints who share the association of the same Gospel or teaching and of the same Holy spirit, who renews, consecrates, and governs their hearts.

[9] We set forth this doctrine for a very necessary reason. We see the infinite dangers that threaten the church with ruin. There is an infinite number of ungodly within the church who oppress it. The

church will abide nevertheless; it exists despite the great multitude of the wicked, and Christ supplies it with the gifts he has promised—the forgiveness of sins, answer to prayer, and the gift of the Holy Spirit. The Creed offers us these consolations that we may not despair but may know all this. [10] It says "the church catholic" lest we take it to mean an outward government of certain nations. It is, rather, made up of men scattered throughout the world who agree on the Gospel and have the same Christ, the same Holy Spirit, and the same sacraments, whether they have the same human traditions or not. The gloss in the *Decrees* says that "the church in the larger sense includes both the godly and the wicked," and that the wicked are part of the church only in name and not in fact, while the godly are part of the church in fact as well as in name. [11] The Fathers say the same thing in many places. For example, Jerome says, "Therefore the sinner who has been defiled by any spot cannot be called part of the church of Christ, nor can he be said to be subject to Christ."

[12] Hypocrites and evil men are indeed associated with the true church as far as outward ceremonies are concerned. But when we come to define the church, we must define that which is the living body of Christ and is the church in fact as well as in name. [13] We must understand what it is that chiefly makes us members, and living members, of the church. If we were to define the church as only an outward organization embracing both the good and the wicked, then men would not understand that the kingdom of Christ is the righteousness of the heart and the gift of the Holy Spirit but would think of it as only the outward observance of certain devotions and rituals. [14] Then, too, what difference will there be between the church and the Old Testament people? Yet Paul distinguishes the church from the Old Testament people by the fact that the church is a spiritual people, separated from the heathen not by civil rites but by being God's

true people, reborn by the Holy Spirit. Among the Old Testament people, those born according to the flesh had promises about physical well-being, political affairs, etc. in addition to the promise about Christ. Because of these promises even the wicked among them were called the people of God inasmuch as God had separated these physical descendants from other nations by certain outward ordinances and promises. Nevertheless, these evil people did not please God. [15] But the Gospel brings not the shadow of eternal things but the eternal blessings themselves, the Holy Spirit and the righteousness by which we are righteous before God.

[16] According to the Gospel, therefore, only those are the true people who accept this promise of the Spirit. Besides the church is the kingdom of Christ, the opposite of the kingdom of the devil. It is evident, moreover, that the wicked are in the power of the devil and are members of the devil's kingdom, as Paul teaches in Eph. 2:2 when he says that the devil "is now at work in the sons of disobedience." Certainly the Pharisees had an outward affiliation with the church (that is, with the saints among the Old Testament people), for they held high positions and they sacrificed and taught. To them Christ says (John 8:44), "You are of your father the devil." Thus the church, which is truly the kingdom of Christ, is, precisely speaking, the congregation of the saints. The wicked are ruled by the devil and are his captives; they are not ruled by the Spirit of Christ.

[17] But why belabor the obvious? If the church, which is truly the kingdom of Christ, is distinguished from the kingdom of the devil, it necessarily follows that since the wicked belong to the kingdom of the devil, they are not the church. In this life, nevertheless, because the kingdom of Christ has not yet been revealed, they are mingled with the church and hold office in the church. [18] The fact that the revelation has not yet come does not make the wicked the kingdom

of Christ. What he quickens by his Spirit is always the same kingdom of Christ, whether it be revealed or hidden under the cross, just as Christ is the same, whether now glorified or previously afflicted. Christ's parables agree with this. [19] He clearly says in Matt. 13:38 that "the good seed means the sons of the kingdom, the weeds are the sons of the evil one." The field, he says, is the world, not the church. Thus John speaks (Matt. 3:12) about the whole Jewish nation and says that the true church will be separated from it. Therefore this passage is more against our opponents than for them since it shows that the true and spiritual people will be separated from the physical people. Christ is talking about the outward appearance of the church when he says that the kingdom of God is like a net (Matt. 13:47) or like ten virgins (Matt. 25:1). He teaches us that the church is hidden under a crowd of wicked men so that this stumbling block may not offend the faithful and so that we may know that the Word and the sacraments are efficacious even when wicked men administer them. Meanwhile he teaches that though these wicked men participate in the outward marks, still they are not the true kingdom of Christ and members of Christ, for they are members of the kingdom of the devil.

[20] We are not dreaming about some Platonic republic, as has been slanderously alleged, but we teach that this church actually exists, made up of true believers and righteous men scattered throughout the world. And we add its marks, the pure teaching of the Gospel and the sacraments. This church is properly called "the pillar of truth" (1 Tim. 3:15), for it retains the pure Gospel and what Paul calls the "foundation" (1 Cor. 3:12), that is, the true knowledge of Christ and faith. Of course, there are also many weak people in it who build on this foundation perishing structures of stubble, that is, unprofitable opinions. But because they do not overthrow the foundation, these are forgiven them or even corrected. [21] The writings of the

holy Fathers show that even they sometimes built stubble on the foundation but that this did not overthrow their faith. Most of what our opponents maintain, on the other hand, does overthrow faith, as when they condemn our doctrine that the forgiveness of sins is received by faith. It is also an open and wicked error when our opponents teach that men merit the forgiveness of sins by their love for God before entering a state of grace. This, too, means to remove Christ as the foundation. Similarly, why will faith be necessary if sacraments justify *ex opere operato*, without a good attitude in the one using them?

22 Just as the church has the promise that it will always have the Holy Spirit, so it also has the warning that there will be ungodly teachers and wolves. But the church, properly speaking, is that which has the Holy Spirit. Though wolves and ungodly teachers may run rampant in the church, they are not, properly speaking, the kingdom of Christ. So Lyra testifies when he says: "The church is not made up of men by reason of their power or position, whether ecclesiastical or secular, because princes and supreme pontiffs as well as those in lesser stations have apostasized from the faith. Therefore the church is made up of those persons in whom there is true knowledge and the confession of faith and truth." What have we said in our Confession that is different from what Lyra says here?

23 Perhaps our opponents demand some such definition of the church as the following. It is the supreme outward monarchy of the whole world in which the Roman pontiff must have unlimited power beyond question or censure. He may establish articles of faith, abolish the Scriptures by his leave, institute devotions and sacrifices, enact whatever laws he pleases, excuse and exempt men from any laws, divine, canonical, or civil, as he wishes. From him the emperor and all kings have received their power and right to rule, and this at

Christ's command; for as the Father subjected everything to him, so now this right has been transferred to the pope. Therefore the pope must be lord of the whole world, of all the kingdoms of the world, and of all public and private affairs. He must have plenary power in both the temporal and the spiritual realm, both swords, the temporal and the spiritual. [24] Now, this definition of the papal kingdom rather than of the church of Christ has as its authors not only the canonists but also Dan. 11:36–39.

[25] If we defined the church that way, we would probably have fairer judges. There are in existence many extravagant and wicked writings about the power of the Roman popc for which no one has ever been brought to trial. We alone are accused, because we preach the blessing of Christ, that we obtain forgiveness of sins through faith in him and not through devotions invented by the pope. [26] Christ, the prophets, and the apostles define the church as anything but such a papal kingdom. [27] Nor should that be transferred to the popes which is the prerogative of the true church: that they are pillars of the truth and that they do not err. How many of them care anything for the Gospel or think it worth reading? Many openly ridicule all religions, or if they accept anything, accept only what agrees with human reason and regard the rest as mythology, like the tragedies of the poets.

[28] In accordance with the Scriptures, therefore, we maintain that the church in the proper sense is the assembly of saints who truly believe the Gospel of Christ and who have the Holy Spirit. Nevertheless, we grant that the many hypocrites and evil men who are mingled with them in this life share an association in the outward marks, are members of the church according to this association in the outward marks, and therefore hold office in the church. When the sacraments are administered by unworthy men, this does not rob them of their efficacy. For they do not represent their own persons

but the person of Christ, because of the church's call, as Christ testifies (Luke 10:16), "He who hears you hears me." When they offer the Word of Christ or the sacraments, they do so in Christ's place and stead. Christ's statement teaches us this in order that we may not be offended by the unworthiness of ministers.

29 On this issue we have spoken out clearly enough in our Confession, where we condemn the Donatists and the Wycliffites, who believed that men sinned if they received the sacraments from unworthy men in the church. For the time being this seemed enough to defend the definition of the church which we had given. Nor do we see how it could be defined otherwise, since the church, properly so called, is termed the body of Christ. It is clear that the wicked belong to the kingdom and body of the devil, who drives them on and holds them captive. All this is clearer than the light of noonday; if our opponents still continue to twist it, we shall not mind replying more fully.

30 Our opponents also condemn the part of the seventh article in which we said, "For the true unity of the church it is enough to agree concerning the teaching of the Gospel and the administration of the sacraments. It is not necessary that human traditions or rites and ceremonies, instituted by men, should be alike everywhere." If we mean "particular rites" they approve our article, but if we mean "universal rites" they disapprove it. 31 We do not quite understand what our opponents mean. We are talking about true spiritual unity, without which there can be no faith in the heart nor righteousness in the heart before God. For this unity, we say, a similarity of human rites, whether universal or particular, is not necessary. The righteousness of faith is not a righteousness tied to certain traditions, as the righteousness of the law was tied to the Mosaic ceremonies, because this righteousness of the heart is something that quickens the heart.

To this quickening human traditions, whether universal or particular, contribute nothing; nor are they wrought by the Holy Spirit, as are chastity, patience, the fear of God, the love of our neighbor, and the works of love.

[32] We certainly had weighty reasons for presenting this article, for it is clear that many foolish opinions about traditions have crept into the church. Some have thought that human traditions are devotions necessary for meriting justification. Later they debated how it happened that they had come to worship God in so many ways, as though these observances were really acts of devotion rather than outward rules of discipline, completely unrelated to the righteousness of the heart or the worship of God. For good and valid reasons, these vary according to the circumstances, one way or another. Similarly, some churches have excommunicated others because of such traditions as the observance of Easter, the use of icons, and the like. From this the uninitiated have concluded that there can be no righteousness of the heart before God without these observances. On this issue there are many foolish books by the summists and others.

[33] But as the different length of day and night does not harm the unity of the church, so we believe that the true unity of the church is not harmed by differences in rites instituted by men, although we like it when universal rites are observed for the sake of tranquility. So in our churches we willingly observe the order of the Mass, the Lord's day, and the other more important feast days. With a very thankful spirit we cherish the useful and ancient ordinances, especially when they contain a discipline that serves to educate and instruct the people and the inexperienced. [34] Now, we are not discussing whether it is profitable to observe them for the sake of tranquility or bodily profit. Another issue is involved. The question is whether the observance of human traditions is an act of worship necessary for righteousness

before God. This must be settled in this controversy, and only then can we decide whether it is necessary for the true unity of the church that human traditions be alike everywhere. If human traditions are not acts of worship necessary for righteousness before God, it follows that somebody can be righteous and a child of God even if he does not observe traditions that have been maintained elsewhere. Thus if the German style of dress is not a devotion to God necessary for righteousness before him, it follows that men can be righteous, children of God, and the church of Christ even though they dress according to the French rather than the German style.

35 Paul clearly teaches this in Colossians (2:16, 17): "Let no one pass judgment on you in questions of food and drink or with regard to a festival or a new moon or a sabbath. These are only a shadow of what is to come; but the substance belongs to Christ." And again (vv. 20–23): "If with Christ you died to the elemental spirits of the universe, why do you live as if you still belonged to the world? Why do you submit to regulations, 'Do not handle, Do not taste, Do not touch' (referring to things which all perish as they are used), according to human precepts and doctrines? These have indeed an appearance of wisdom in promoting rigor of devotion and self-abasement." 36 What he means is this. The righteousness of the heart is a spiritual thing that quickens men's hearts. It is evident that human traditions do not quicken the heart, are not works of the Holy Spirit (like love of neighbor, chastity, etc.), and are not means by which God moves the heart to believe (like the divinely instituted Word and sacraments). Rather, they are customs that do not pertain to the heart and "perish as they are used." Therefore we must not believe that they are necessary for righteousness before God. He says the same in Rom. 14:17, "The kingdom of God does not mean food and drink but righteousness and peace and joy in the Holy Spirit."

[37] But it is not necessary to cite a great deal of evidence since it is obvious throughout the Scriptures and we have assembled much of it in the latter part of our Confession. Later on we must raise again and discuss more fully the issue in this controversy, namely, the question whether human traditions are acts of devotion necessary for righteousness before God.

[38] Our opponents say that universal traditions should be observed because they are supposed to have been handed down by the apostles. How devout they are! Apostolic rites they want to keep, apostolic doctrine they do not want to keep. [39] We should interpret those rites just as the apostles themselves did in their writings. They did not want us to believe that we are justified by such rites or that such rites are necessary for righteousness before God. They did not want to impose such a burden on consciences, nor to make the observance of days, food, and the like a matter of righteousness or of sin. [40] In fact, Paul calls such opinions "doctrines of demons." To determine the apostles' wish and intention, therefore, we must consult their writings, not merely their example. They observed certain days, not because such observance was necessary for justification but to let the people know when to assemble. When they assembled, they also observed other rites and a sequence of lessons. Frequently the people continued to observe certain Old Testament customs, which the apostles adapted in modified form to the Gospel history, like the Passover and Pentecost, so that by these examples as well as by instruction they might transmit to posterity the memory of these great events. [41] But if they were transmitted as something necessary for justification, why did the bishops later change them in so many ways? If they were of divine right, it was unlawful for men to assume the right to change them.

[42] Before the Council of Nicaea some people celebrated Easter at one time and others at another, but this difference did no harm to faith. Later on came the arrangement by which our Passover falls at a different time from the Jewish Passover. The apostles had commanded their churches to celebrate the Passover with the brethren who had been converted from Judaism, and so, after the Council of Nicaea, certain nations held tenaciously to the custom of using the Jewish time. But as the words of this decree show, the apostles did not want to impose an ordinance on the churches. For they say that no one should mind if his brethren do not correctly compute the time in celebrating Easter. The text of the decree is preserved in Epiphanius: "Do not calculate, but whenever your brethren of the circumcision do, celebrate it at the same time with them; even if they have made a mistake, do not let this bother you." According to Epiphanius, these words are from an apostolic decree about Easter; from them the discerning reader can easily judge that the apostles wanted to disabuse the people of the foolish notion of having to observe a set time, since they tell them not to be bothered even if there has been a mistake in the calculations.

[43] There were some in the East who maintained that because of this apostolic decree the Passover should be celebrated with the Jews; they were called Audians, from the originator of this idea. In his refutation of them Epiphanius praises the decree and says that it contains nothing contrary to the faith or the rule of the church, and he criticizes the Audians for misunderstanding it. He interprets it the same way that we do; for the apostles did not intend it to refer to the time when Easter should be celebrated, but for the sake of harmony they wanted others to follow the example of the chief brethren who had been converted from Judaism but kept their customs. [44] The apostles wisely admonished the reader neither to destroy evangelical liberty

nor to impose a necessity upon consciences, since they tell him not to be bothered even if there has been a mistake in the calculations.

[45] Many similar instances can be gathered from the histories in which it appears that a difference in human observances does not harm the unity of the faith. But why discuss it? Our opponents completely misunderstand the meaning of the righteousness of faith and of the kingdom of God if they regard as necessary a uniformity of observances in food, days, clothing, and similar matters without divine command. [46] But see what religious men our opponents are! They require uniform human ceremonies for the unity of the church while they themselves have changed the ordinance of Christ in the use of the Lord's Supper, which certainly was previously a universal ordinance. But if universal ordinances are necessary, why do they change the ordinance of Christ's Supper, which is not human but divine? But on this whole controversy we shall have a few things to say later.

[47] They have approved the entire eighth article. There we confess that hypocrites and evil men have been mingled with the church and that the sacraments are efficacious even when evil men administer them, for ministers act in Christ's stead and do not represent their own persons, according to the word (Luke 10:16), "He who hears you hears me." [48] We should forsake wicked teachers because they no longer function in the place of Christ, but are antichrists. Christ says (Matt. 7:15), "Beware of false prophets"; Paul says (Gal. 1:9), "If anyone is preaching to you a gospel contrary to that which you received, let him be accursed."

[49] Christ has also warned us in his parables on the church that when we are offended by the personal conduct of priests or people, we should not incite schisms, as the Donatists wickedly did. [50] We regard as utterly seditious those who have incited schisms because

they denied to priests the right to hold property or other possessions. The right to hold property is a civil ordinance. It is legitimate for Christians to use civil ordinances just as it is legitimate for them to use the air, light, food, and drink. For as this universe and the fixed movements of the stars are truly ordinances of God and are preserved by God, so lawful governments are ordinances of God and are preserved and defended by God against the devil.

[Article X. The Holy Supper]

[1] They approve the tenth article, where we confess our belief that in the Lord's Supper the body and blood of Christ are truly and substantially present and are truly offered with those things that are seen, the bread and the wine, to those who receive the sacrament. After careful examination and consideration of it, we firmly defend this belief. For since Paul says that the bread is "a participation in the Lord's body," it would follow that the bread would not be a participation in the body of Christ but only in his spirit if the Lord's body were not truly present.

[2] We know that not only the Roman Church affirms the bodily presence of Christ, but that the Greek Church has taken and still takes this position. Evidence for this is their canon of the Mass, in which the priest clearly prays that the bread may be changed and become the very body of Christ. And Vulgarius, who seems to us to be a sensible writer, says distinctly that "the bread is not merely a figure but is truly changed into flesh." [3] There is a long exposition of John 15 in Cyril which teaches that Christ is offered to us bodily in the Supper. He says: "We do not deny that we are joined to Christ spiritually by true faith and sincere love. But we do deny that we have no kind of connection with him according to the flesh, and we say that this would be completely foreign to the sacred Scriptures. Who has ever doubted that Christ is a vine in this way and that we are truly

branches, deriving life from him for ourselves? Listen to Paul say, 'We are all one body in Christ' (Rom. 12:5); 'We who are many are one body, for we all partake of the same loaf' (1 Cor. 10:17). Does he think perhaps that we do not know the power of the mystical benediction? Since this is in us, does it not also cause Christ to dwell in us bodily through the communication of the flesh of Christ?" A little later he says, "Therefore we must consider that Christ is in us, not only according to the habit which we understand as love, but also by a natural participation," etc.

[4] We have quoted all of this here, not to begin an argument on this subject (his Imperial Majesty does not disapprove this article), but to make clear to all our readers that we defend the doctrine received in the whole church—that in the Lord's Supper the body and blood of Christ are truly and substantially present and are truly offered with those things that are seen, bread and wine. We are talking about the presence of the living Christ, knowing that "death no longer has dominion over him."

Luther's Large Catechism

[Fifth Part:] The Sacrament of the Altar

[1] As we treated Holy Baptism under three headings, so we must deal with the second sacrament in the same way, stating what it is, what its benefits are, and who is to receive it. All these are established from the words by which Christ instituted it. [2] So everyone who wishes to be a Christian and go to the sacrament should be familiar with them. For we do not intend to admit to the sacrament and administer it to those who do not know what they seek or why they come. The words are these:

[3] *"Our Lord Jesus Christ on the night when he was betrayed took bread, gave thanks, broke it, and gave it to his disciples and said, 'Take,*

eat; this is my body, which is given for you. Do this in remembrance of me.'"

"In the same way also he took the cup, after supper, gave thanks, and gave it to them, saying, 'This cup is the new testament in my blood, which is poured out for you for the forgiveness of sins. Do this, as often as you drink it, in remembrance of me.'"

[4] We have no wish on this occasion to quarrel and dispute with those who blaspheme and desecrate this sacrament; but as in the case of Baptism, we shall first learn what is of greatest importance, namely, God's Word and ordinance or command, which is the chief thing to be considered. For the Lord's Supper was not invented or devised by any man. It was instituted by Christ without man's counsel or deliberation. [5] Therefore, just as the Ten Commandments, the Lord's Prayer, and the Creed retain their nature and value even if we never keep, pray, or believe them, so also does this blessed sacrament remain unimpaired and inviolate even if we use and handle it unworthily. [6] Do you think God cares so much about our faith and conduct that he would permit them to affect his ordinance? No, all temporal things remain as God has created and ordered them, regardless of how we treat them. [7] This must always be emphasized, for thus we can thoroughly refute all the babbling of the seditious spirits who regard the sacraments, contrary to the Word of God, as human performances.

[8] Now, what is the Sacrament of the Altar? Answer: It is the true body and blood of the Lord Christ in and under the bread and wine which we Christians are commanded by Christ's word to eat and drink. [9] As we said of Baptism that it is not mere water, so we say here that the sacrament is bread and wine, but not mere bread or wine such as is served at the table. It is bread and wine comprehended in God's Word and connected with it.

[10] It is the Word, I maintain, which distinguishes it from mere bread and wine and constitutes it a sacrament which is rightly called Christ's body and blood. It is said, *"Accedat verbum ad elementum et fit sacramentum,"* that is, "When the Word is joined to the external element, it becomes a sacrament." This saying of St. Augustine is so accurate and well put that it is doubtful if he has said anything better. The Word must make the element a sacrament; otherwise it remains a mere element. [11] Now, this is not the word and ordinance of a prince or emperor, but of the divine Majesty at whose feet every knee should bow and confess that it is as he says and should accept it with all reverence, fear, and humility.

[12] With this Word you can strengthen your conscience and declare: "Let a hundred thousand devils, with all the fanatics, rush forward and say, 'How can bread and wine be Christ's body and blood?' Still I know that all the spirits and scholars put together have less wisdom than the divine Majesty has in his little finger. [13] Here we have Christ's word, 'Take, eat; this is my body.' 'Drink of it, all of you, this is the new covenant in my blood,' etc. Here we shall take our stand and see who dares to instruct Christ and alter what he has spoken. [14] It is true, indeed, that if you take the Word away from the elements or view them apart from the Word, you have nothing but ordinary bread and wine. But if the words remain, as is right and necessary, then in virtue of them they are truly the body and blood of Christ. For as we have it from the lips of Christ, so it is; he cannot lie or deceive."

[15] Hence it is easy to answer all kinds of questions which now trouble men—for example, whether even a wicked priest can administer the sacrament, and like questions. [16] Our conclusion is: Even though a knave should receive or administer it, it is the true sacrament (that is, Christ's body and blood) just as truly as when one uses

it most worthily. For it is not founded on the holiness of men but on the Word of God. As no saint on earth, yes, no angel in heaven can transform bread and wine into Christ's body and blood, so likewise no one can change or alter the sacrament, even if it is misused. [17] For the Word by which it was constituted a sacrament is not rendered false because of an individual's unworthiness or unbelief. Christ does not say, "If you believe, or if you are worthy, you receive my body and blood," but, "Take, eat and drink, this is my body and blood." Likewise, he says, "Do this," namely, what I now do, what I institute, what I give you and bid you take. [18] This is as much as to say, "No matter whether you are unworthy or worthy, you here have Christ's body and blood by virtue of these words which are coupled with the bread and wine." [19] Mark this and remember it well. For upon these words rest our whole argument, protection, and defense against all errors and deceptions that have ever arisen or may yet arise.

[20] We have briefly considered the first part, namely, the essence of this sacrament. Now we come to its power and benefit, the purpose for which the sacrament was really instituted, for it is most necessary that we know what we should seek and obtain there. [21] This is plainly evident from the words just quoted, "This is my body and blood, given and poured out *for you* for the forgiveness of sins." [22] In other words, we go to the sacrament because we receive there a great treasure, through and in which we obtain the forgiveness of sins. Why? Because the words are there through which this is imparted! Christ bids me eat and drink in order that the sacrament may be mine and may be a source of blessing to me as a sure pledge and sign—indeed, as the very gift he has provided for me against my sins, death, and all evils.

[23] Therefore, it is appropriately called the food of the soul since it nourishes and strengthens the new man. While it is true that through

Baptism we are first born anew, our human flesh and blood have not lost their old skin. There are so many hindrances and temptations of the devil and the world that we often grow weary and faint, at times even stumble. [24] The Lord's Supper is given as a daily food and sustenance so that our faith may refresh and strengthen itself and not weaken in the struggle but grow continually stronger. [25] For the new life should be one that continually develops and progresses. [26] Meanwhile it must suffer much opposition. The devil is a furious enemy; when he sees that we resist him and attack the old man, and when he cannot rout us by force, he sneaks and skulks about everywhere, trying all kinds of tricks, and does not stop until he has finally worn us out so that we either renounce our faith or yield hand and foot and become indifferent or impatient. [27] For such times, when our heart feels too sorely pressed, this comfort of the Lord's Supper is given to bring us new strength and refreshment.

[28] Here again our clever spirits comfort themselves with their great learning and wisdom, bellowing and blustering, "How can bread and wine forgive sins or strengthen faith?" Yet they know that we do not claim this of bread and wine—since in itself bread is bread—but of that bread and wine which are Christ's body and blood and with which the words are coupled. These and no other, we say, are the treasure through which forgiveness is obtained. [29] This treasure is conveyed and communicated to us in no other way than through the words, "given and poured out for you." Here you have both truths, that it is Christ's body and blood and that these are yours as your treasure and gift. [30] Christ's body can never be an unfruitful, vain thing, impotent and useless. Yet, however great the treasure may be in itself, it must be comprehended in the Word and offered to us through the Word, otherwise we could never know of it or seek it.

[31] Therefore it is absurd to say that Christ's body and blood are not given and poured out for us in the Lord's Supper and hence that we cannot have forgiveness of sins in the sacrament. Although the work was accomplished and forgiveness of sins was acquired on the cross, yet it cannot come to us in any other way than through the Word. How should we know that this has been accomplished and offered to us if it were not proclaimed by preaching, by the oral Word? Whence do they know of forgiveness, and how can they grasp and appropriate it, except by steadfastly believing the Scriptures and the Gospel? [32] Now, the whole Gospel and the article of the Creed, "I believe in the holy Christian church, the forgiveness of sins," are embodied in this sacrament and offered to us through the Word. Why, then, should we allow this treasure to be torn out of the sacrament? Our opponents must still confess that these are the very words which we hear everywhere in the Gospel. They can say that these words in the sacrament are of no value just as little as they dare say that the whole Gospel or Word of God apart from the sacrament is of no value.

[33] So far we have treated the sacrament from the standpoint both of its essence and of its effect and benefit. It remains for us to consider who it is that receives this power and benefit. Briefly, as we said above concerning Baptism and in many other places, the answer is: It is he who believes what the words say and what they give, for they are not spoken or preached to stone and wood but to those who hear them, those to whom Christ says, "Take and eat," etc. [34] And because he offers and promises forgiveness of sins, it cannot be received except by faith. This faith he himself demands in the Word when he says, "Given *for you*" and "poured out *for you*," as if he said, "This is why I give it and bid you eat and drink, that you may take it as your own and enjoy it." [35] Whoever lets these words be addressed

to him and believes that they are true has what the words declare. But he who does not believe has nothing, for he lets this gracious blessing be offered to him in vain and refuses to enjoy it. The treasure is opened and placed at everyone's door, yes, upon everyone's table, but it is also your responsibility to take it and confidently believe that it is just as the words tell you.

[36] This, now, is the preparation required of a Christian for receiving this sacrament worthily. Since this treasure is fully offered in the words, it can be grasped and appropriated only by the heart. Such a gift and eternal treasure cannot be seized with the hand. [37] Fasting and prayer and the like may have their place as an external preparation and children's exercise so that one's body may behave properly and reverently toward the body and blood of Christ. But what is given in and with the sacrament cannot be grasped and appropriated by the body. This is done by the faith of the heart which discerns and desires this treasure.

[38] Enough has been said now for all ordinary instruction on the essentials of this sacrament. What may be further said belongs to another occasion.

[39] In conclusion, now that we have the right interpretation and doctrine of the sacrament, there is great need also of an admonition and entreaty that so great a treasure, which is daily administered and distributed among Christians, may not be heedlessly passed by. What I mean is that those who claim to be Christians should prepare themselves to receive this blessed sacrament frequently. [40] For we see that men are becoming listless and lazy about its observance. A lot of people who heard the Gospel, now that the pope's nonsense has been abolished and we are freed from his oppression and authority, let a year, or two, three, or more years go by without receiving the sacrament, as if they were such strong Christians that they have

no need of it. [41] Some let themselves be kept and deterred from it because we have taught that no one should go unless he feels a hunger and thirst impelling him to it. Some pretend that it is a matter of liberty, not of necessity, and that it is enough if they simply believe. Thus the majority go so far that they have become quite barbarous, and ultimately despise both the sacrament and the Word of God.

[42] Now it is true, we repeat, that no one should under any circumstances be coerced or compelled, lest we institute a new slaughter of souls. Nevertheless, let it be understood that people who abstain and absent themselves from the sacrament over a long period of time are not to be considered Christians. Christ did not institute it to be treated merely as a spectacle, but commanded his Christians to eat and drink and thereby remember him.

[43] Indeed, true Christians who cherish and honor the sacrament will of their own accord urge and impel themselves to come. However, in order that the common people and the weak, who also would like to be Christians, may be induced to see the reason and the need for receiving the sacrament, we shall devote a little attention to this point. [44] As in other matters pertaining to faith, love, and patience it is not enough simply to teach and instruct, but there must also be daily exhortation, so on this subject we must be persistent in preaching, lest people become indifferent and bored. For we know from experience that the devil always sets himself against this and every other Christian activity, hounding and driving people from it as much as he can.

[45] In the first place, we have a clear text in the words of Christ, "*Do this* in remembrance of me." These are words of precept and command, enjoining all who would be Christians to partake of the sacrament. They are words addressed to disciples of Christ; hence whoever would be one of them, let him faithfully hold to this

sacrament, not from compulsion, coerced by men, but to obey and please the Lord Christ. [46] However, you may say, "But the words are added, 'as often as you do it'; so he compels no one, but leaves it to our free choice." [47] I answer: That is true, but it does not say that we should never partake. Indeed, the very words, "as often as you do it," imply that we should do it often. And they are added because Christ wishes the sacrament to be free, not bound to a special time like the Passover, which the Jews were obliged to eat only once a year, precisely on the evening of the fourteenth day of the first full moon, without variation of a single day. Christ means to say: "I institute a Passover or Supper for you, which you shall enjoy not just on this one evening of the year, but frequently, whenever and wherever you will, according to everyone's opportunity and need, being bound to no special place or time" [48] (although the pope afterward perverted it and turned it back into a Jewish feast).

[49] Thus you see that we are not granted liberty to despise the sacrament. When a person, with nothing to hinder him, lets a long period of time elapse without ever desiring the sacrament, I call that despising it. If you want such liberty, you may just as well take the further liberty not to be a Christian; then you need not believe or pray, for the one is just as much Christ's commandment as the other. But if you wish to be a Christian, you must from time to time satisfy and obey this commandment. [50] For this commandment should ever move you to examine your inner life and reflect: "See what sort of Christian I am! If I were one, I would surely have at least a little longing to do what my Lord has commanded me to do."

[51] Indeed, since we show such an aversion toward the sacrament, men can easily sense what sort of Christians we were under the papacy when we attended the sacrament merely from compulsion and fear of men's commandments, without joy and love and even

without regard for Christ's commandment. [52] But we neither force nor compel anyone, nor need anyone partake of the sacrament to serve or please us. What should move and impel you is the fact that Christ desires it, and it pleases him. You should not let yourself be forced by men either to faith or to any good work. All we are doing is to urge you to do what you ought to do, not for our sake but for your own. He invites and incites you; if you despise this, you must answer for it yourself.

[53] This is the first point, especially for the benefit of the cold and indifferent, that they may come to their senses and wake up. It is certainly true, as I have found in my own experience, and as everyone will find in his own case, that if a person stays away from the sacrament, day by day he will become more and more callous and cold, and eventually spurn it altogether. [54] To avoid this, we must examine our heart and conscience and act like a person who really desires to be right with God. The more we do this, the more will our heart be warmed and kindled, and it will not grow entirely cold.

[55] But suppose you say, "What if I feel that I am unfit?" Answer: This also is my temptation, especially inherited from the old order under the pope when we tortured ourselves to become so perfectly pure that God might not find the least blemish in us. Because of this we became so timid that everyone was thrown into consternation, saying, "Alas, I am not worthy!" [56] Then nature and reason begin to contrast our unworthiness with this great and precious blessing, and it appears like a dark lantern in contrast to the bright sun, or as dung in contrast to jewels. Because nature and reason see this, such people refuse to go to the sacrament and wait until they become prepared, until one week passes into another and one half year into yet another. [57] If you choose to fix your eye on how good and pure you are, to

work toward the time when nothing will prick your conscience, you will never go.

[58] For this reason we must make a distinction among men. Those who are shameless and unruly must be told to stay away, for they are not fit to receive the forgiveness of sins since they do not desire it and do not want to be good. [59] The others, who are not so callous and dissolute but would like to be good, should not absent themselves, even though in other respects they are weak and frail. As St. Hilary has said, "Unless a man has committed such a sin that he has forfeited the name of Christian and has to be expelled from the congregation, he should not exclude himself from the sacrament," lest he deprive himself of life. [60] No one will make such progress that he does not retain many common infirmities in his flesh and blood.

[61] People with such misgivings must learn that it is the highest wisdom to realize that this sacrament does not depend upon our worthiness. We are not baptized because we are worthy and holy, nor do we come to confession pure and without sin; on the contrary, we come as poor, miserable men, precisely because we are unworthy. The only exception is the person who desires no grace and absolution and has no intention to amend his life.

[62] He who earnestly desires grace and consolation should compel himself to go and allow no one to deter him, saying, "I would really like to be worthy, but I come not on account of any worthiness of mine, but on account of thy Word, because thou hast commanded it and I want to be thy disciple, no matter how insignificant my worthiness." [63] This is difficult, for we always have this obstacle and hindrance to contend with, that we concentrate more upon ourselves than upon the words that proceed from Christ's lips. Nature would like to act in such a way that it may rest and rely firmly upon itself; otherwise it refuses to take a step. Let this suffice for the first point.

[64] In the second place, a promise is attached to the commandment, as we heard above, which should most powerfully draw and impel us. Here stand the gracious and lovely words, "This is my body, given *for you*," "This is my blood, poured out *for you* for the forgiveness of sins." [65] These words, I have said, are not preached to wood or stone but to you and me; otherwise Christ might just as well have kept quiet and not instituted a sacrament. Ponder, then, and include yourself personally in the "you" so that he may not speak to you in vain.

[66] In this sacrament he offers us all the treasure he brought from heaven for us, to which he most graciously invites us in other places, as when he says in Matt. 11:28, "Come to me, all who labor and are heavy-laden, and I will refresh you." [67] Surely it is a sin and a shame that, when he tenderly and faithfully summons and exhorts us to our highest and greatest good, we act so distantly toward it, neglecting it so long that we grow quite cold and callous and lose all desire and love for it. [68] We must never regard the sacrament as a harmful thing from which we should flee, but as a pure, wholesome, soothing medicine which aids and quickens us in both soul and body. For where the soul is healed, the body has benefited also. Why, then, do we act as if the sacrament were a poison which would kill us if we ate of it?

[69] Of course, it is true that those who despise the sacrament and lead unchristian lives receive it to their harm and damnation. To such people nothing can be good or wholesome, just as when a sick person willfully eats and drinks what is forbidden him by the physician. [70] But those who feel their weakness, who are anxious to be rid of it and desire help, should regard and use the sacrament as a precious antidote against the poison in their systems. For here in the sacrament you receive from Christ's lips the forgiveness of sins, which contains and conveys God's grace and Spirit with all his gifts,

protection, defense, and power against death and the devil and all evils.

[71] Thus you have on God's part both the commandment and the promise of the Lord Christ. Meanwhile, on your part, you ought to be impelled by your own need, which hangs around your neck and which is the very reason for this command and invitation and promise. Christ himself says, "Those who are well have no need of a physician, but those who are sick," that is, those who labor and are heavy-laden with sin, fear of death, and the assaults of the flesh and the devil. [72] If you are heavy-laden and feel your weakness, go joyfully to the sacrament and receive refreshment, comfort, and strength. [73] If you wait until you are rid of your burden in order to come to the sacrament purely and worthily, you must stay away from it forever. [74] In such a case Christ pronounces the judgment, "If you are pure and upright, you have no need of me and I have no need of you." Therefore they alone are unworthy who neither feel their infirmities nor admit to being sinners.

[75] Suppose you say, "What shall I do if I cannot feel this need or experience hunger and thirst for the sacrament?" Answer: For persons in such a state of mind that they cannot feel it, I know no better advice than to suggest that they put their hands to their bosom and ask whether they are made of flesh and blood. If you find that you are, then for your own good turn to St. Paul's Epistle to the Galatians and hear what are the fruits of the flesh: "The works of the flesh are plain: adultery, immorality, impurity, licentiousness, idolatry, sorcery, enmity, strife, jealousy, anger, selfishness, dissension, party spirit, envy, murder, drunkenness, carousing, and the like."

[76] If you cannot feel the need, therefore, at least believe the Scriptures. They will not lie to you, and they know your flesh better than you yourself do. Yes, and St. Paul concludes in Rom. 7:18, "For

I know that nothing good dwells within me, that is, in my flesh." If St. Paul can speak thus of his flesh, let us not pretend to be better or more holy. [77] But the fact that we are insensitive to our sin is all the worse, for it is a sign that ours is a leprous flesh which feels nothing though the disease rages and rankles. [78] As we have said, even if you are so utterly dead in sin, at least believe the Scriptures, which pronounce this judgment upon you. In short, the less you feel your sins and infirmities, the more reason you have to go to the sacrament and seek a remedy.

[79] Again, look about you and see whether you are also in the world. If you do not know, ask your neighbors about it. If you are in the world, do not think that there will be any lack of sins and needs. Just begin to act as if you want to become good and cling to the Gospel, and see whether you will not acquire enemies who harm, wrong, and injure you and give you occasion for sin and wrong-doing. If you have not experienced this, then take it from the Scriptures, which everywhere give this testimony about the world.

[80] Besides the flesh and the world, you will surely have the devil about you. You will not entirely trample him under foot because our Lord Christ himself could not entirely avoid him. [81] Now, what is the devil? Nothing else than what the Scriptures call him, a liar and a murderer.

A liar who seduces the heart from God's Word and blinds it, making you unable to feel your needs or come to Christ. A murderer who begrudges you every hour of your life. [82] If you could see how many daggers, spears, and arrows are at every moment aimed at you, you would be glad to come to the sacrament as often as possible. The only reason we go about so securely and heedlessly is that we neither acknowledge nor believe that we are in the flesh, in this wicked world, or under the kingdom of the devil.

[83] Try this, therefore, and practice it well. Just examine yourself, look around a little, cling to the Scriptures. If even then you feel nothing, you have all the more need to lament both to God and to your brother. Take others' advice and seek their prayers, and never give up until the stone is removed from your heart. [84] Then your need will become apparent, and you will perceive that you have sunk twice as low as any other poor sinner and are much in need of the sacrament to combat your misery. This misery, unfortunately, you do not see, though God grants his grace that you may become more sensitive to it and more hungry for the sacrament. This happens especially because the devil so constantly besieges you and lies in wait to trap and destroy you, soul and body, so that you cannot be safe from him one hour. How quickly can he bring you into misery and distress when you least expect it!

[85] Let this serve as an exhortation, then, not only for us who are grown and advanced in years, but also for the young people who ought to be brought up in Christian doctrine and a right understanding of it. With such training we may more easily instill the Ten Commandments, the Creed, and the Lord's Prayer into the young so that they will receive them with joy and earnestness, practice them from their youth, and become accustomed to them. [86] For it is clearly useless to try to change old people. We cannot perpetuate these and other teachings unless we train the people who come after us and succeed us in our office and work, so that they in turn may bring up their children successfully. Thus the Word of God and the Christian church will be preserved. [87] Therefore let every head of a household remember that it is his duty, by God's injunction and command, to teach or have taught to his children the things they ought to know. Since they are baptized and received into the Christian church, they should also enjoy this fellowship of the sacrament so that they may

serve us and be useful. For they must all help us to believe, to love, to pray, and to fight the devil.

Here follows an exhortation to confession.

A Brief Exhortation to Confession

[1] Concerning confession, we have always taught that it should be voluntary and purged of the pope's tyranny. We have been set free from his coercion and from the intolerable burden he imposed upon the Christian church. Up to now, as we all know from experience, there has been no law quite so oppressive as that which forced everyone to make confession on pain of the gravest mortal sin. [2] Moreover, it so greatly burdened and tortured consciences with the enumeration of all kinds of sin that no one was able to confess purely enough. [3] Worst of all, no one taught or understood what confession is and how useful and comforting it is. Instead, it was made sheer anguish and a hellish torture since people had to make confession even though nothing was more hateful to them. [4] These three things have now been removed and made voluntary so that we may confess without coercion or fear, and we are released from the torture of enumerating all sins in detail. Moreover, we have the advantage of knowing how to use confession beneficially for the comforting and strengthening of our conscience.

[5] Everyone knows this now. Unfortunately, men have learned in only too well; they do whatever they please and take advantage of their freedom, acting as if they will never need or desire to go to confession any more. We quickly understand whatever benefits us, and we grasp with uncommon ease whatever in the Gospel is mild and gentle. But such pigs, as I have said, are unworthy to appear in the presence of the Gospel or to have any part of it. They ought to remain under the pope and submit to being driven and tormented to confess, fast, etc., more than ever before. For he who will not believe

the Gospel, live according to it, and do what a Christian ought to do, should enjoy none of its benefits. [6] What would happen if you wished to enjoy the Gospel's benefits but did nothing about it and paid nothing for it? For such people we shall provide no preaching, nor will they have our permission to share and enjoy any part of our liberty, but we shall let the pope or his like bring them back into subjection and coerce them like the tyrant he is. The rabble who will not obey the Gospel deserve just such a jailer as God's devil and hangman. [7] To others who hear it gladly, however, we must preach, exhorting, encouraging, and persuading them not to lose this precious and comforting treasure which the Gospel offers. Therefore we must say something about confession to instruct and admonish the simple folk.

[8] To begin with, I have said that in addition to the confession which we are discussing here there are two other kinds, which have an even greater right to be called the Christians' common confession. I refer to the practice of confessing to God alone or to our neighbor alone, begging for forgiveness. These two kinds are expressed in the Lord's Prayer when we say, "Forgive us our debts, as we forgive our debtors," etc. [9] Indeed, the whole Lord's Prayer is nothing else than such a confession. For what is our prayer but a confession that we neither have nor do what we ought and a plea for grace and a happy conscience? This kind of confession should and must take place incessantly as long as we live. For this is the essence of a genuinely Christian life, to acknowledge that we are sinners and to pray for grace.

[10] Similarly the second confession, which each Christian makes toward his neighbor, is included in the Lord's Prayer. We are to confess our guilt before one another and forgive one another before we come into God's presence to beg for forgiveness. Now, all of us are

debtors one to another, therefore we should and we may confess publicly in everyone's presence, no one being afraid of anyone else. [11] For it is true, as the proverb says, "If one man is upright, so are they all"; no one does to God or his neighbor what he ought. However, besides our universal guilt there is also a particular one, when a person has provoked another to anger and needs to beg his pardon. [12] Thus we have in the Lord's Prayer a twofold absolution: our debts both to God and to our neighbor are forgiven when we forgive our neighbor and become reconciled with him.

[13] Besides this public, daily, and necessary confession, there is also the secret confession which takes place privately before a single brother. When some problem or quarrel sets us at one another's throats and we cannot settle it, and yet we do not find ourselves sufficiently strong in faith, we may at any time and as often as we wish lay our complaint before a brother, seeking his advice, comfort, and strength. [14] This kind of confession is not included in the commandment like the other two but is left to everyone to use whenever he needs it. Thus by divine ordinance Christ himself has entrusted absolution to his Christian church and commanded us to absolve one another from sins. So if there is a heart that feels its sin and desires consolation, it has here a sure refuge when it hears in God's Word that through a man God looses and absolves him from his sins.

[15] Note, then, as I have often said, that confession consists of two parts. The first is my work and act, when I lament my sin and desire comfort and restoration for my soul. The second is a work which God does, when he absolves me of my sins through a word placed in the mouth of a man. This is the surpassingly grand and noble thing that makes confession so wonderful and comforting. [16] In the past we placed all the emphasis on our work alone, and we were only concerned whether we had confessed purely enough. We neither noticed

nor preached the very necessary second part; it was just as if our confession were simply a good work with which we could satisfy God. Where the confession was not made perfectly and in complete detail, we were told that the absolution was not valid and the sin was not forgiven. [17] Thereby the people were driven to the point that everyone inevitably despaired of confessing so purely (which was impossible), and nobody could feel his conscience at peace or have confidence in his absolution. Thus the precious confession was not only made useless to us but it also became burdensome and bitter, to the manifest harm and destruction of souls.

[18] We should therefore take care to keep the two parts clearly separate. We should set little value on our work but exalt and magnify God's Word. We should not act as if we wanted to perform a magnificent work to present to him, but simply to accept and receive something from him. You dare not come and say how good or how wicked you are. [19] If you are a Christian, I know this well enough anyway; if you are not, I know it still better. But what you must do is to lament your need and allow yourself to be helped so that you may attain a happy heart and conscience.

[20] Further, no one dare oppress you with requirements. Rather, whoever is a Christian, or would like to be one, has here the faithful advice to go and obtain this precious treasure. If you are no Christian, and desire no such comfort, we shall leave you to another's power. [21] Hereby we abolish the pope's tyranny, commandments, and coercion since we have no need of them. For our teaching, as I have said, is this: If anybody does not go to confession willingly and for the sake of absolution, let him just forget about it. Yes, and if anybody goes about relying on the purity of his confession, let him just stay away from it. [22] We urge you, however, to confess and express your needs, not for the purpose of performing a work but to hear what

God wishes to say to you. The Word or absolution, I say, is what you should concentrate on, magnifying and cherishing it as a great and wonderful treasure to be accepted with all praise and gratitude.

[23] If all this were clearly explained, and meanwhile if the needs which ought to move and induce us to confession were clearly indicated, there would be no need of coercion and force. A man's own conscience would impel him and make him so anxious that he would rejoice and act like a poor miserable beggar who hears that a rich gift, of money or clothes, is to be given out at a certain place; he would need no bailiff to drive and beat him but would run there as fast as he could so as not to miss the gift. [24] Suppose, now, that the invitation were changed into a command that all beggars should run to the place, no reason being given and no mention of what they were to look for or receive. How else would the beggar go but with repugnance, not expecting to receive anything but just letting everyone see how poor and miserable he is? Not much joy or comfort would come from this, but only a greater hostility to the command.

[25] In the same way the pope's preachers have in the past kept silence about this wonderful, rich alms and this indescribable treasure; they have simply driven men together in hordes just to show what impure and filthy people they were. Who could thus go to confession willingly? [26] We, on the contrary, do not say that men should look to see how full of filthiness you are, making of you a mirror for contemplating themselves. Rather we advise: If you are poor and miserable, then go and make use of the healing medicine. [27] He who feels his misery and need will develop such a desire for confession that he will run toward it with joy. But those who ignore it and do not come of their own accord, we let go their way. However, they ought to know that we do not regard them as Christians.

[28] Thus we teach what a wonderful, precious, and comforting thing confession is, and we urge that such a precious blessing should not be despised, especially when we consider our great need. If you are a Christian, you need neither my compulsion nor the pope's command at any point, but you will compel yourself and beg me for the privilege of sharing in it. [29] However, if you despise it and proudly stay away from confession, then we must come to the conclusion that you are no Christian and that you ought not receive the sacrament. For you despise what no Christian ought to despise, and you show thereby that you can have no forgiveness of sin. And this is a sure sign that you also despise the Gospel.

[30] In short, we approve of no coercion. However, if anyone refuses to hear and heed the warning of our preaching, we shall have nothing to do with him, nor may he have any share in the Gospel. If you are a Christian, you should be glad to run more than a hundred miles for confession, not under compulsion but rather coming and compelling us to offer it. [31] For here the compulsion must be inverted; we must come under the command and you must come into freedom. We compel no man, but allow ourselves to be compelled, just as we are compelled to preach and administer the sacrament.

[32] Therefore, when I urge you to go to confession, I am simply urging you to be a Christian. If I bring you to this point, I have also brought you to confession. Those who really want to be good Christians, free from their sins, and happy in their conscience, already have the true hunger and thirst. [33] They snatch at the bread just like a hunted hart, burning with heat and thirst, as Ps. 42:2 says, "As a heart longs for flowing streams, so longs my soul for thee, O God." That is, as a hart trembles with eagerness for a fresh spring, so I yearn and tremble for God's Word, absolution, the sacrament, etc. [34] In this way, you see, confession would be rightly taught, and such

a desire and love for it would be aroused that people would come running after us to get it, more than we would like. We shall let the papists torment and torture themselves and other people who ignore such a treasure and bar themselves from it. [35] As for ourselves, however, let us lift our hands in praise and thanks to God that we have attained to this blessed knowledge of confession.

APPENDIX D

LCMS World Mission Report

"Historical Country Work List"
LCMS World Mission

Introduction

As of January 1, 2009, LCMS World Mission is working, has working partnerships, or has historical work in a total of 88 countries, including the United States.

Keys to understanding the Tables:

The following statements define the "Relationship Status" between LCMS World Mission and the country in which it supports mission, education, and human care work. This Status is indicated by a numerical value in the "Status" column of each table:

Status 1—Denotes direct work by expatriate personnel of LCMS World Mission and trained national workers.

Status 2—Denotes work carried on with expatriate personnel and/or trained national workers with an existing indigenous or official partner church.

Status 3—Denotes work carried on through partner outreach—that is, ministry is carried on by an entity with resources and support from LCMS World Mission.

Status 4—Denotes historical work carried on by the LCMS.

Status 5—Denotes a working relationship exists, but there is no current or historical work or resources from LCMS World Mission.

Dates in the "Year" column refer to the year when LCMS World Mission formally began its support of ministry in that country or when the relationship was established.

Two numbers for a country in the "Year" column indicate that LCMS World Mission began work in that country at two separate times, the second date coming after a period when LCMS World Mission had withdrawn from that field for a year or more.

Countries-Year Work/Relationship Begun-Status†
(Grouped By Decade)

Decade	Country	Continent	Year	Status	Year became a "Partner Church"
1840-49	United States	North America	1847	1	
1850-59	None				
1860-69	None				
1870-79	None				
1880-89	Denmark	Eurasia	1882	5	1882
1890-99	India	Asia	1895	2	1859
	England	Eurasia	1896/2004	2	?
1900-09	Brazil	Latin America	1900	2	1980
	Argentina	Latin America	1905	2	1986
1910-19	Cuba (Isle of Pines)	Latin America	1911/93	2	
	China	Asia	1913/90	2	
1920-29	Finland	Eurasia	1928		1928-1998
	Sri Lanka	Asia	1927	2	2001
	France	Eurasia	2002	2	1927
	Belgium	Eurasia		5	1927
1930-39	Nigeria	Africa	1936	2	1963
	Paraguay	Latin America	1938	2	1995
1940-49	Mexico	Latin America	1940	2	1940
	Panama	Latin America	1941	1	
	Poland	Eurasia	1943/94	2	
	Philippines	Asia	1946	2	1971
	Guatemala	Latin America	1947	1	
	Australia	Asia	1948	3	
	Papua New Guinea	Asia	1948	2	1971
	Japan	Asia	1948	2	1976
1950-59	Lebanon	Eurasia	1950	4	
	Hong Kong	Asia	1950	2	1977
	El Salvador	Latin America	1958	4	
	Taiwan	Asia	1951	2	1966
	Venezuela	Latin America	1951	2	?
	Portugal	Eurasia	1956	3	
	South Korea	Asia	1958	2	1971
	Ghana	Africa	1958	2	1971
1960-69	Chile	Latin America	1960	2	1960
	Uruguay	Latin America	1960	3	
	Ghana	Africa	1960	2	1971
	Honduras	Latin America	1961	4	
1970-79	Germany	Eurasia	1972	2	?
	Eritrea	Africa	1975/94	4	
	Haiti	Latin America	1978		

	Liberia	Africa	1978	1	
	Guam	Asia	1978	Int'l Cong.	
1980-89	Togo	Africa	1980	1	
	South Africa	Africa	1982	2	1987?/1995?
	Sierra Leone	Africa	1983	1	
	Botswana	Africa	1982	2	
	Congo-Kinshasa (DRC)	Africa	1984	3	
	Thailand	Asia	1986	1	
	Macau	Asia	1988	1	
	Canada	North America	1989	4	1989?
1990-99	Czech Repub.	Eurasia	1990	2	
	Hungary	Eurasia	1991	2	
	Slovakia	Eurasia	1991	2	
	Ivory Coast	Africa	1991	1	
	Russia	Eurasia	1992	2	1998
	Kazakhstan	Asia	1993	1	
	Puerto Rico	Latin America	1993	1	
	Jamaica	Latin America	1993	1	
	Uganda	Africa	1995	2	
	Indonesia	Asia	1995	2	
	Vietnam	Asia	1995	1	
	Latvia	Eurasia	1996	2	2001
	Lithuania	Eurasia	1996	2	2001
	Estonia	Eurasia	1996	4	
	Guinea	Africa	1996	1	
	Benin	Africa	1996	3	
	Kenya	Africa	1998	2	2004
	Sudan	Africa	1998	2	
	Kyrgyzstan	Asia	1998	1	
	Bolivia	Latin America	1998	5	
	Laos	Asia	1999	2	
	Myanmar	Asia	1999	2	
	Spain	Latin America	1999	3	
	Angola	Latin America	1997	3	
2000-09	Ethiopia	Africa	2000	2	
	Burkina Faso	Africa	2000	1	
	Belarus	Eurasia	2001	2	
	The Gambia	Africa	2001	3	
	Cambodia	Asia	2001	2	
	Pakistan	Eurasia	2002	3	
	Afghanistan	Eurasia	2002	3	
	Tanzania	Africa	2002	2	
	Grand Cayman Islands	Latin America	2002	Int'l Cong.	
	Georgia	Eurasia	2004	2	
	Dominican Republic	Latin America	2004	1	

	Mongolia	Eurasia	2004	1	
	Madagascar	Africa	2005	3	
	North Korea	Asia	2006	3	
	Peru	Latin America	2007	2	
	Senegal	Africa	2007	5	
	Mali	Africa	2009	5	(Relocation of missionaries in the works)

†As of 5/12/09.

Receipts by District from Congregations and District to Synod
For Calendar Years 1973 and 2007

Year End	District Name	Increase (Decrease)	Feb 1, 2007 to Jan 31, 2008: District to Synod	% of Total to Synod	Congregation to District	% Congr to District to Synod	Feb 1, 1973 to Jan 31, 1974: District to Synod	% of Total to Synod	Congregation to District	% Congr to District to Synod
31-Dec	Atlantic	(115,661)	62,899	0.32%	689,276	9.13%	178,560	0.75%	758,421	23.54%
31-Dec	Cal-Nev-Hawaii	(286,679)	207,321	1.07%	2,209,546	9.38%	494,000	2.08%	1,056,255	46.77%
15-Jan	Eastern	(466,000)	110,000	0.57%	879,600	12.51%	576,000	2.43%	1,006,195	57.25%
31-Jan	English	(846,880)	277,231	1.43%	1,341,637	20.66%	1,124,111	4.74%	1,729,890	64.98%
31-Jan	Florida-Georgia	40,000	540,000	2.78%	2,661,575	20.29%	500,000	2.11%	906,531	55.16%
15-Jan	Illinois-Central	(402,450)	552,000	2.84%	1,923,529	28.70%	954,450	4.03%	1,312,286	72.73%
31-Jan	Illinois-Northern	(356,237)	843,763	4.34%	2,852,445	29.58%	1,200,000	5.06%	2,324,436	51.63%
15-Jan	Illinois-Southern	(239,207)	299,266	1.54%	997,552	30.00%	538,473	2.27%	756,352	71.19%
31-Mar	Indiana	(192,907)	999,000	5.14%	2,668,768	37.43%	1,191,907	5.03%	1,803,174	66.10%
31-Dec	Iowa East	(440,000)	185,000	0.95%	1,308,310	14.14%	625,000	2.64%	935,469	66.81%
31-Jan	Iowa West	(427,618)	787,652	4.05%	1,969,130	40.00%	1,215,270	5.13%	1,537,904	79.02%
15-Jan	Kansas	(29,980)	748,020	3.85%	1,867,919	40.05%	778,000	3.28%	1,246,819	62.40%
31-Jan	Michigan	382,101	2,806,101	14.44%	5,579,963	50.29%	2,424,000	10.23%	3,553,864	68.21%
15-Jan	Mid-South	275,700	528,200	2.72%	1,817,871	29.06%	252,500	1.07%	540,045	46.76%
15-Jan	Minnesota-North	159,166	613,306	3.16%	1,459,366	42.03%	454,140	1.92%	959,864	47.31%
31-Dec	Minnesota-South	(335,542)	1,367,295	7.04%	2,734,589	50.00%	1,702,837	7.18%	2,354,344	72.33%
30-Jun	Missouri	(657,066)	707,934	3.64%	3,042,411	23.27%	1,365,000	5.76%	2,346,412	58.17%
31-Jan	Montana	62,345	131,345	0.68%	524,570	25.04%	69,000	0.29%	220,514	31.29%
31-Jan	Nebraska	111,081	1,500,000	7.72%	2,886,085	51.97%	1,388,919	5.86%	1,911,363	72.67%
31-Mar	New England	88,303	113,303	0.58%	576,641	19.65%	25,000	0.11%	420,885	5.94%
31-Jan	New Jersey	(38,800)	61,200	0.31%	446,846	13.70%	100,000	0.42%	393,403	25.42%
31-Jan	North Dakota	132,657	351,558	1.81%	790,225	44.49%	218,901	0.92%	454,120	48.20%
31-Dec	Northwest	(325,352)	230,148	1.18%	1,990,565	11.56%	555,500	2.34%	1,251,361	44.39%
15-Jan	Ohio	(266,189)	363,707	1.87%	1,749,595	20.79%	629,896	2.66%	1,085,325	58.04%
31-Dec	Oklahoma	(75,775)	205,005	1.06%	1,069,224	19.17%	280,780	1.18%	651,413	43.10%
31-Dec	Pacific Southwest	(290,298)	250,000	1.29%	2,444,183	10.23%	540,298	2.28%	1,517,397	35.61%
31-Jan	Rocky Mountain	8,406	278,500	1.43%	1,546,596	18.01%	270,094	1.14%	908,728	29.72%
31-Aug	SELC	146,800	190,800	0.98%	569,628	33.50%	44,000	0.19%	218,156	20.17%
14-Jan	South Dakota	(15,000)	285,000	1.47%	967,985	29.44%	300,000	1.27%	548,101	54.73%
31-Dec	Southeastern	224,901	503,821	2.59%	2,519,923	19.99%	278,920	1.18%	1,025,623	27.20%
15-Jan	Southern	(184,000)	119,000	0.61%	1,087,514	10.94%	303,000	1.28%	538,856	56.23%
15-Jan	Texas	1,029,545	1,829,545	9.42%	6,788,984	26.95%	800,000	3.38%	1,955,084	40.92%
31-Dec	Wisconsin-North	(251,121)	901,393	4.64%	2,277,932	39.57%	1,152,514	4.86%	1,483,969	77.66%
31-Jan	Wisconsin-South	(779,878)	315,349	1.62%	2,540,633	12.41%	1,095,227	4.62%	1,872,096	58.50%
15-Jan	Wyoming	89,150	164,150	0.84%	678,938	24.18%	75,000	0.32%	225,231	33.30%
		(4,272,485)	19,428,812	100%	67,459,554	28.80%	23,701,297	100%	41,809,886	56.69%
Total Decrease (22 districts)		(7,022,640)								
Total Increase: 13 districts		2,750,155					Total Congregational Offerings $285,424,594			

Note: This report was prepared on the district fiscal year basis, February 1, 2008 - January 31, 2009

APPENDIX F

Report of Mission 21st Century Task Force

The Commission on Theology and Church Relations Statement of 1991 states, "Each of us has received from God's hand grace upon grace, all flowing from the sacrificial service of the One who laid down His life for us on the cross. We cannot, therefore, leave the work of God's mission to 'the church' in general or to 'others' who may appear more gifted for the task or to 'the pastor.' What an honor it is to follow in the footsteps of God's Servant-Son, and to share with others the love He has so freely and fully bestowed on us! Each of us is a personal letter from Christ to the world (2 Cor. 3:2–3), telling all who will listen of His grace, mercy and power." With the CTCR we have affirmed:

- **Mission begins in the heart of God**
- **God's mission is necessary because of sin**
- **God's mission centers in Jesus Christ**
- **God's mission is empowered by the Holy Spirit**
- **God's mission is to and for everyone**
- **God's mission is our mission**
- **God's mission is my mission**
- **God's mission is urgent**

While we as a synod and in many of our congregations have declared our mission to be reaching our communities and the world for Jesus Christ, our history in North America over the past 30 plus years gives a much different message. We continue to decline in membership in the midst of a population that is rapidly growing.

We believe it is time for the LCMS in convention under our theme of **One Mission ABLAZE** to return to faithfulness as a missional church in North America. Mission 21st Century is a matter of faithfulness to our Scriptural and Confessional teachings and our commitment to reach each community with the Good News of Jesus Christ.

To be in mission is to affirm our history. Our forefathers came to the new world with a commitment to Confessional Lutheranism and they sent pastors and missionaries to the unchurched. They established new congregations where God's people gathered for Word and Sacrament and the building up of the Saints.

To be in mission is to look forward. It is to heed our Lord's admonition to "put our hands to the plow" (Luke 9:57–62) and to see people "like sheep without a shepherd" (Matthew 9:36–38). It is to see fields white unto the harvest. It is to invest the talents He gives us, expecting to provide Him the increase (Matt. 25:14–30). It is to speak of salvation in Jesus Christ, knowing that the Holy Spirit causes tongues to confess "Jesus is Lord!" (1 Cor. 12:3) It is to understand that as "royal priests," we are ambassadors for Jesus Christ (2 Cor. 3:2–3; 2 Cor. 5:20–21).

To be in mission is to be realistic. It is to recognize that our numbers are growing smaller while the number of people without Christ grows larger. It is to understand that almost half the children of the 1950s left the church—and fewer of their children and grandchildren are in the church today. It is acknowledging that our churches exist in the midst of an unchurched culture and that our church buildings have become sanctuaries to which we escape rather than mission training centers from which we move out into our community. It is to realize that many people no longer speak our language. It is to admit that things are different in our communities today and they will never be what we remember them to be.

To be in mission is to use the precious gifts that God has given us. We are people of the Means of Grace. God's Word is the norm of our teachings that points us to His unfailing love for us in Jesus Christ. We are His people washed in the forgiving water of baptism and regularly nourished with the body and blood of our Lord in the Sacrament.

To be in mission is to recognize the urgency. We are a people who teach and confess that "Christ will come again," yet we live as if it will not be soon. In 1992 we approved The Mission Blueprint for the Nineties which declared North America to be a world mission field; yet our actions have continued to think of missions as across the sea or "over there." Our statements on mission have been forward looking yet our numbers continue to decline. Only 25% of our congregations have a specific plan for how to reach their community for Jesus Christ.

To be in mission is to involve all members. The Mission 21st Century Task Force calls on the people and congregations of the Synod to be faithful in mission to the home next door. We urge each of us to see our home as a center for mission activity where each baptized believer is a missionary. The task force renews the "Blueprint" call to each congregation to measure the size of their congregation "not by the number of members in attendance but by the number of members active in mission."

To be in mission is to evaluate all that we do. The Mission 21st Century Task Force calls on all entities of the Synod—congregations, districts, national offices, boards and commissions, schools, colleges, universities, seminaries, mission societies, Recognized Service Organizations—to reevaluate everything they are doing in light of being mission outposts in a mission field."

RECOMMENDATIONS:

First: The work of reaching our communities for Jesus Christ is the work of all the baptized people of God. God's call is for each of us to think of ourselves as Christian missionaries who are participants in God's command to make disciples of all people. We pray that the Spirit of God will move over this convention and then over each of our congregations to renew in us a spirit of Christian vocation as God's ambassadors to the world around us. We encourage every congregation to return to a study of the 1991 CTCR Theological Statement of Mission that we might face the future together drawing on the Word of God and our understanding of that Word as described in the Confessions to be a movement for change in North America.

To be strong **we must confess our shortcomings.** We can not ignore or deny the decline in our membership. We have hurt one another by the things we have done and we have failed our God and his desire that all would be saved by the things we have left undone. "We have not loved our neighbor as our self" and we have not reached out to those in the shadow of our churches who do not know Jesus Christ as Lord and Savior.

We can come to the task with hope as we **celebrate where we have done missions well.** We thank God for our commitment as a church to send missionaries into foreign fields where today thousands are coming to faith in Christ through our efforts of the past. Today some of those partner churches are sending missionaries to North America to work with us in reaching diverse cultures. We have learned from our foreign mission work how we can be missionaries to the person next door.

God's Mission Is My Mission and God's Mission Is Urgent.

Secondly: The task force realizes that to be confessional and missional is a difficult responsibility. To be confessional is to present the truth of the Gospel without compromise and to be missional is to be willing to engage cultures that are different from us. In an unchurched, diverse culture we are challenged with Peter to "give the reason for the hope that we have with gentleness and respect" (1 Peter 3:15). The strategies we have learned in bringing Christ to other parts of the world are also applicable to bringing Christ to this foreign mission field called North America. Our foreign missionaries have taught us that to bring Jesus Christ to an unchurched people we have to:

- **Learn the culture**
- **Learn the language**
- **Train the leaders**
- **Grow the mission**

We are a **diverse people** today who live in a land of great diversity. We are a nation today of languages and cultures that we once only experienced in pictures. Today they are our neighbors. The world is literally at our front door and God has privileged us to be His missionaries to our community. We are a nation that will continue to change dramatically over the next decades. Whether Los Angeles, New York, or Des Moines, Iowa, we are a society of many people, languages and cultures. We are a people described as "builders," "boomers," "busters," and now Generations "X," "Y," and "Z."

The task is huge and the challenge is great. Our Lord's promise to His first missionaries is His promise to us as well, "All authority in heaven and on earth has been given to Me. . . . And surely I will be with you always, to the very end of the age."

GOD'S MISSION IS MY MISSION AND GOD'S MISSION IS URGENT.

Our Third learning is that for us to be a missional church, each congregation will need to see itself as a mission outpost. As a synod we join together to send missionaries to foreign lands but in North America the task of mission is not the synod's task nor that of the districts. Each congregation is in the middle of the mission field and we encourage each one of our 6,100 congregations to see themselves as a mission outpost in their mission field. An outpost is there to encourage and protect the missionary while training and sending the missionary from that place into the mission field.

This task is much more than placing a sign at the end of the driveway. This vision becomes reality when each of our congregations looks at its community with **mission eyes.** It calls for an awareness on the part of each of us that the people living in our community do not have a relationship with Jesus Christ and He is not a part of their daily lives. As an outpost congregations will provide Bible study and classes that teach the very tenets of our faith **together with** the tools for evangelism. It calls for a "can do" attitude that looks at the strengths of the congregation that can be used for outreach. It calls for each congregation to look into its community and identify ways it can become involved in its mission field.

Congregations as mission outposts have available the **resources** of the districts to teach missionary methods, provide additional training and demonstrate the strength that is theirs when they network with other congregations, social service agencies, schools and other community resources. Through LCEF and CEF our congregations can do demographic studies of their mission field to better understand their opportunities. One of the great strengths of our ministry is the presence of our schools, preschools, elementary and high schools. Throughout our history our schools have been valuable resources to reach our community and today they are often an untapped missionary tool. Today about 59% of our congregations operate schools with 289,100 students during the 2002–2003 school year. The influence of these schools was instrumental in 4,208 children and 3,308 adults being baptized. During the same year over half of the children came from non-Lutheran homes with 16% claiming no church home.

Congregations as mission outposts are the key factor in the starting of new congregations. Studies have proven that more people are reached through new church starts than through existing congregations. While we celebrate the longevity of many of our congregations, the trend is that congregations by the time they reach their fortieth or fiftieth anniversary are on the decline and have lost their missionary effectiveness. One of the most effective ways to be in mission is to look with missionary eyes at new communities of growth and new cultural groups that can be reached with the planting of a new missionary outpost. When existing congregations help to plant new missions both congregations regain a missionary zeal.

GOD'S MISSION IS MY MISSION AND GOD'S MISSION IS URGENT.

Finally the task force has learned that if we are going to be a missionary church with every congregation as a mission outpost, we need to evaluate and change how we train our professional workers. We celebrate the education of our pastors as theologians and shepherds of God's people. Our seminary education is strongly focused on shepherding, which prepares the pastor to preach and teach the Word, counsel with both Law and Gospel and assure that the congregation remains true to the Confessions and the right administration of the Sacraments. Today most seminarians graduate with only one course or none at all in missions. For our congregations to become mission outposts in an unchurched culture, the task force is recommending to the convention and the seminaries that courses in mission be required of all graduates.

The task force also noted that many of our active pastors have not had the opportunity to continue their training after graduation and they too were trained in a shepherding model of ministry. While the task force recognizes that shepherding is a vital part of the ministry of any congregation, our active pastors also need the opportunity for continuing education in missionary methods and in relating the Gospel to a diverse culture in an unchurched society.

The same training is required of all those preparing for church work professions. Currently missionary training in our universities is very limited and most of our teachers, DCEs and other rostered workers with the exception possibly of Directors of Outreach have very little if any missionary training. Congregations and schools will be better served as missionary outposts by called workers who have missionary training and team-building experience.

The task force also encourages the colleges and seminaries to explore courses that prepare our professional church work graduates to see as a primary part of their ministry the training of God's people to serve in their neighborhood mission field. The request comes in two forms. First, as part of their preparations, these future workers be encouraged to see one of their congregational roles as being trainers to equip laity to work in partnership in the mission outreach of the congregation. Second, that these future workers, especially pastors, also be offered courses that equip them to teach and serve in team ministry with the laity.

One message the task force heard loud and strong from our congregation members is, "Teach us how." We declare the world outside the congregation as the mission field and we need to train our professional workers and our members how to be missionaries. These overtures will come to the convention when Committee 5, Higher Education, comes before you.

GOD'S MISSION IS MY MISSION AND GOD'S MISSION IS URGENT.

With this training is the use of technology. We are a church body that prides itself in our history with the use of technology. The Lutheran Church—Missouri Synod was in the forefront of technology evangelism with the use of radio and The Lutheran Hour, and television with This is the Life. Visionary leaders brought us into the Twentieth Century technology with great enthusiasm. As we look to the Twenty-first Century we enter into a new world of technology. Some of us sit in this convention with our wireless pocket PCs or will return to our hotel room tonight and log on to the internet. We carry our cell phones and celebrate wireless Internet.

The world before us is exciting and frightening, challenging and frustrating. There is great cause for hope as we see some examples of what is happening within LCMS congregations who are blazing the trail for us.